THE TRIAL

A GRAPHIC NOVEL

FRANZ KAFKA'S

THE TRIAL

A GRAPHIC NOVEL

ILLUSTRATED BY
CHANTAL MONTELLIER

ADAPTED AND TRANSLATED BY
DAVID ZANE MAIROWITZ

STERLING

New York / London
www.sterlingpublishing.com

Published by Sterling Publishing Co., Inc.
387 Park Avenue South, New York, NY 10016

© 2008 SelfMadeHero

First published 2008
by SelfMadeHero
A division of Metro Media Ltd
5 Upper Wimpole Street
London W1G 6BP
www.selfmadehero.com

Illustrated by Chantal Montellier
Translated and adapted by David Zane Mairowitz
Cover Designer: Jeff Willis
Designers: Andy Huckle, Kurt Young
Kafka introduction/biography by Robert Collins
Editorial: Dan Lockwood
Editorial Assistance: Lizzie Spratt
Originating Publisher: Emma Hayley

With thanks to Andrzej Klimowski, Doug Wallace, and Jane Goodsir
With special thanks to Robert Crumb

Distributed in Canada by Sterling Publishing
C/o Canadian Manda Group, 165 Dufferin Street,
Toronto, Ontario, Canada M6K 3H6

Library of Congress Cataloging-in-Publication Data

Montellier, Chantal.
    The Trial: A graphic adaptation of Franz Kafka's novel. Illustrated by
Chantal Montellier; translated and adapted by David Zane Mairowitz.
        p. cm.—(Illustrated Classics)
    ISBN-13: 978-1-4114-1591-1 (pbk.)
    ISBN-10: 1-4114-1591-4 (pbk.)
    1. Graphic novels. I. Mairowitz, David Zane, 1943- II. Kafka, Franz, 1883-1924.
Der Proces. III. Title.
PN6747.M66T75 2008
741.5'944—dc22

                                                        2007045050

For information about custom editions, special sales, premium and corporate
purchases, please contact Sterling Special Sales Department at 800-805-5489 or
specialsales@sterlingpub.com.

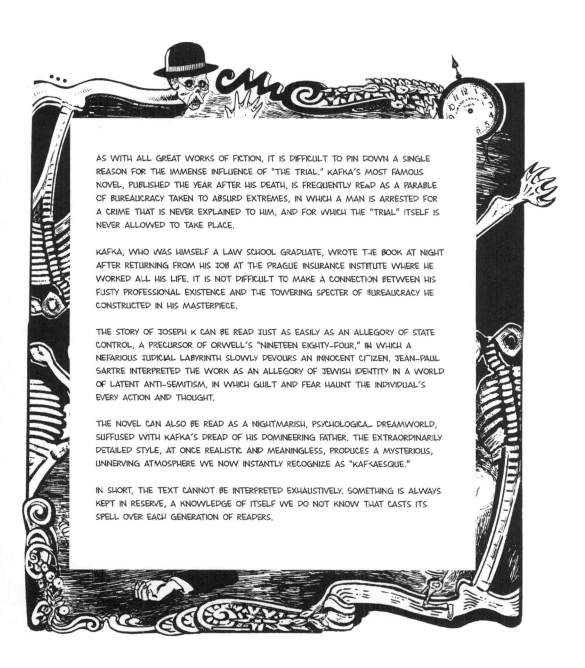

AS WITH ALL GREAT WORKS OF FICTION, IT IS DIFFICULT TO PIN DOWN A SINGLE REASON FOR THE IMMENSE INFLUENCE OF "THE TRIAL." KAFKA'S MOST FAMOUS NOVEL, PUBLISHED THE YEAR AFTER HIS DEATH, IS FREQUENTLY READ AS A PARABLE OF BUREAUCRACY TAKEN TO ABSURD EXTREMES, IN WHICH A MAN IS ARRESTED FOR A CRIME THAT IS NEVER EXPLAINED TO HIM, AND FOR WHICH THE "TRIAL" ITSELF IS NEVER ALLOWED TO TAKE PLACE.

KAFKA, WHO WAS HIMSELF A LAW SCHOOL GRADUATE, WROTE THE BOOK AT NIGHT AFTER RETURNING FROM HIS JOB AT THE PRAGUE INSURANCE INSTITUTE WHERE HE WORKED ALL HIS LIFE. IT IS NOT DIFFICULT TO MAKE A CONNECTION BETWEEN HIS FUSTY PROFESSIONAL EXISTENCE AND THE TOWERING SPECTER OF BUREAUCRACY HE CONSTRUCTED IN HIS MASTERPIECE.

THE STORY OF JOSEPH K CAN BE READ JUST AS EASILY AS AN ALLEGORY OF STATE CONTROL, A PRECURSOR OF ORWELL'S "NINETEEN EIGHTY-FOUR," IN WHICH A NEFARIOUS JUDICIAL LABYRINTH SLOWLY DEVOURS AN INNOCENT CITIZEN. JEAN-PAUL SARTRE INTERPRETED THE WORK AS AN ALLEGORY OF JEWISH IDENTITY IN A WORLD OF LATENT ANTI-SEMITISM, IN WHICH GUILT AND FEAR HAUNT THE INDIVIDUAL'S EVERY ACTION AND THOUGHT.

THE NOVEL CAN ALSO BE READ AS A NIGHTMARISH, PSYCHOLOGICAL DREAMWORLD, SUFFUSED WITH KAFKA'S DREAD OF HIS DOMINEERING FATHER. THE EXTRAORDINARILY DETAILED STYLE, AT ONCE REALISTIC AND MEANINGLESS, PRODUCES A MYSTERIOUS, UNNERVING ATMOSPHERE WE NOW INSTANTLY RECOGNIZE AS "KAFKAESQUE."

IN SHORT, THE TEXT CANNOT BE INTERPRETED EXHAUSTIVELY. SOMETHING IS ALWAYS KEPT IN RESERVE, A KNOWLEDGE OF ITSELF WE DO NOT KNOW THAT CASTS ITS SPELL OVER EACH GENERATION OF READERS.

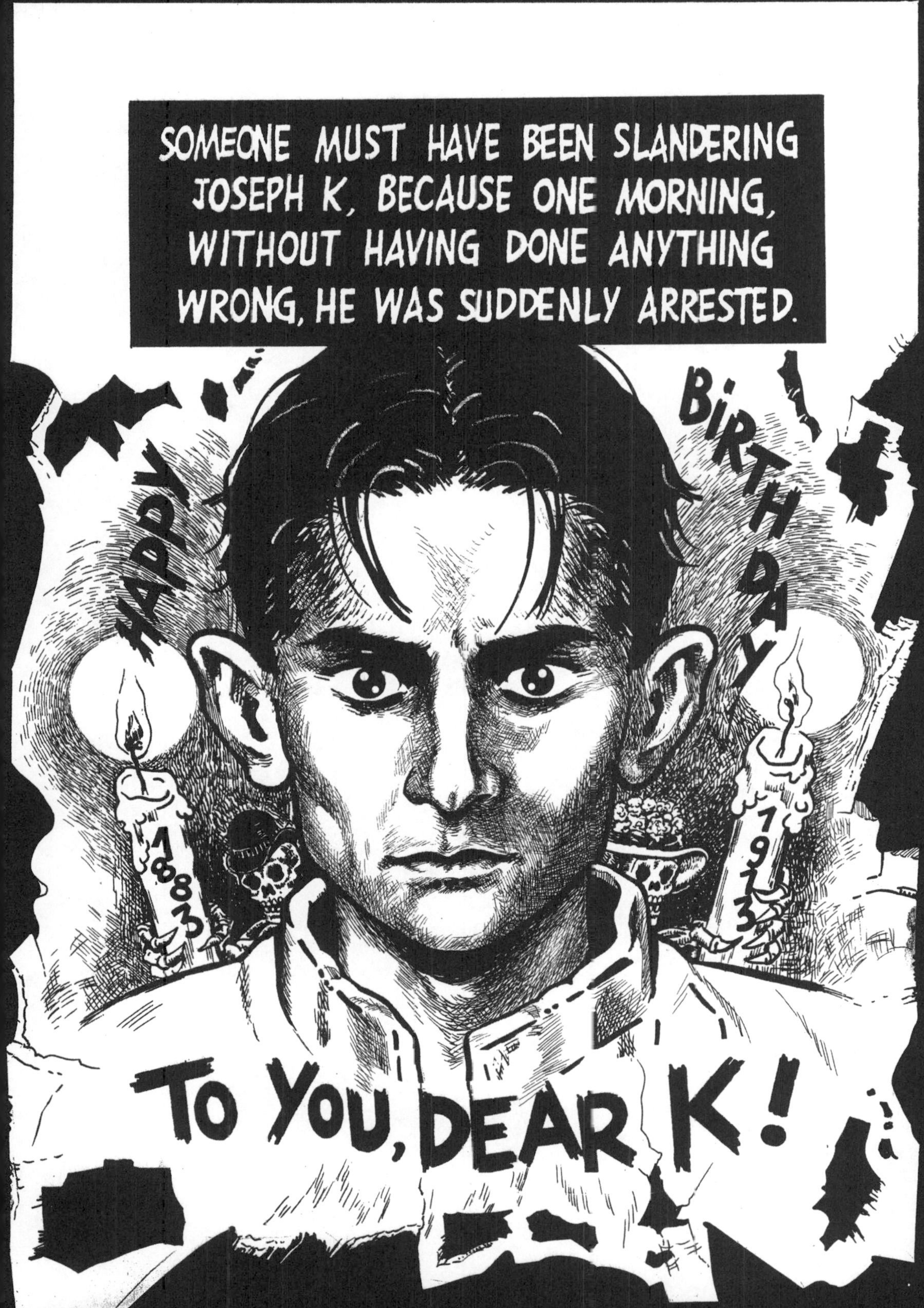

SOMEONE MUST HAVE BEEN SLANDERING JOSEPH K, BECAUSE ONE MORNING, WITHOUT HAVING DONE ANYTHING WRONG, HE WAS SUDDENLY ARRESTED.
HAPPY BIRTHDAY
1883
1913
TO YOU, DEAR K!

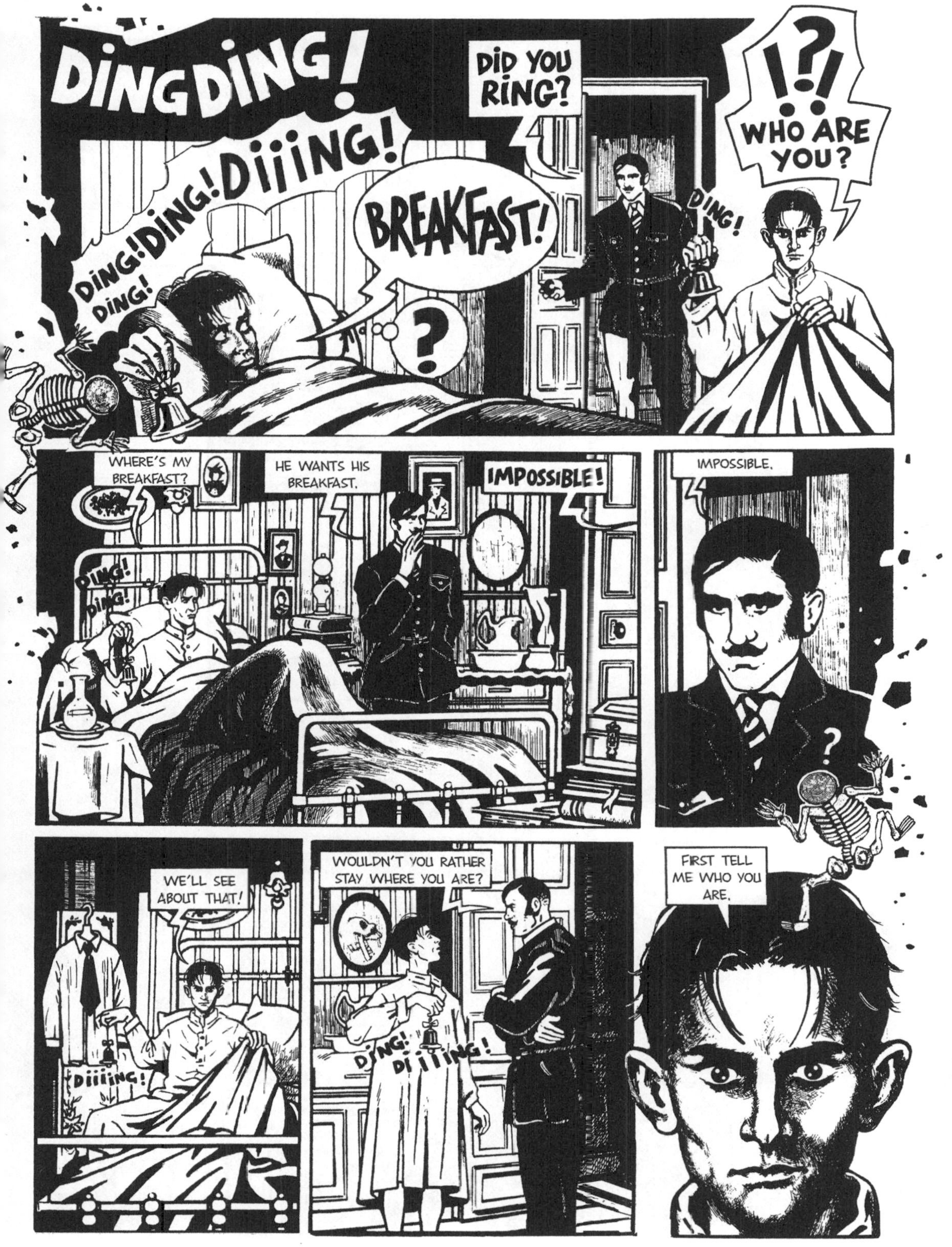
DINGDING!
DING! DING!
DING! DING! DIIING!
BREAKFAST!
?
DID YOU RING?
DING!
!?! WHO ARE YOU?
WHERE'S MY BREAKFAST?
DING! DING!
HE WANTS HIS BREAKFAST.
IMPOSSIBLE!
IMPOSSIBLE.
?
WE'LL SEE ABOUT THAT!
DIIING!
WOULDN'T YOU RATHER STAY WHERE YOU ARE?
DING! DIIING!
FIRST TELL ME WHO YOU ARE.

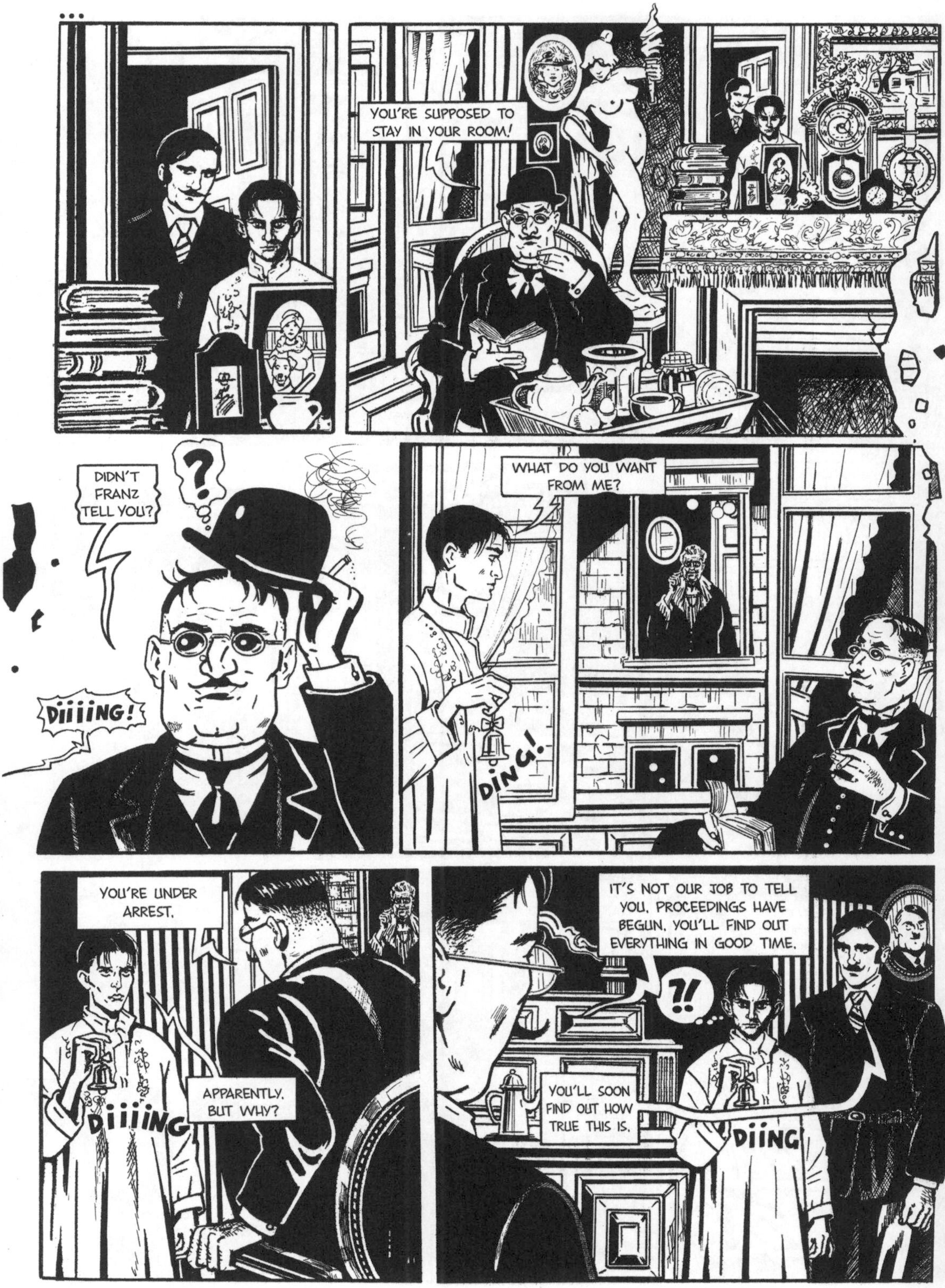
...
YOU'RE SUPPOSED TO STAY IN YOUR ROOM!
DIDN'T FRANZ TELL YOU?
?
DIiiiNG!
WHAT DO YOU WANT FROM ME?
DING!
YOU'RE UNDER ARREST.
APPARENTLY. BUT WHY?
DIiiiNG
IT'S NOT OUR JOB TO TELL YOU. PROCEEDINGS HAVE BEGUN. YOU'LL FIND OUT EVERYTHING IN GOOD TIME.
?!
YOU'LL SOON FIND OUT HOW TRUE THIS IS.
DIiNG

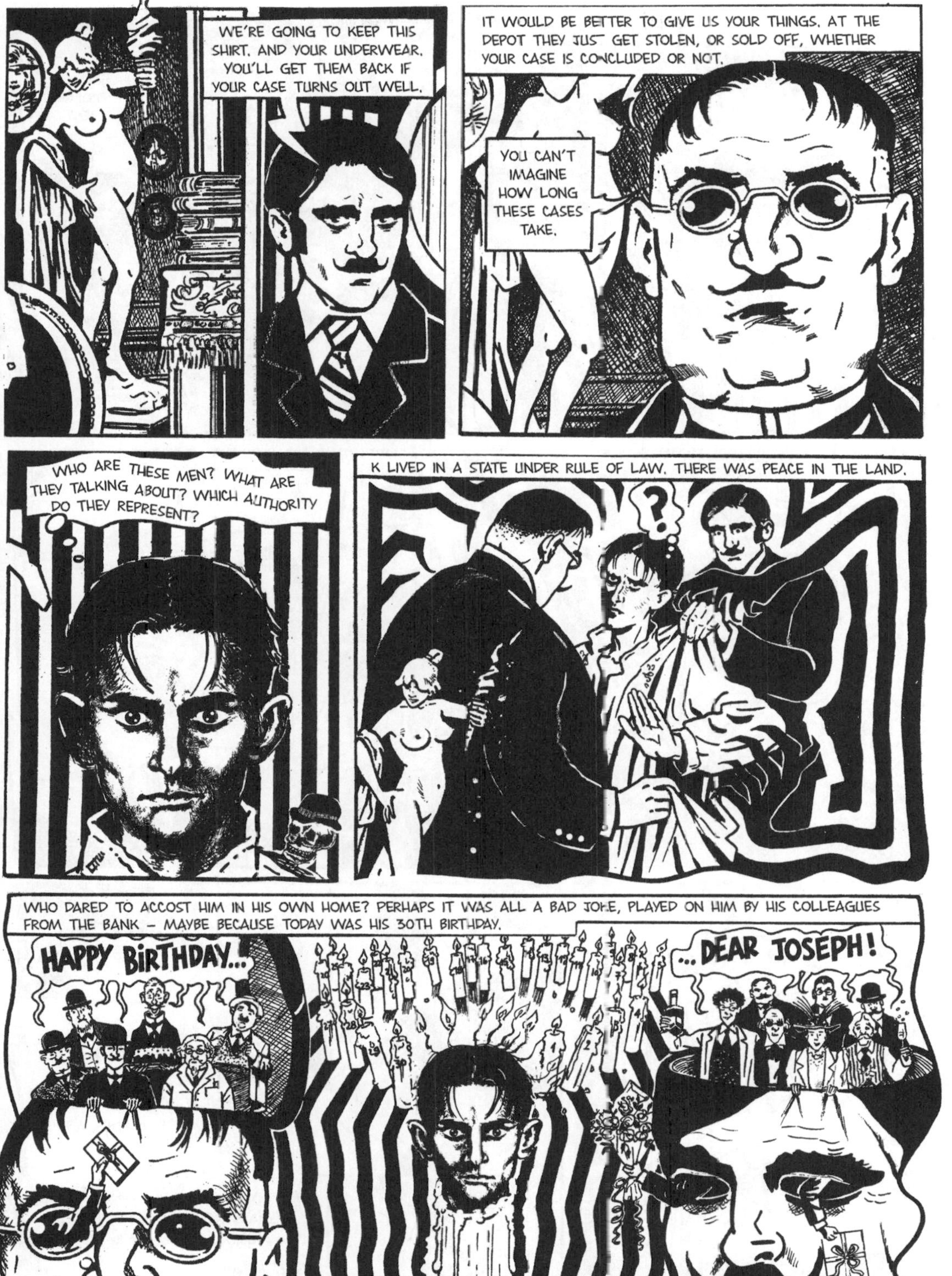

WE'RE GOING TO KEEP THIS SHIRT, AND YOUR UNDERWEAR. YOU'LL GET THEM BACK IF YOUR CASE TURNS OUT WELL.
IT WOULD BE BETTER TO GIVE US YOUR THINGS. AT THE DEPOT THEY JUST GET STOLEN, OR SOLD OFF, WHETHER YOUR CASE IS CONCLUDED OR NOT.
YOU CAN'T IMAGINE HOW LONG THESE CASES TAKE.
WHO ARE THESE MEN? WHAT ARE THEY TALKING ABOUT? WHICH AUTHORITY DO THEY REPRESENT?
K LIVED IN A STATE UNDER RULE OF LAW. THERE WAS PEACE IN THE LAND.
?
WHO DARED TO ACCOST HIM IN HIS OWN HOME? PERHAPS IT WAS ALL A BAD JOKE, PLAYED ON HIM BY HIS COLLEAGUES FROM THE BANK – MAYBE BECAUSE TODAY WAS HIS 30TH BIRTHDAY.
HAPPY BIRTHDAY...
...DEAR JOSEPH!

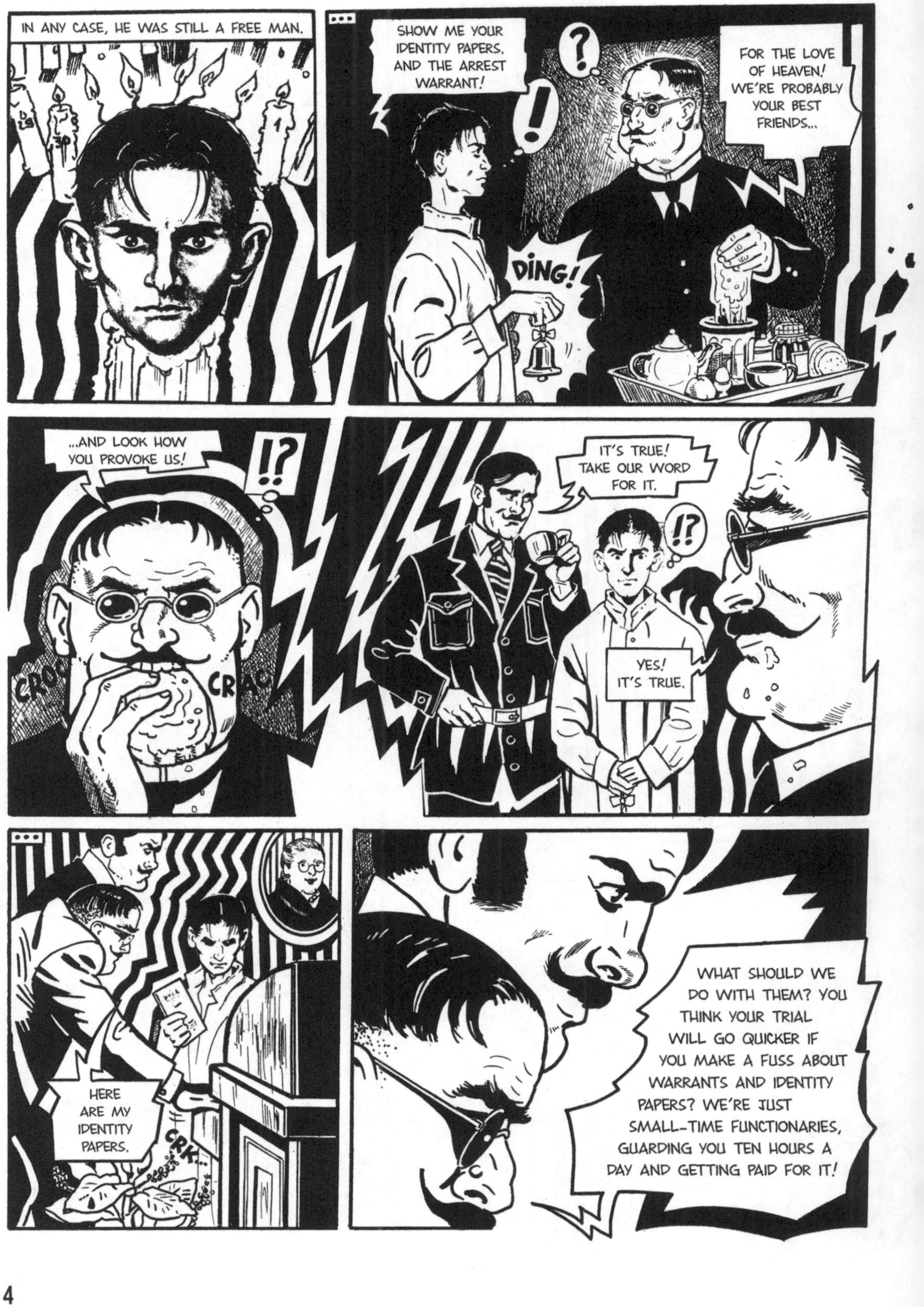
IN ANY CASE, HE WAS STILL A FREE MAN.
SHOW ME YOUR IDENTITY PAPERS, AND THE ARREST WARRANT!
?
!
FOR THE LOVE OF HEAVEN! WE'RE PROBABLY YOUR BEST FRIENDS...
DING!
...AND LOOK HOW YOU PROVOKE US!
!?
CROC
CRAC
IT'S TRUE! TAKE OUR WORD FOR IT.
!?
YES! IT'S TRUE.
HERE ARE MY IDENTITY PAPERS.
CRK...
WHAT SHOULD WE DO WITH THEM? YOU THINK YOUR TRIAL WILL GO QUICKER IF YOU MAKE A FUSS ABOUT WARRANTS AND IDENTITY PAPERS? WE'RE JUST SMALL-TIME FUNCTIONARIES, GUARDING YOU TEN HOURS A DAY AND GETTING PAID FOR IT!

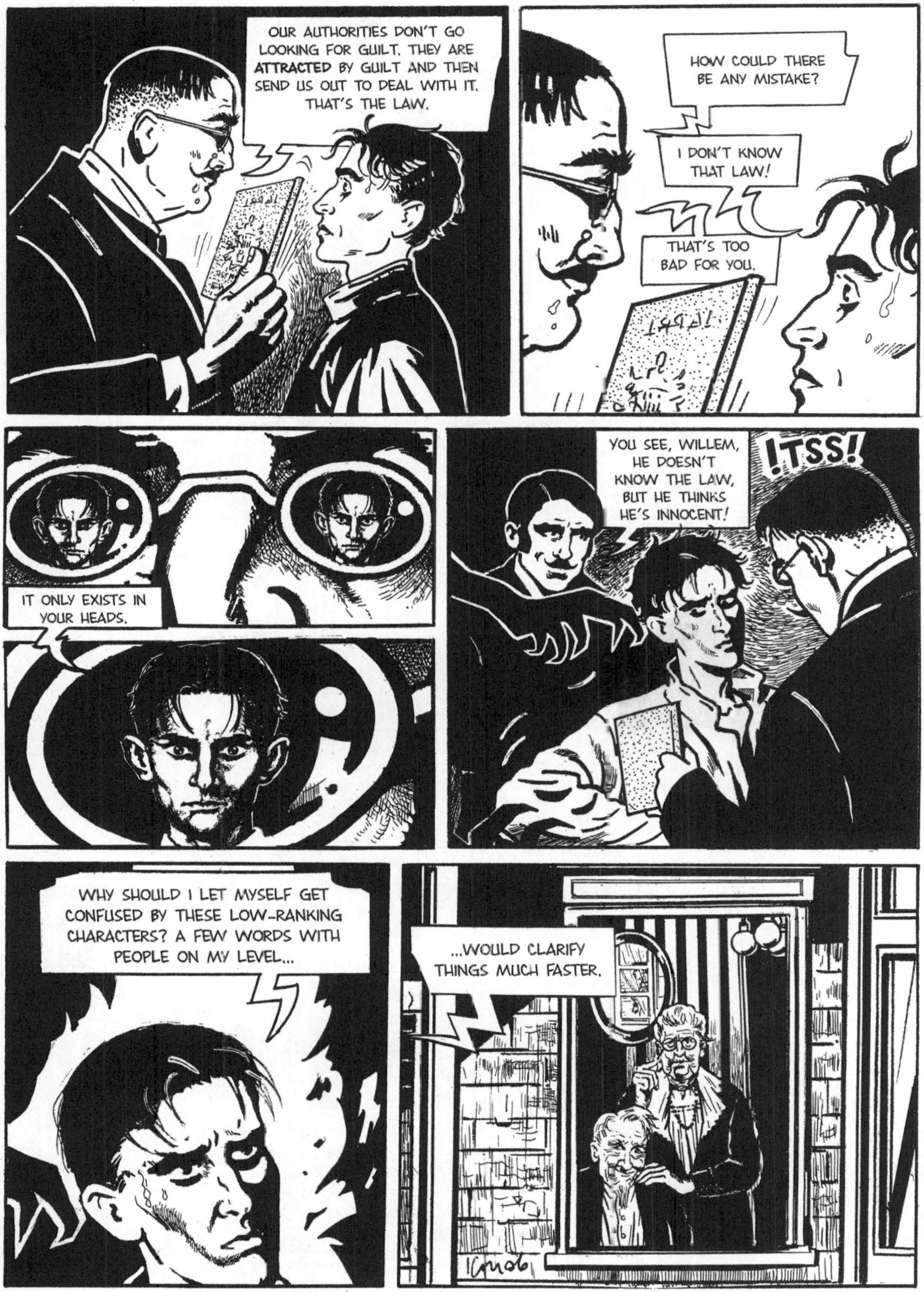
OUR AUTHORITIES DON'T GO LOOKING FOR GUILT. THEY ARE **ATTRACTED** BY GUILT AND THEN SEND US OUT TO DEAL WITH IT. THAT'S THE LAW.
HOW COULD THERE BE ANY MISTAKE?
I DON'T KNOW THAT LAW!
THAT'S TOO BAD FOR YOU.
IT ONLY EXISTS IN YOUR HEADS.
YOU SEE, WILLEM, HE DOESN'T KNOW THE LAW, BUT HE THINKS HE'S INNOCENT!
!TSS!
WHY SHOULD I LET MYSELF GET CONFUSED BY THESE LOW-RANKING CHARACTERS? A FEW WORDS WITH PEOPLE ON MY LEVEL...
...WOULD CLARIFY THINGS MUCH FASTER.

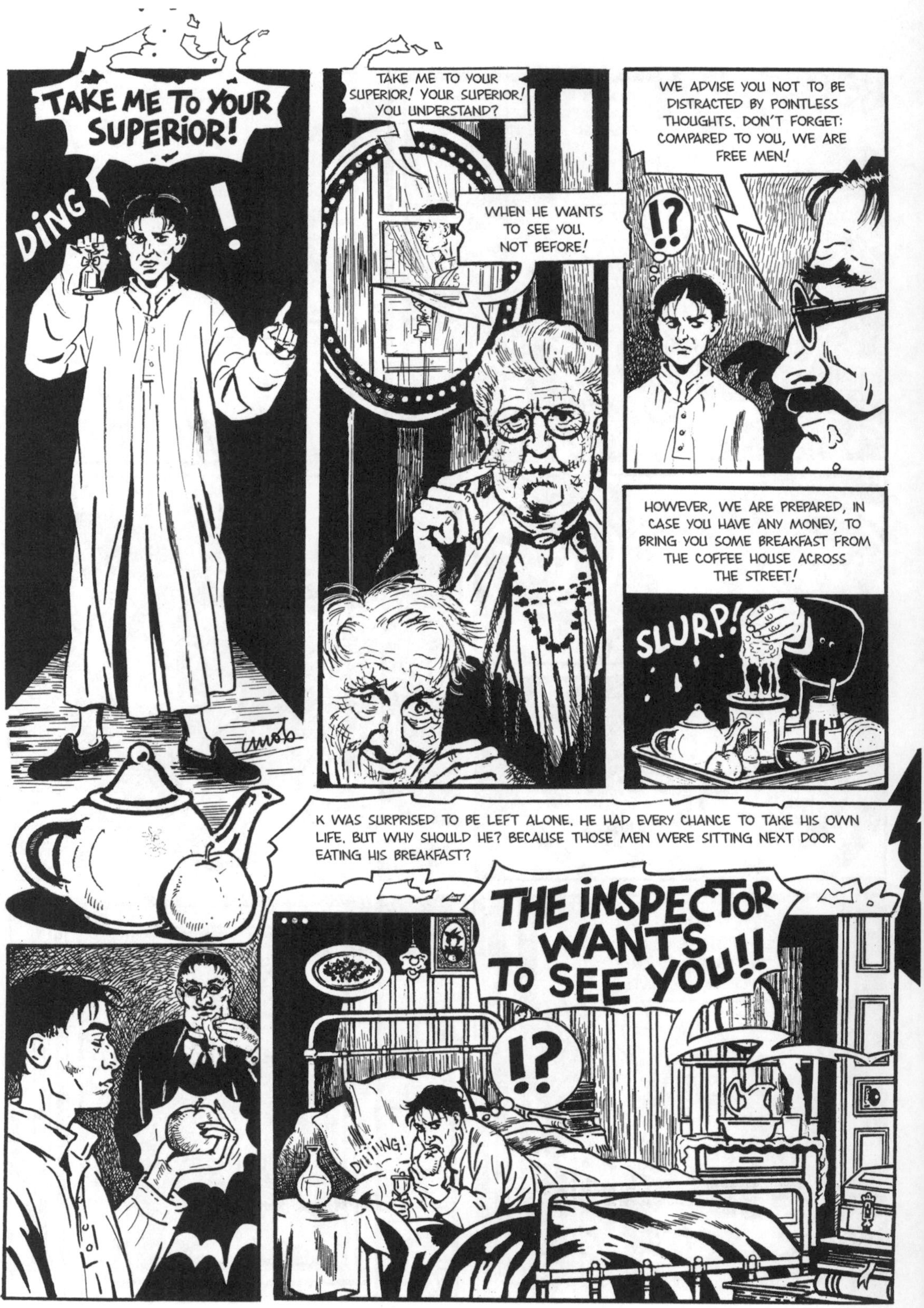
TAKE ME TO YOUR SUPERIOR!
DING
!
TAKE ME TO YOUR SUPERIOR! YOUR SUPERIOR! YOU UNDERSTAND?
WHEN HE WANTS TO SEE YOU. NOT BEFORE!
WE ADVISE YOU NOT TO BE DISTRACTED BY POINTLESS THOUGHTS. DON'T FORGET: COMPARED TO YOU, WE ARE FREE MEN!
!?
HOWEVER, WE ARE PREPARED, IN CASE YOU HAVE ANY MONEY, TO BRING YOU SOME BREAKFAST FROM THE COFFEE HOUSE ACROSS THE STREET!
SLURP!
K WAS SURPRISED TO BE LEFT ALONE. HE HAD EVERY CHANCE TO TAKE HIS OWN LIFE. BUT WHY SHOULD HE? BECAUSE THOSE MEN WERE SITTING NEXT DOOR EATING HIS BREAKFAST?
THE INSPECTOR WANTS TO SEE YOU!!
!?
DIIIING!

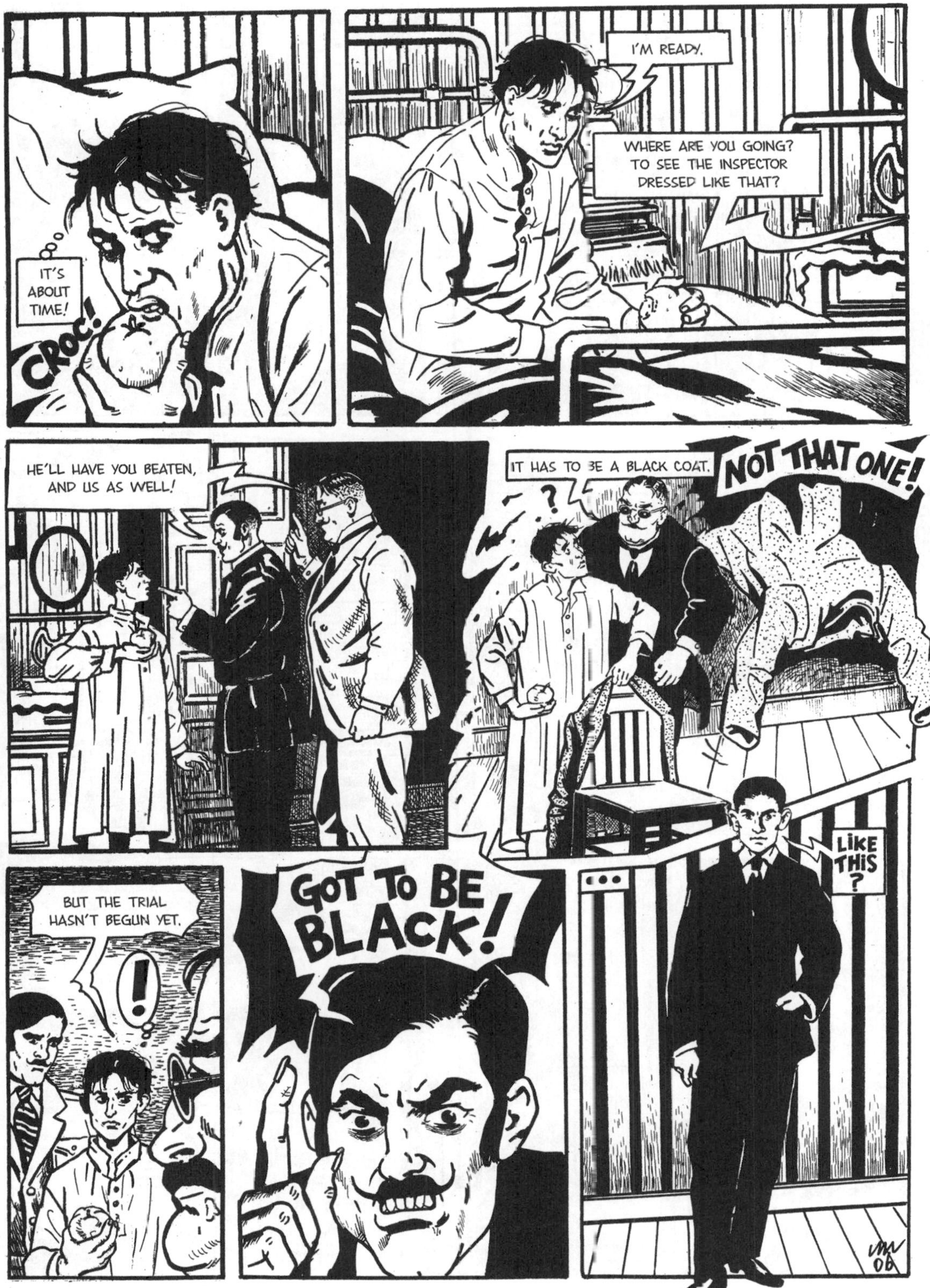
IT'S ABOUT TIME!
CROC!
I'M READY.
WHERE ARE YOU GOING? TO SEE THE INSPECTOR DRESSED LIKE THAT?
HE'LL HAVE YOU BEATEN, AND US AS WELL!
IT HAS TO BE A BLACK COAT.
?
NOT THAT ONE!
BUT THE TRIAL HASN'T BEGUN YET.
!
GOT TO BE BLACK!
LIKE THIS?

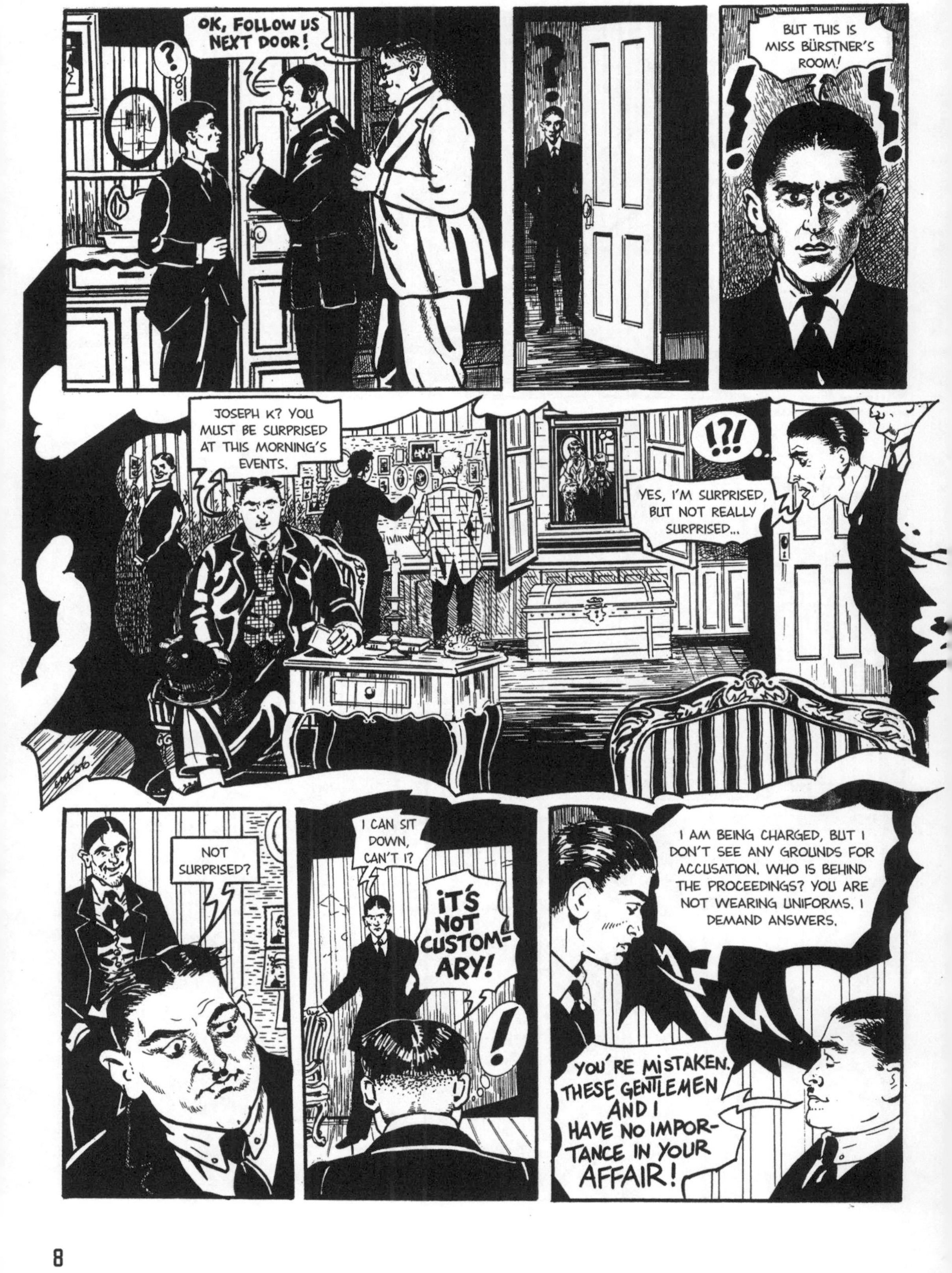
?
OK, FOLLOW US NEXT DOOR!
?
BUT THIS IS MISS BÜRSTNER'S ROOM!
!
!
JOSEPH K? YOU MUST BE SURPRISED AT THIS MORNING'S EVENTS.
!?!
YES, I'M SURPRISED, BUT NOT REALLY SURPRISED...
NOT SURPRISED?
I CAN SIT DOWN, CAN'T I?
IT'S NOT CUSTOMARY!
!
I AM BEING CHARGED, BUT I DON'T SEE ANY GROUNDS FOR ACCUSATION. WHO IS BEHIND THE PROCEEDINGS? YOU ARE NOT WEARING UNIFORMS. I DEMAND ANSWERS.
YOU'RE MISTAKEN. THESE GENTLEMEN AND I HAVE NO IMPORTANCE IN YOUR AFFAIR!

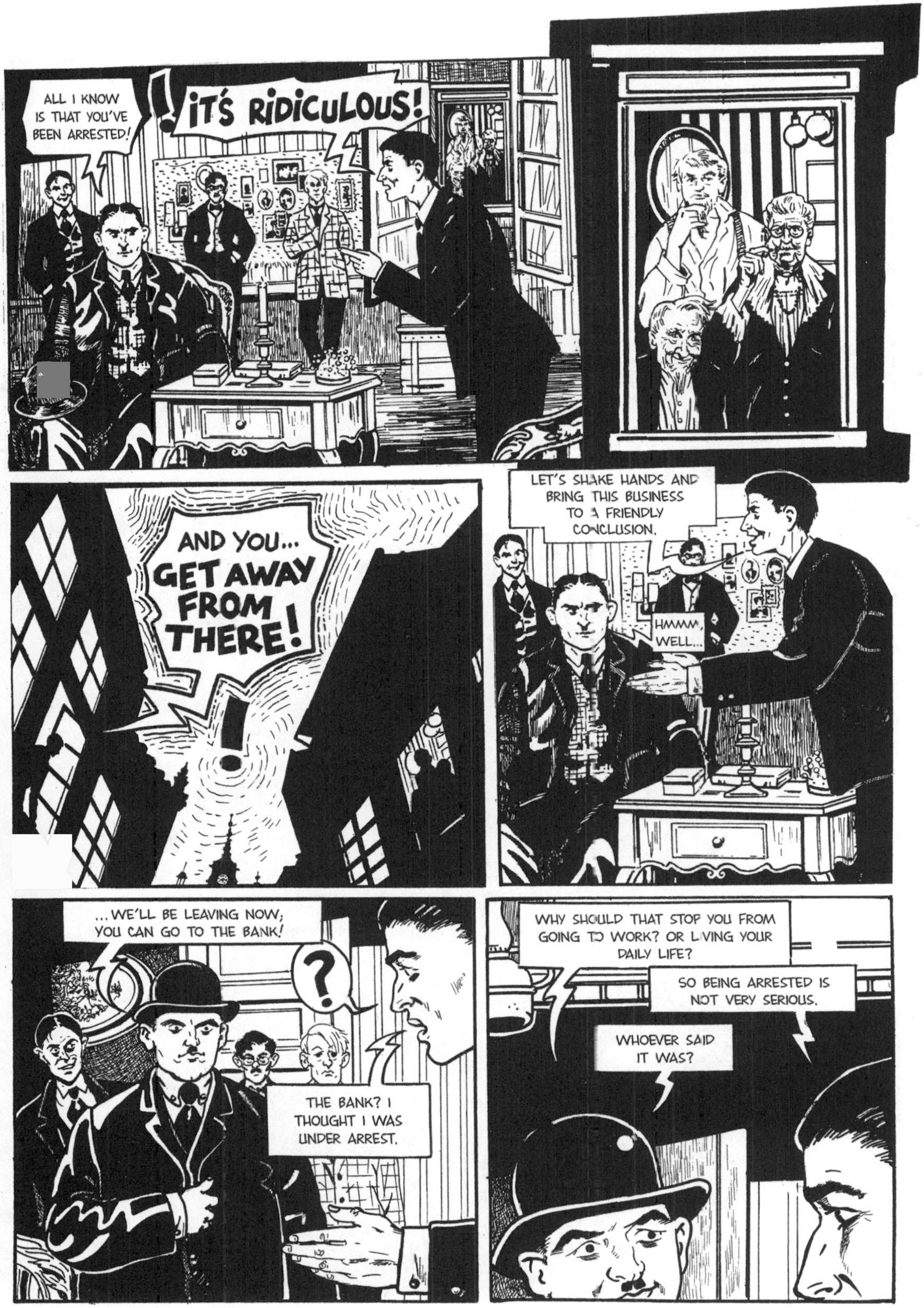
ALL I KNOW IS THAT YOU'VE BEEN ARRESTED!
IT'S RIDICULOUS!
AND YOU... GET AWAY FROM THERE!
LET'S SHAKE HANDS AND BRING THIS BUSINESS TO A FRIENDLY CONCLUSION.
HMMM, WELL...
...WE'LL BE LEAVING NOW; YOU CAN GO TO THE BANK!
?
THE BANK? I THOUGHT I WAS UNDER ARREST.
WHY SHOULD THAT STOP YOU FROM GOING TO WORK? OR LIVING YOUR DAILY LIFE?
SO BEING ARRESTED IS NOT VERY SERIOUS.
WHOEVER SAID IT WAS?

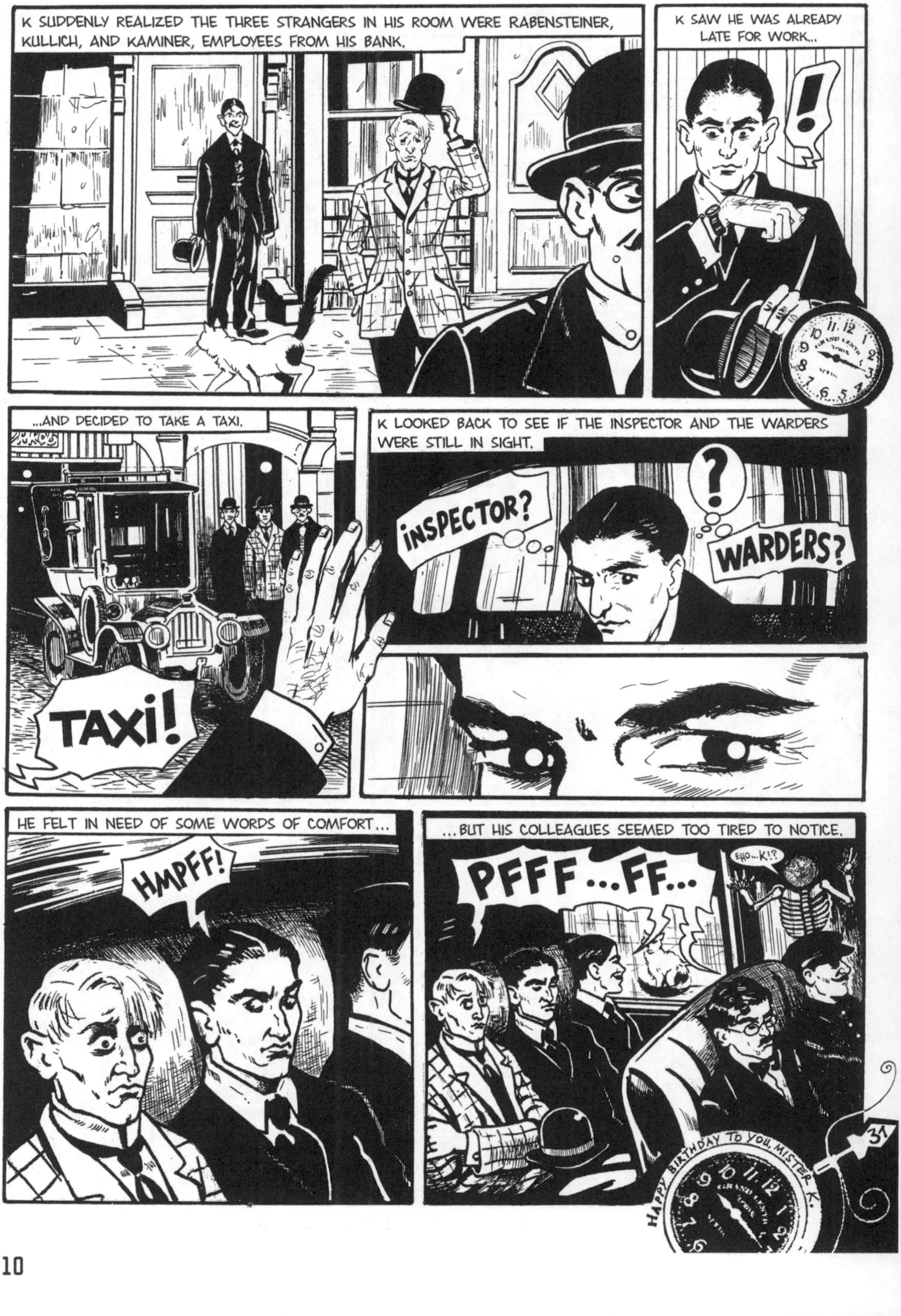
K SUDDENLY REALIZED THE THREE STRANGERS IN HIS ROOM WERE RABENSTEINER, KULLICH, AND KAMINER, EMPLOYEES FROM HIS BANK.
K SAW HE WAS ALREADY LATE FOR WORK...
!
...AND DECIDED TO TAKE A TAXI.
TAXI!
K LOOKED BACK TO SEE IF THE INSPECTOR AND THE WARDERS WERE STILL IN SIGHT.
INSPECTOR?
?
WARDERS?
HE FELT IN NEED OF SOME WORDS OF COMFORT...
HMPFF!
...BUT HIS COLLEAGUES SEEMED TOO TIRED TO NOTICE.
PFFF...FF...
EHO...K!?
HAPPY BIRTHDAY TO YOU, MISTER K.
31

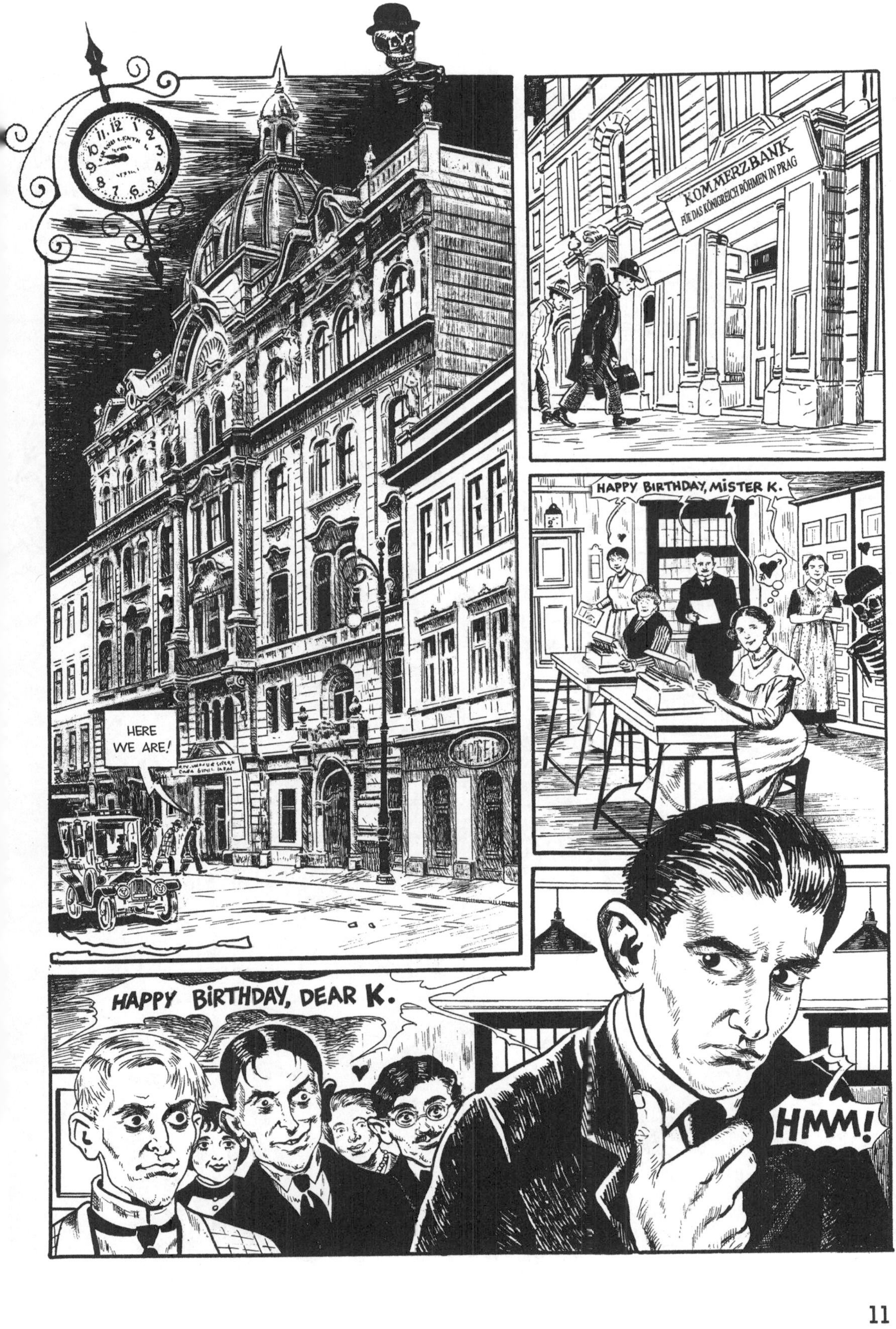
HERE WE ARE!
KOMMERZBANK
FÜR DAS KÖNIGREICH BÖHMEN IN PRAG
HAPPY BIRTHDAY, MISTER K.
HAPPY BIRTHDAY, DEAR K.
HMM!

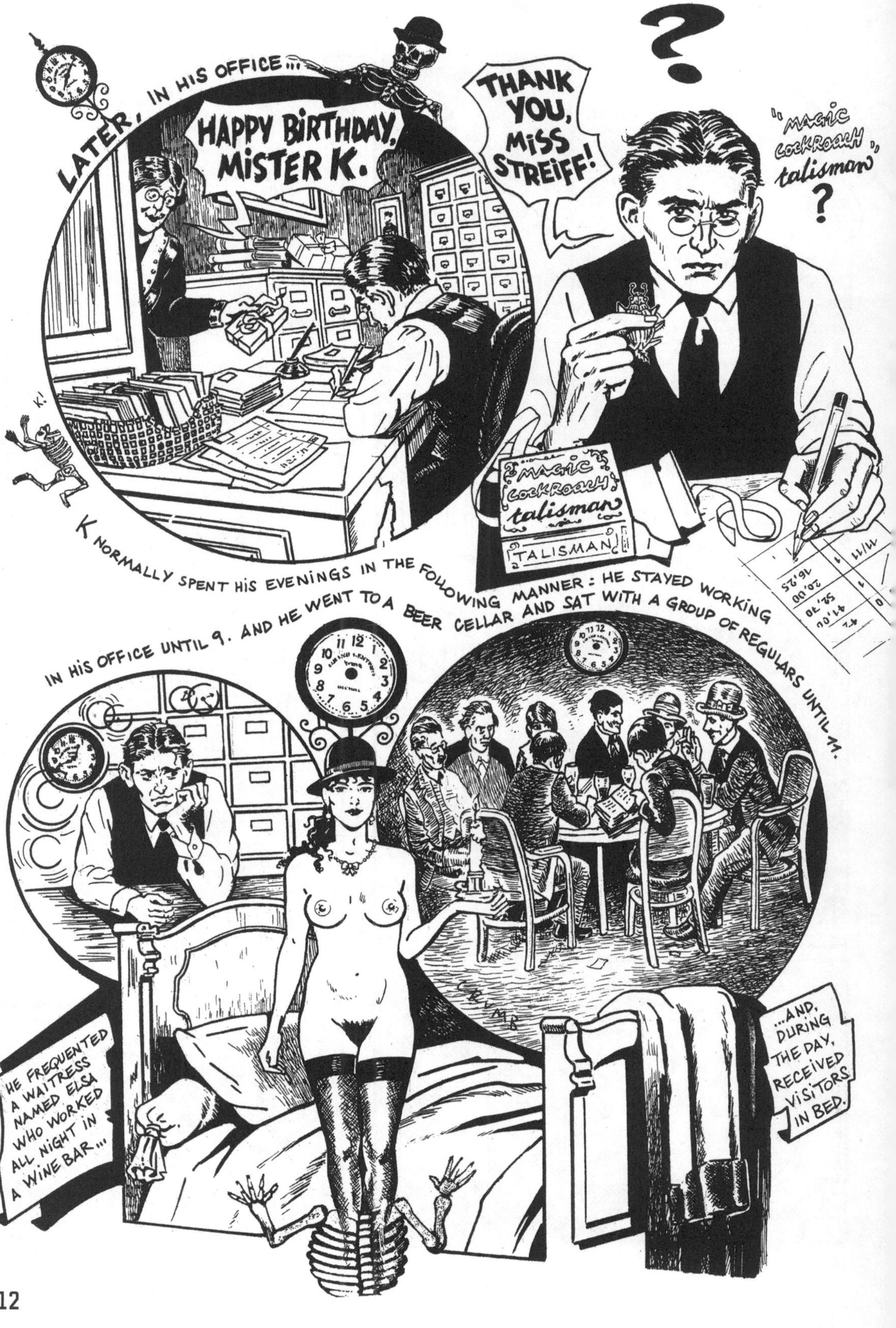
LATER, IN HIS OFFICE...
HAPPY BIRTHDAY, MISTER K.
THANK YOU, MISS STREIFF!
?
"MAGIC COCKROACH" talisman?
K!
MAGIC COCKROACH talisman
TALISMAN
K NORMALLY SPENT HIS EVENINGS IN THE FOLLOWING MANNER: HE STAYED WORKING IN HIS OFFICE UNTIL 9. AND HE WENT TO A BEER CELLAR AND SAT WITH A GROUP OF REGULARS UNTIL 11.
HE FREQUENTED A WAITRESS NAMED ELSA WHO WORKED ALL NIGHT IN A WINE BAR...
...AND, DURING THE DAY, RECEIVED VISITORS IN BED.
CRUMB

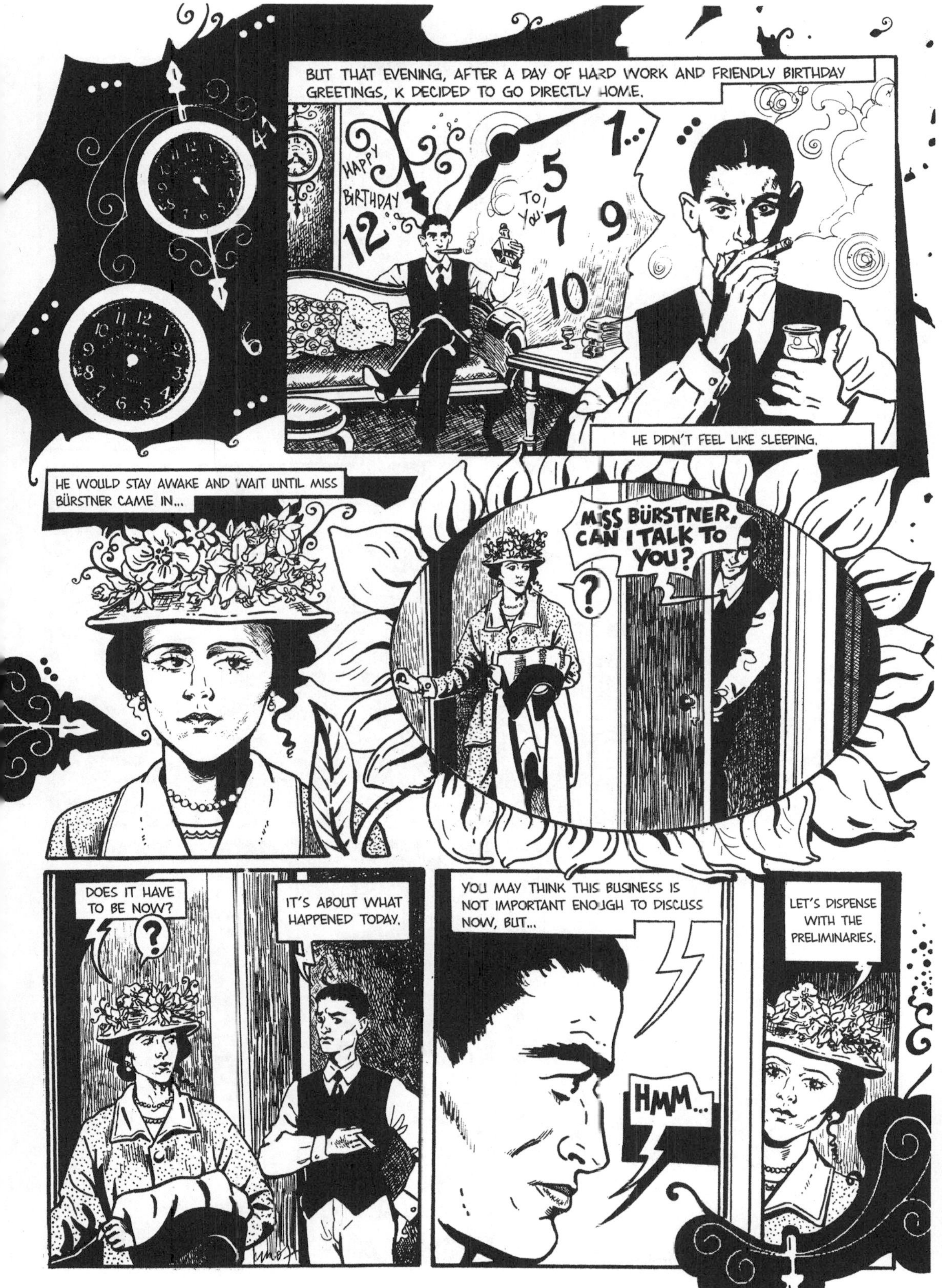
BUT THAT EVENING, AFTER A DAY OF HARD WORK AND FRIENDLY BIRTHDAY GREETINGS, K DECIDED TO GO DIRECTLY HOME.
HAPPY BIRTHDAY
TO YOU
HE DIDN'T FEEL LIKE SLEEPING.
HE WOULD STAY AWAKE AND WAIT UNTIL MISS BÜRSTNER CAME IN...
MISS BÜRSTNER, CAN I TALK TO YOU?
?
DOES IT HAVE TO BE NOW?
?
IT'S ABOUT WHAT HAPPENED TODAY.
YOU MAY THINK THIS BUSINESS IS NOT IMPORTANT ENOUGH TO DISCUSS NOW, BUT...
HMM...
LET'S DISPENSE WITH THE PRELIMINARIES.

THIS MORNING THERE WERE PEOPLE IN YOUR ROOM!
IN MY ROOM!?
!
YES! MY THINGS HAVE BEEN MOVED AROUND.
!!?
I FORBID YOU TO ENTER MY ROOM WHEN I'M NOT HERE!
...
HMM
BUT IT WASN'T ME. IT WAS THE... INQUIRY COMMISSION.
INQUIRY COMMISSION? FOR YOU?
YOU THINK I'M INNOCENT?
INNOCENT? I CAN'T SAY. AN INQUIRY COMMISSION IS USUALLY FOR IMPORTANT CRIMINALS.
BUT YOU'RE AT LIBERTY.
...HMM!
THERE'S SOMETHING ATTRACTIVE ABOUT A COURT OF LAW, DON'T YOU THINK? WHAT WAS IT LIKE THIS MORNING?
I'LL SHOW YOU.

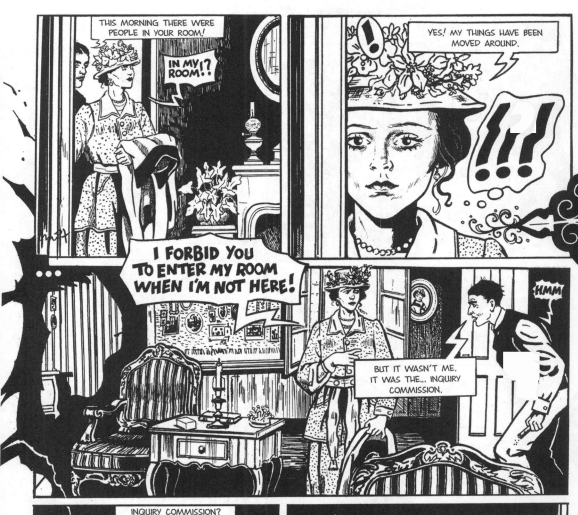

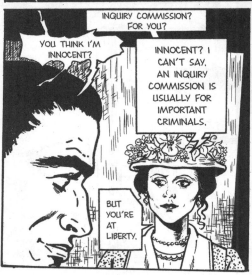

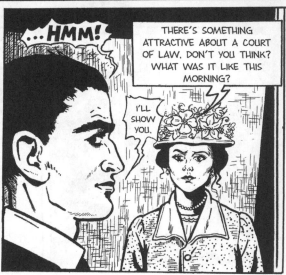

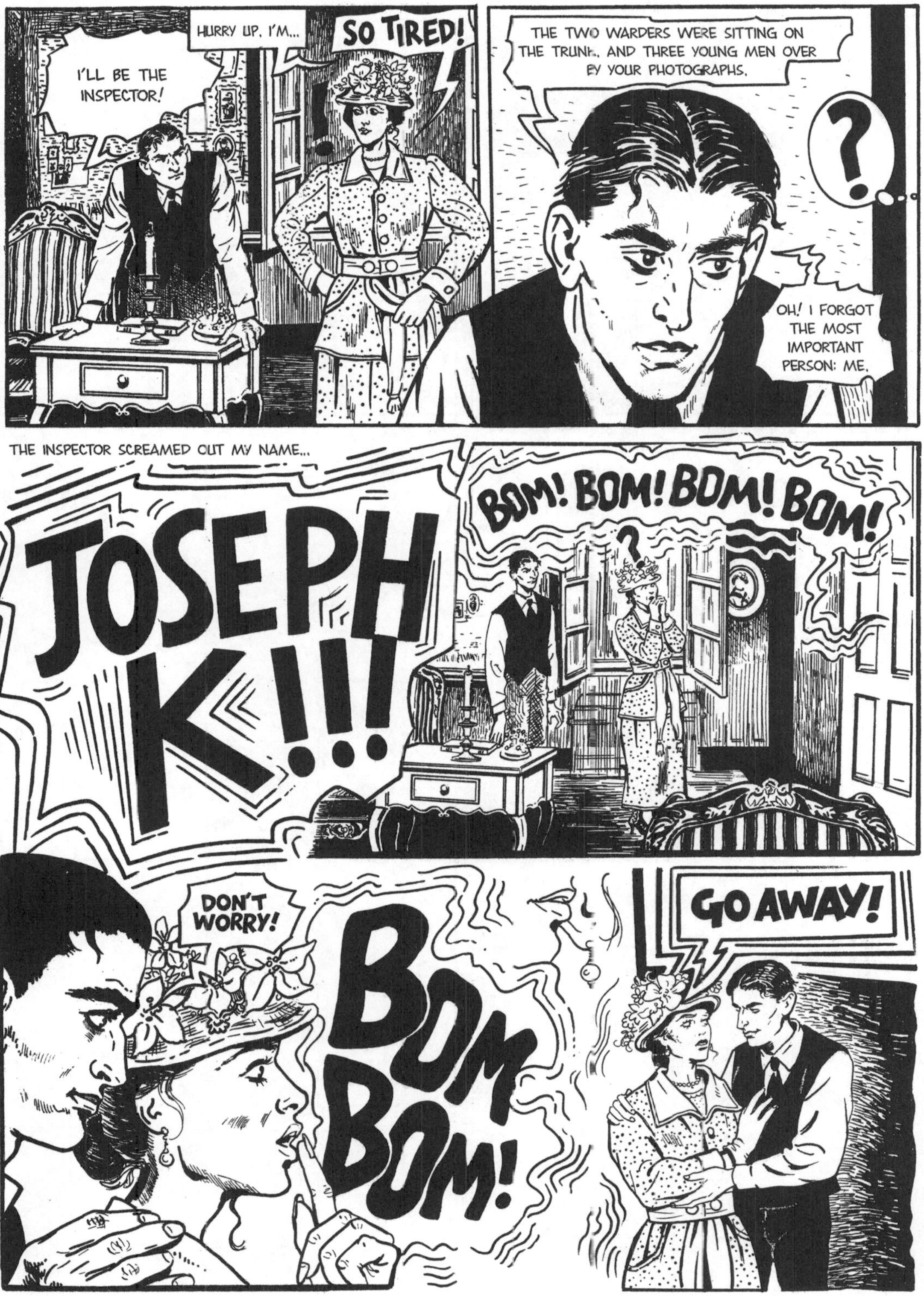
I'LL BE THE INSPECTOR!
HURRY UP, I'M...
SO TIRED!
THE TWO WARDERS WERE SITTING ON THE TRUNK, AND THREE YOUNG MEN OVER BY YOUR PHOTOGRAPHS.
?
OH! I FORGOT THE MOST IMPORTANT PERSON: ME.
THE INSPECTOR SCREAMED OUT MY NAME...
JOSEPH K!!!
BOM! BOM! BOM! BOM!
?
DON'T WORRY!
BOM BOM!
GO AWAY!

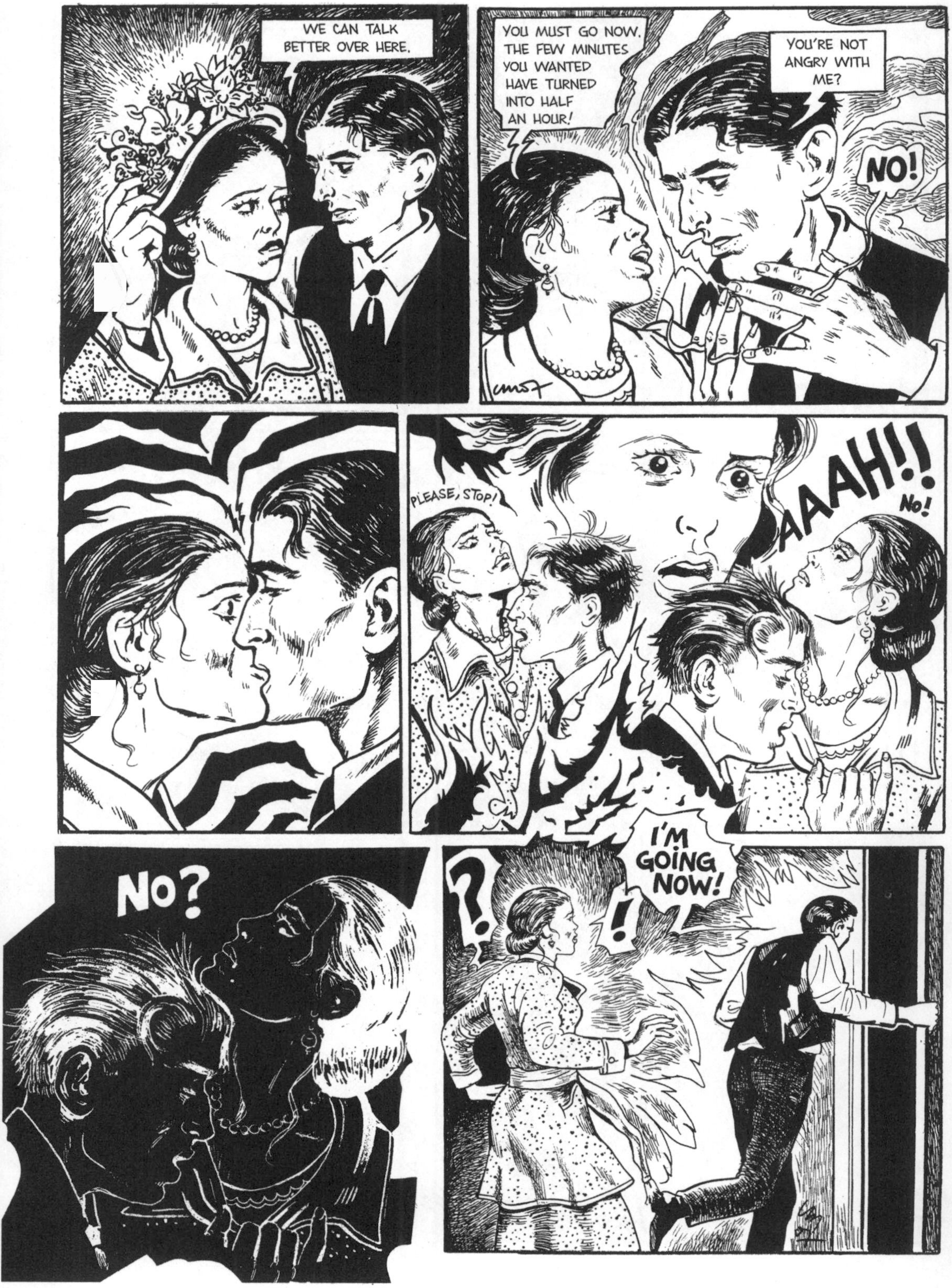
WE CAN TALK BETTER OVER HERE.
YOU MUST GO NOW. THE FEW MINUTES YOU WANTED HAVE TURNED INTO HALF AN HOUR!
YOU'RE NOT ANGRY WITH ME?
NO!
PLEASE, STOP!
AAAH!!
NO!
NO?
?
!
I'M GOING NOW!

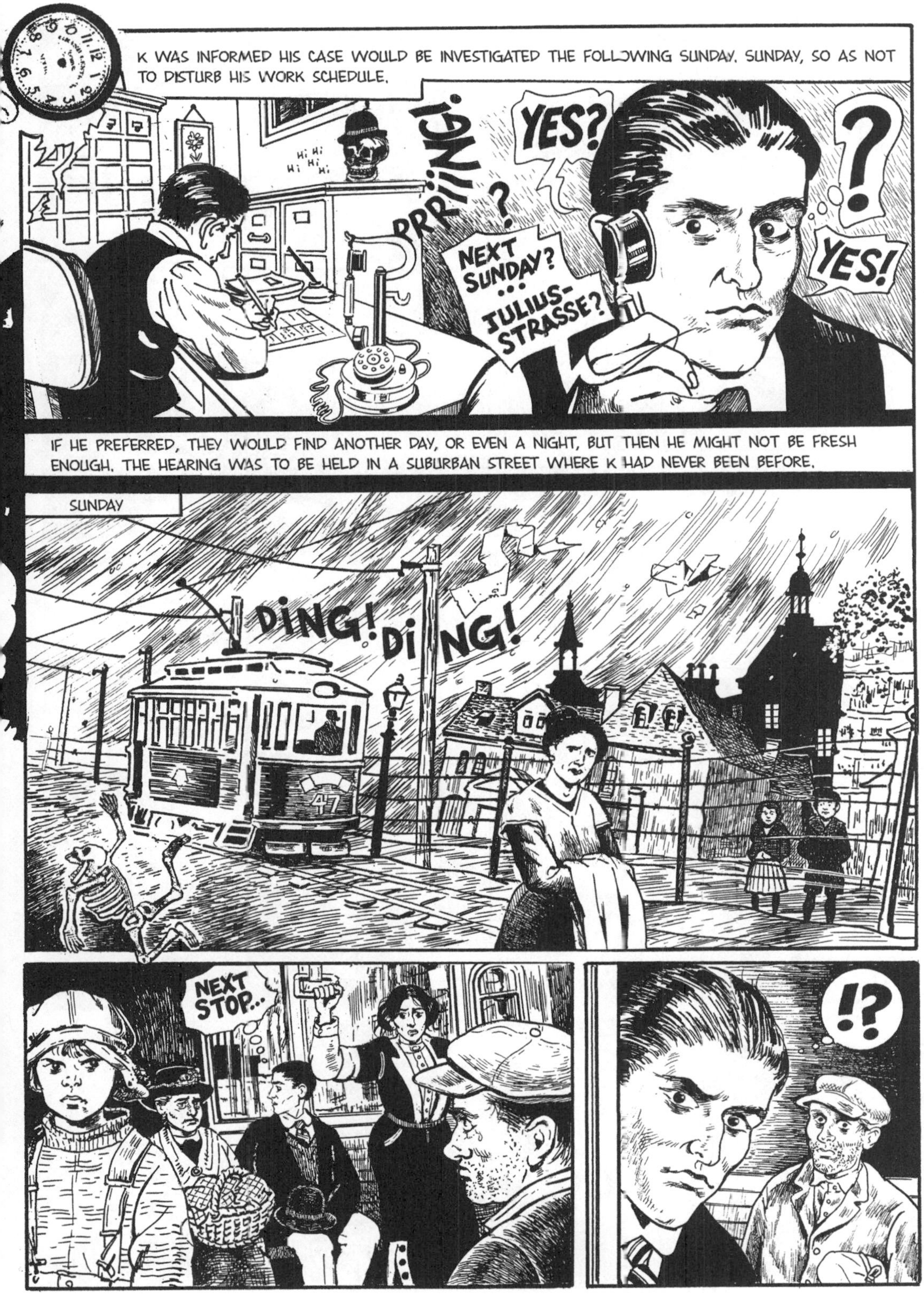
K WAS INFORMED HIS CASE WOULD BE INVESTIGATED THE FOLLOWING SUNDAY. SUNDAY, SO AS NOT TO DISTURB HIS WORK SCHEDULE.
HI HI HI HI HI
PRRÏÏNG!
YES?
?
NEXT SUNDAY? ... JULIUS-STRASSE?
?
YES!
IF HE PREFERRED, THEY WOULD FIND ANOTHER DAY, OR EVEN A NIGHT, BUT THEN HE MIGHT NOT BE FRESH ENOUGH. THE HEARING WAS TO BE HELD IN A SUBURBAN STREET WHERE K HAD NEVER BEEN BEFORE.
SUNDAY
DING! DING!
47
NEXT STOP...
!?

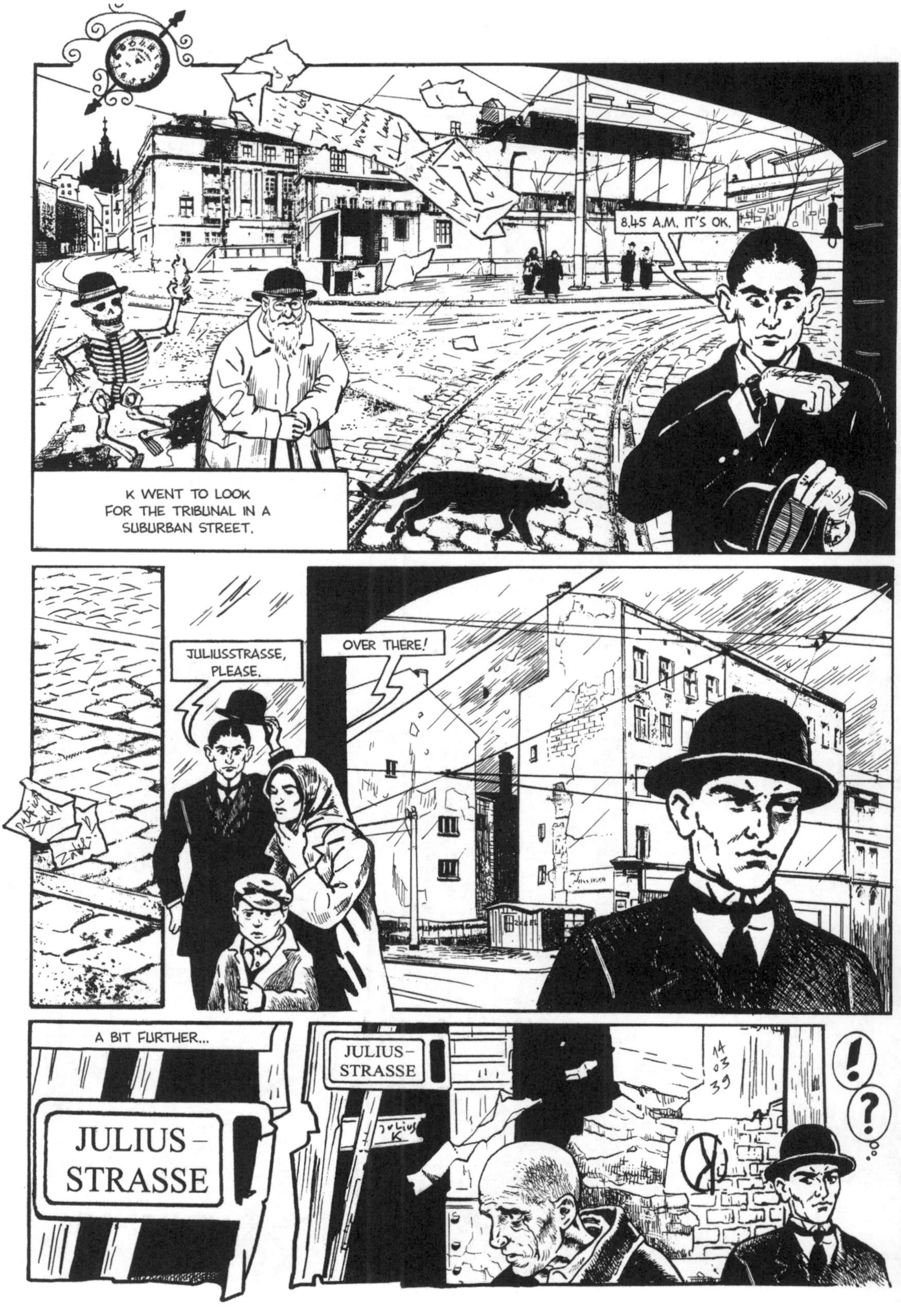
8.45 A.M. IT'S OK.
K WENT TO LOOK FOR THE TRIBUNAL IN A SUBURBAN STREET.
JULIUSSTRASSE, PLEASE.
OVER THERE!
A BIT FURTHER...
JULIUS-STRASSE
JULIUS-STRASSE
14 03 39
!
?

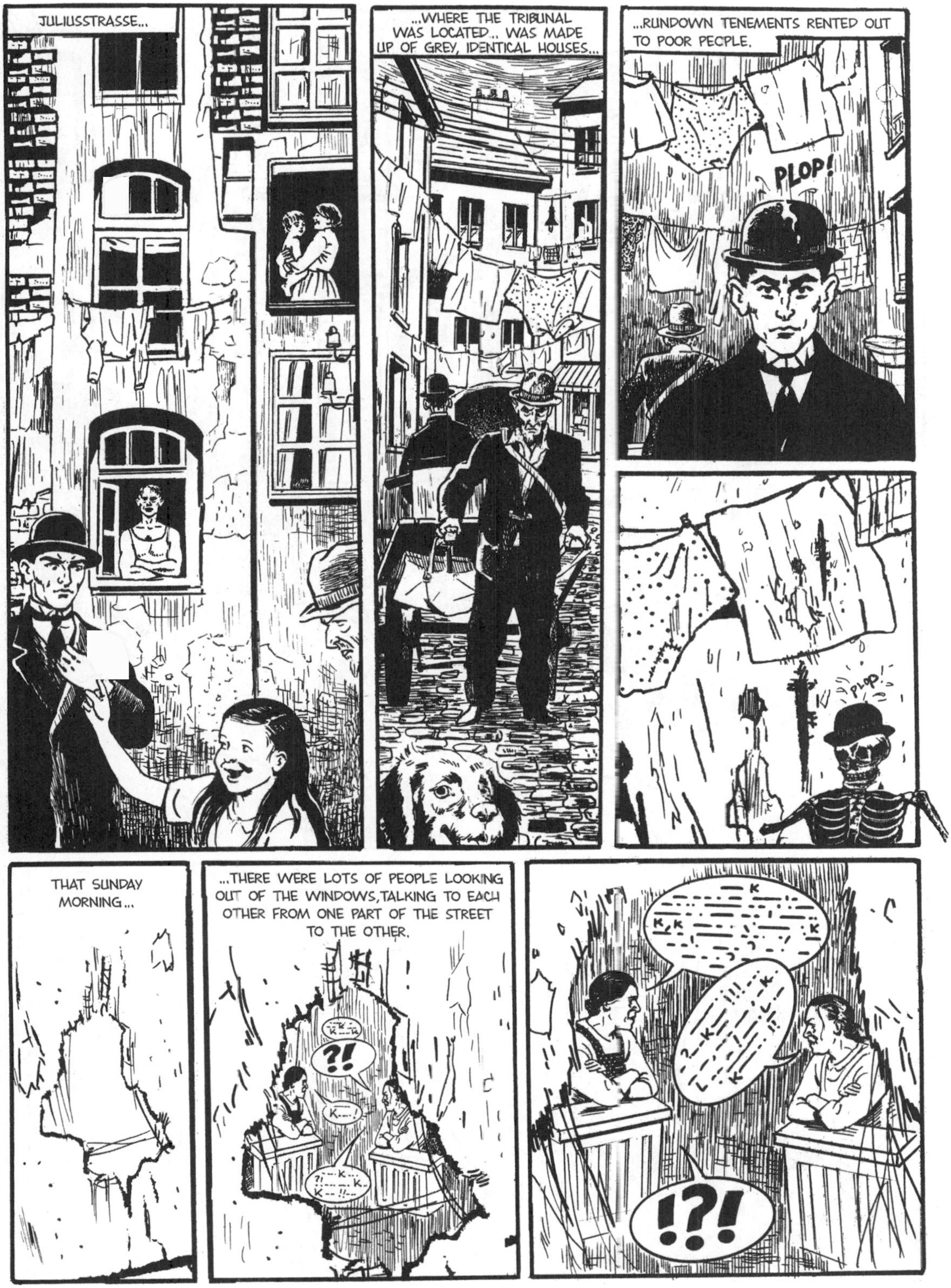
JULIUSSTRASSE...
...WHERE THE TRIBUNAL WAS LOCATED... WAS MADE UP OF GREY, IDENTICAL HOUSES...
...RUNDOWN TENEMENTS RENTED OUT TO POOR PEOPLE.
PLOP!
PLOP!
THAT SUNDAY MORNING...
...THERE WERE LOTS OF PEOPLE LOOKING OUT OF THE WINDOWS, TALKING TO EACH OTHER FROM ONE PART OF THE STREET TO THE OTHER.
?!
!?!

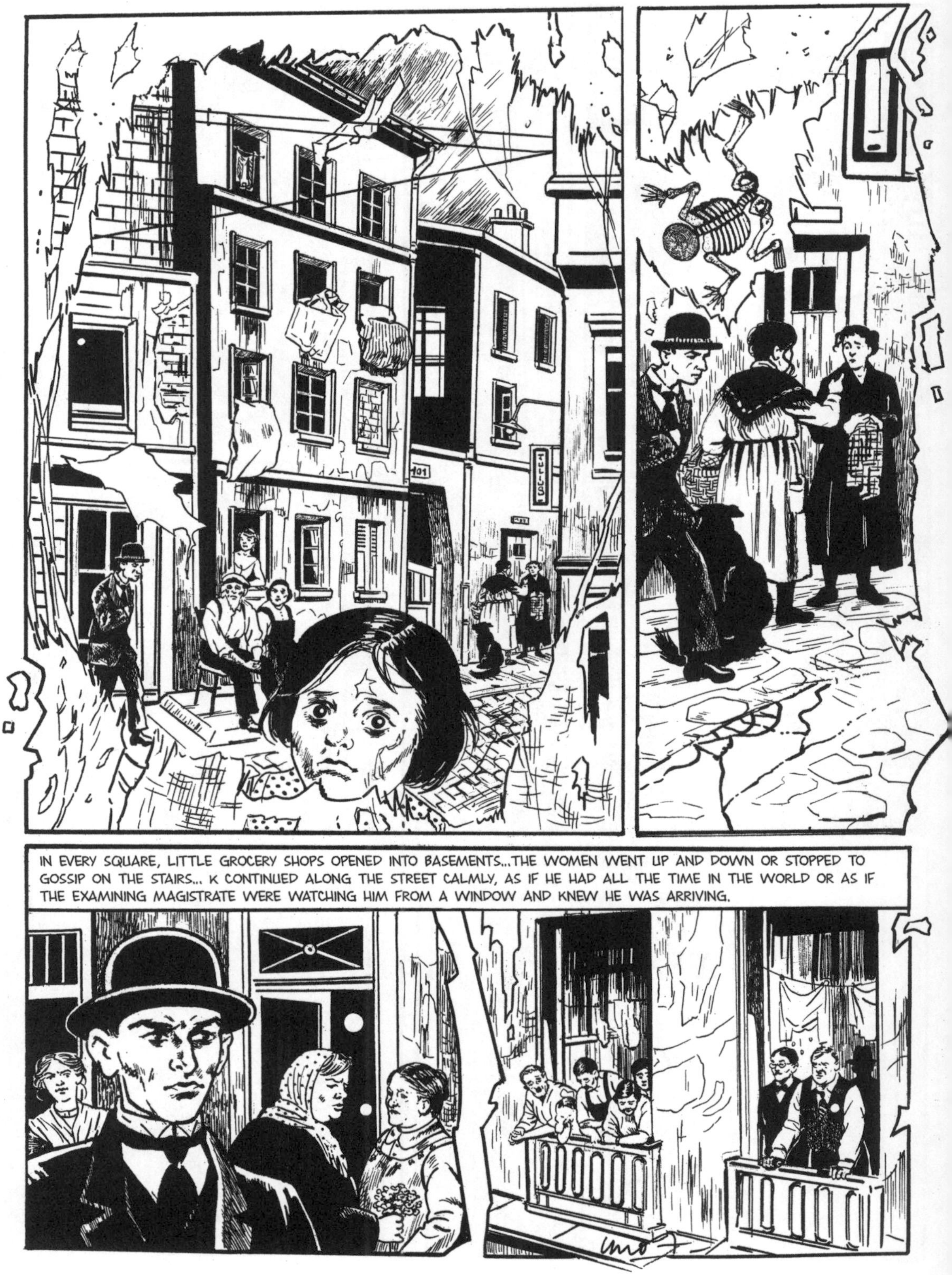
IN EVERY SQUARE, LITTLE GROCERY SHOPS OPENED INTO BASEMENTS...THE WOMEN WENT UP AND DOWN OR STOPPED TO GOSSIP ON THE STAIRS... K CONTINUED ALONG THE STREET CALMLY, AS IF HE HAD ALL THE TIME IN THE WORLD OR AS IF THE EXAMINING MAGISTRATE WERE WATCHING HIM FROM A WINDOW AND KNEW HE WAS ARRIVING.

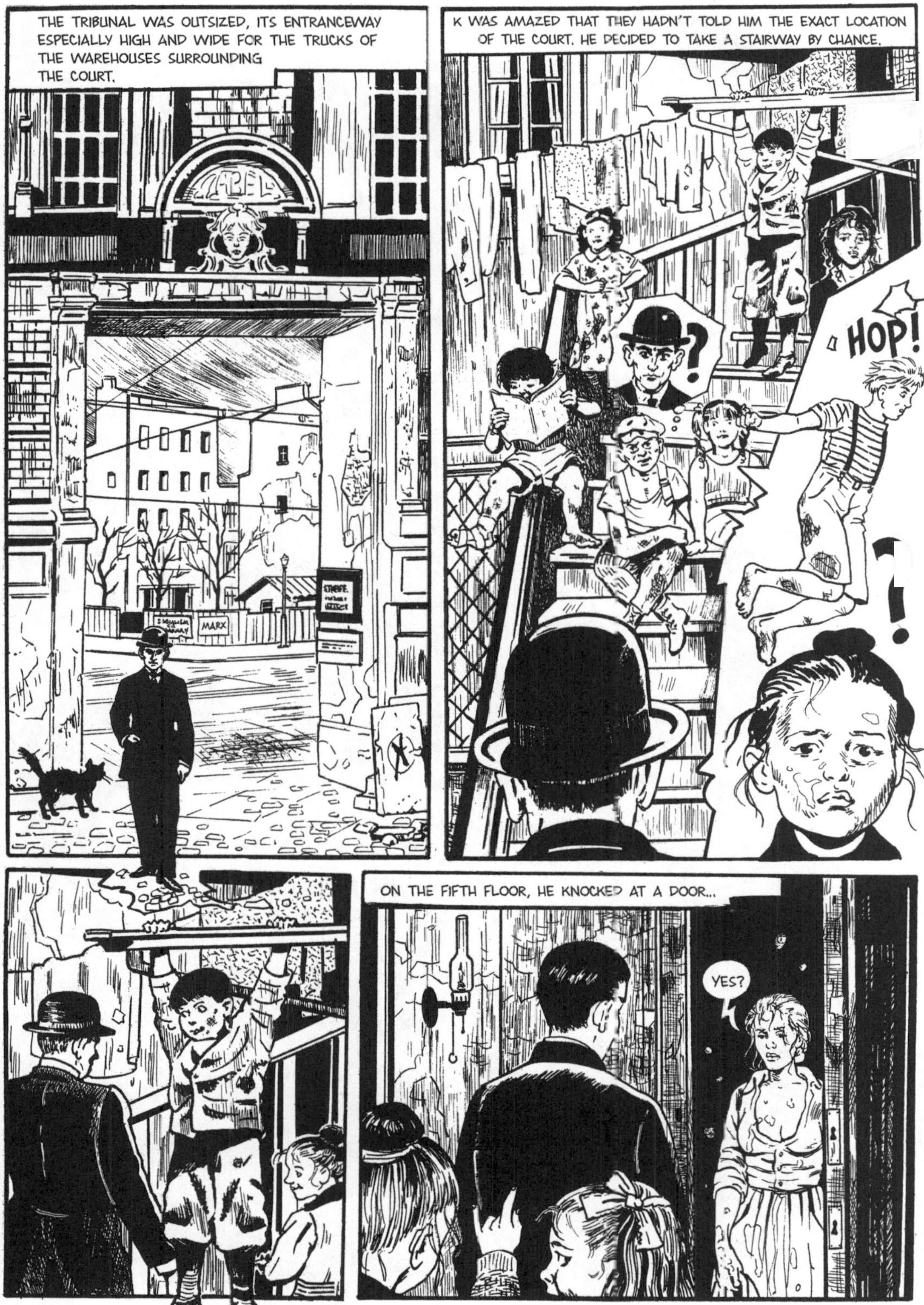
THE TRIBUNAL WAS OUTSIZED, ITS ENTRANCEWAY ESPECIALLY HIGH AND WIDE FOR THE TRUCKS OF THE WAREHOUSES SURROUNDING THE COURT.
MARX
K WAS AMAZED THAT THEY HADN'T TOLD HIM THE EXACT LOCATION OF THE COURT. HE DECIDED TO TAKE A STAIRWAY BY CHANCE.
?
HOP!
?
!
ON THE FIFTH FLOOR, HE KNOCKED AT A DOOR...
YES?

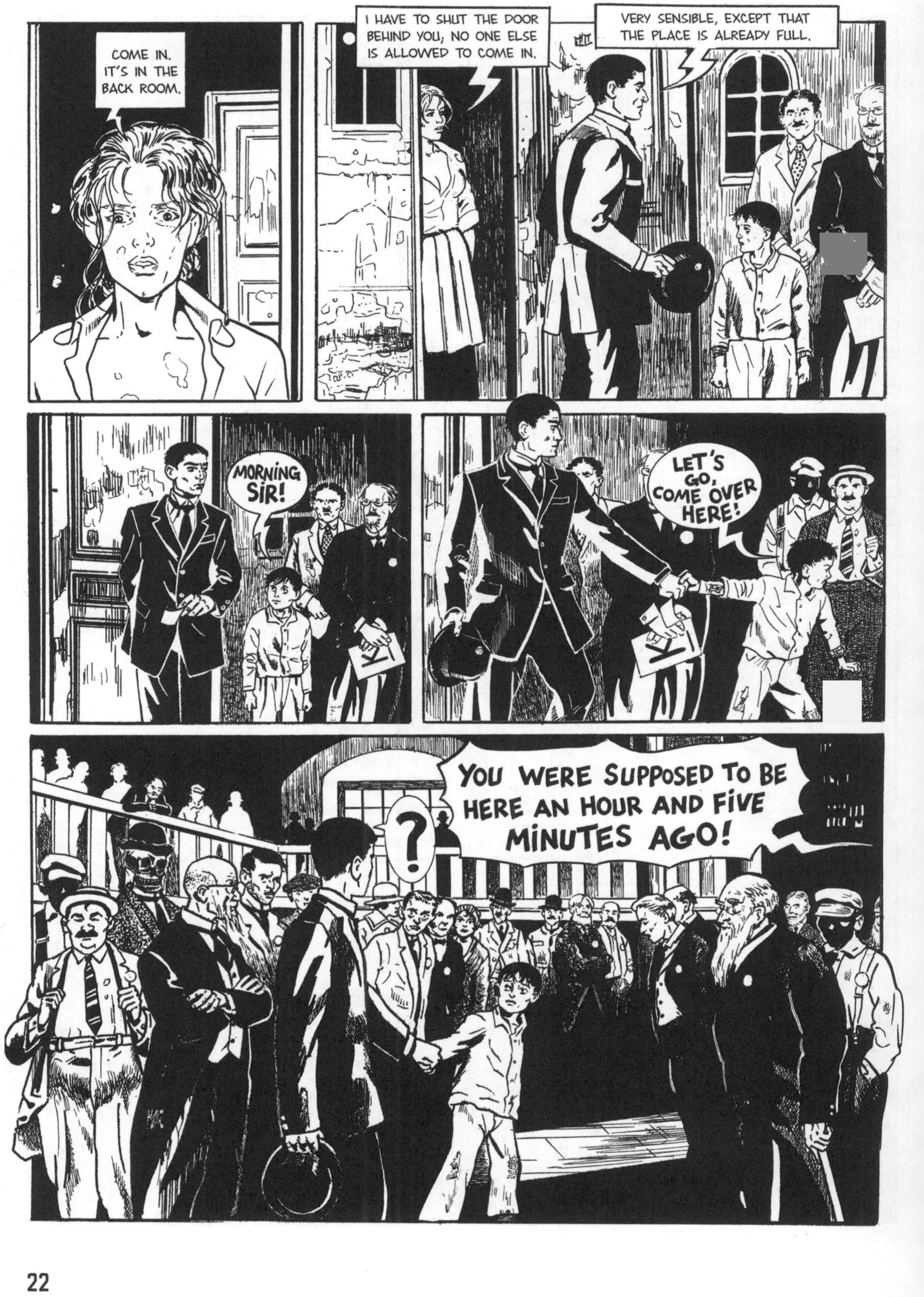
COME IN. IT'S IN THE BACK ROOM.
I HAVE TO SHUT THE DOOR BEHIND YOU; NO ONE ELSE IS ALLOWED TO COME IN.
VERY SENSIBLE, EXCEPT THAT THE PLACE IS ALREADY FULL.
MORNING SIR!
LET'S GO, COME OVER HERE!
?
YOU WERE SUPPOSED TO BE HERE AN HOUR AND FIVE MINUTES AGO!

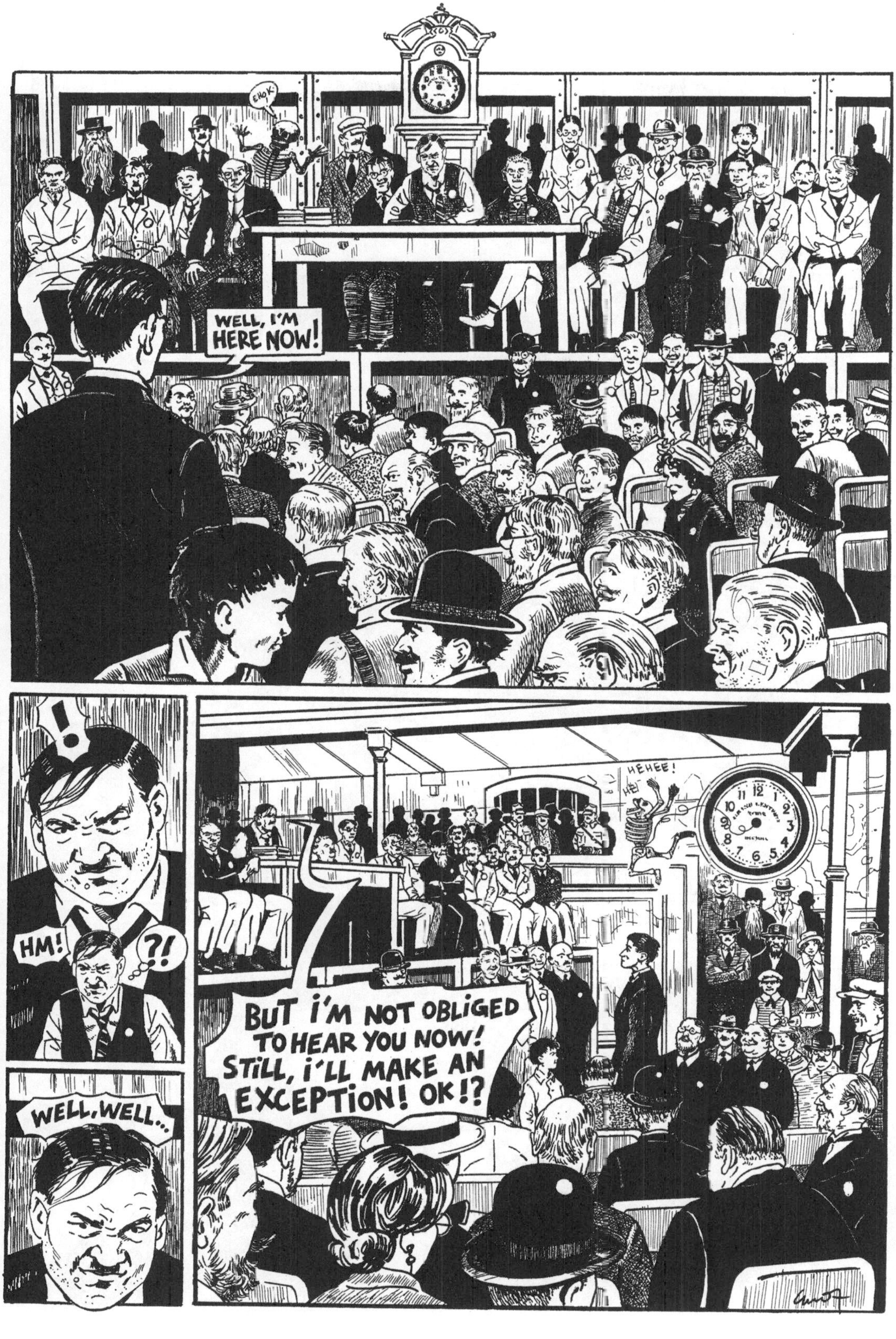
EHOK!
WELL, I'M HERE NOW!
!
HM!
?!
HEHEE!
HE!
BUT I'M NOT OBLIGED TO HEAR YOU NOW! STILL, I'LL MAKE AN EXCEPTION! OK!?
WELL, WELL...

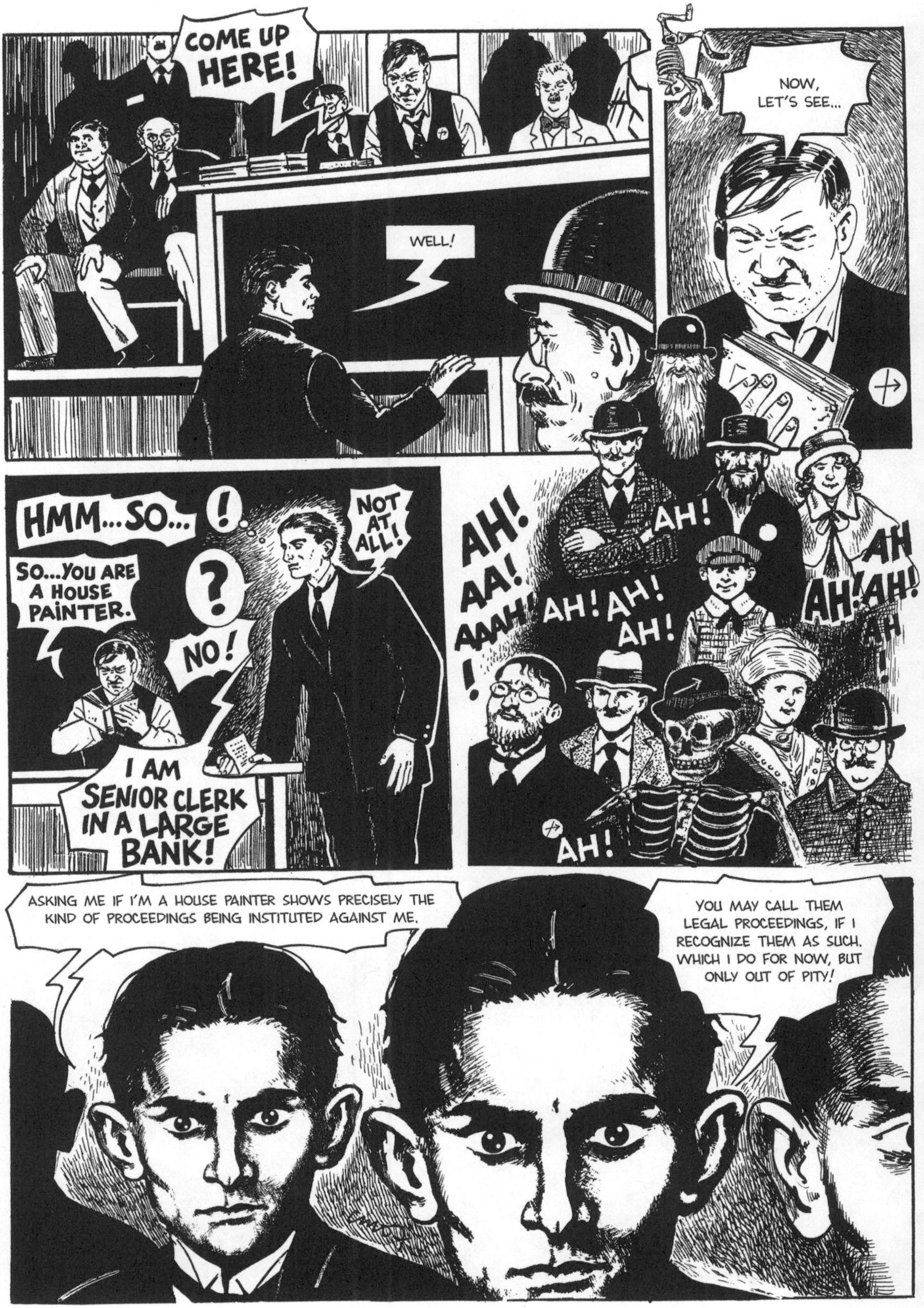
COME UP HERE!
WELL!
NOW, LET'S SEE...
HMM...SO...
!
SO...YOU ARE A HOUSE PAINTER.
?
NOT AT ALL!
NO!
I AM SENIOR CLERK IN A LARGE BANK!
AH! AA! AAAH!
AH!
AH! AH! AH!
AH AH! AH! AH!
AH!
ASKING ME IF I'M A HOUSE PAINTER SHOWS PRECISELY THE KIND OF PROCEEDINGS BEING INSTITUTED AGAINST ME.
YOU MAY CALL THEM LEGAL PROCEEDINGS, IF I RECOGNIZE THEM AS SUCH. WHICH I DO FOR NOW, BUT ONLY OUT OF PITY!

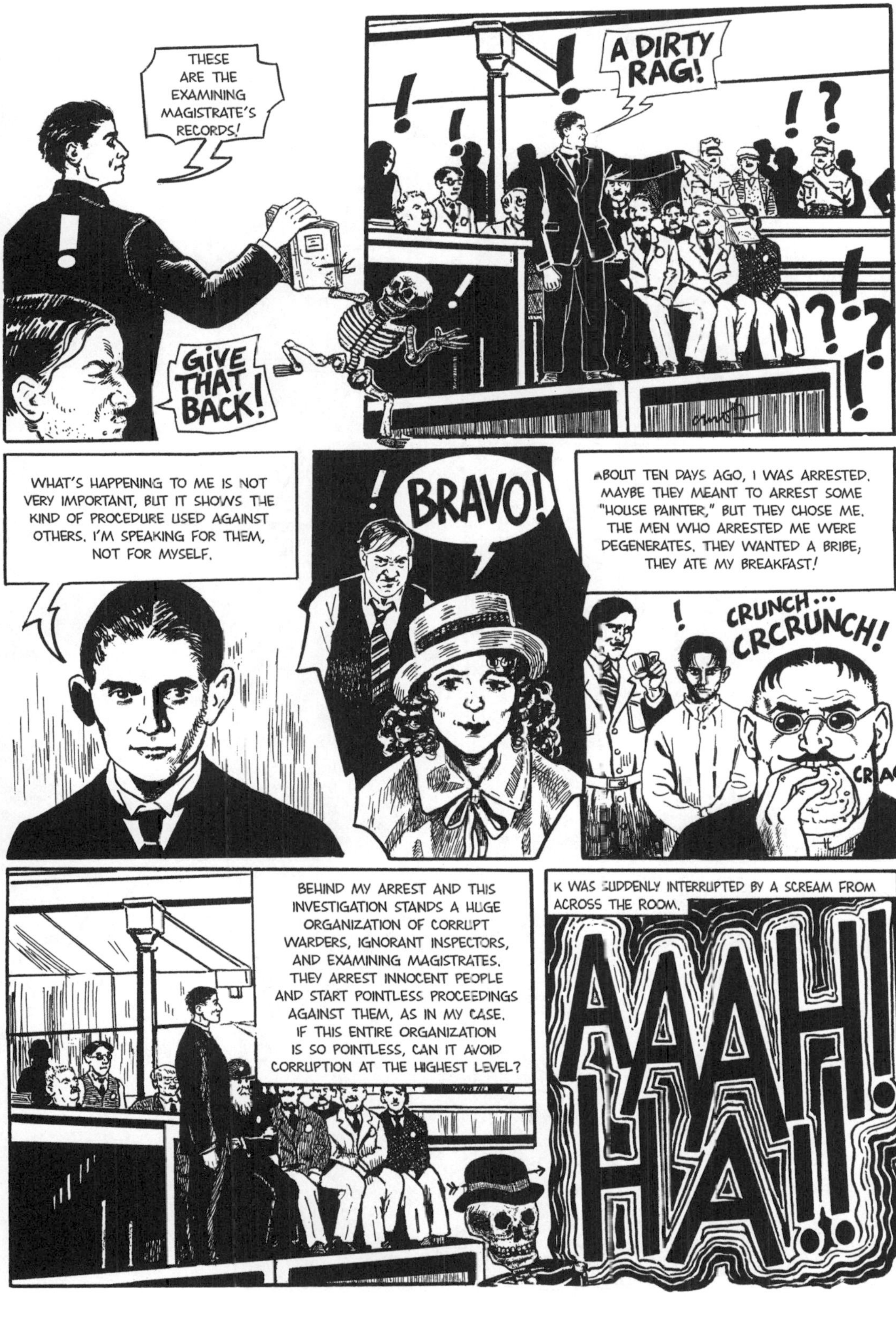
THESE ARE THE EXAMINING MAGISTRATE'S RECORDS!
GIVE THAT BACK!
A DIRTY RAG!
WHAT'S HAPPENING TO ME IS NOT VERY IMPORTANT, BUT IT SHOWS THE KIND OF PROCEDURE USED AGAINST OTHERS. I'M SPEAKING FOR THEM, NOT FOR MYSELF.
BRAVO!
ABOUT TEN DAYS AGO, I WAS ARRESTED. MAYBE THEY MEANT TO ARREST SOME "HOUSE PAINTER," BUT THEY CHOSE ME. THE MEN WHO ARRESTED ME WERE DEGENERATES. THEY WANTED A BRIBE; THEY ATE MY BREAKFAST!
CRUNCH... CRCRUNCH!
CRAC
BEHIND MY ARREST AND THIS INVESTIGATION STANDS A HUGE ORGANIZATION OF CORRUPT WARDERS, IGNORANT INSPECTORS, AND EXAMINING MAGISTRATES. THEY ARREST INNOCENT PEOPLE AND START POINTLESS PROCEEDINGS AGAINST THEM, AS IN MY CASE. IF THIS ENTIRE ORGANIZATION IS SO POINTLESS, CAN IT AVOID CORRUPTION AT THE HIGHEST LEVEL?
K WAS SUDDENLY INTERRUPTED BY A SCREAM FROM ACROSS THE ROOM.
AAAH! HA!!!

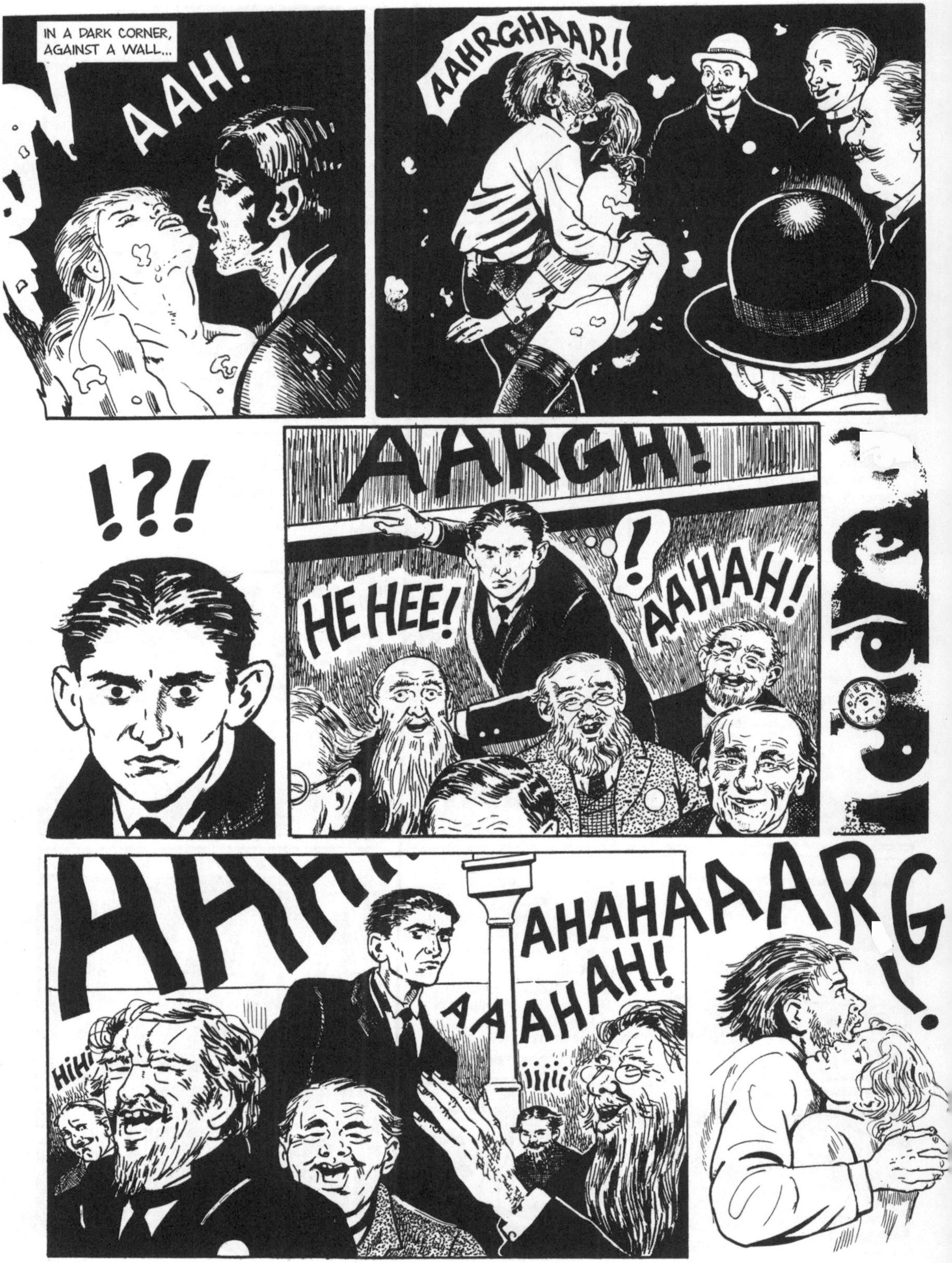
IN A DARK CORNER, AGAINST A WALL...
AAH!
AAHRGHAAR!
!?!
AARGH!
HE HEE!
?
AAHAH!
AAHAHAAARG!
AHAHA
AAAHAH!
HiHi
iiiii

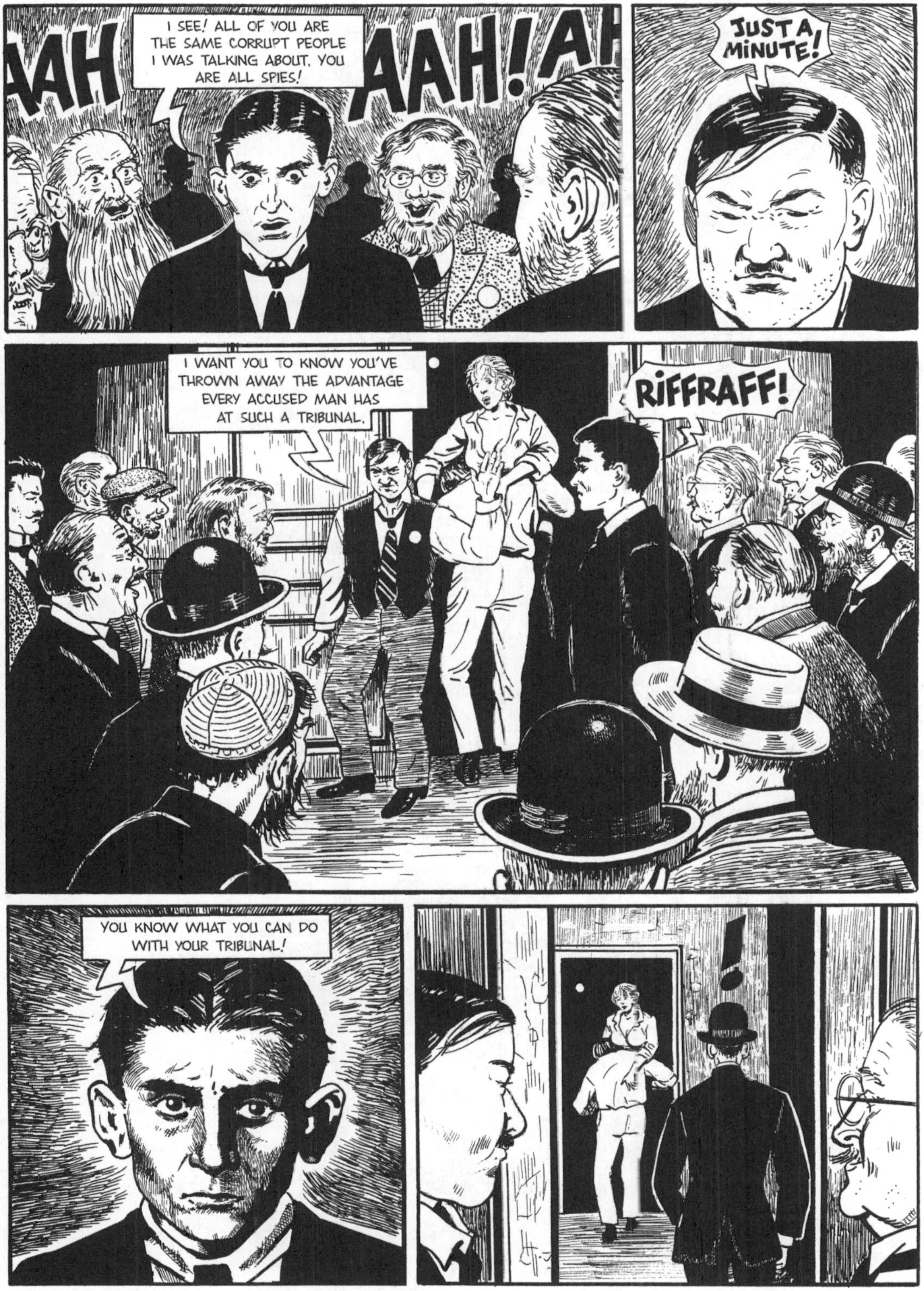
AAH
I SEE! ALL OF YOU ARE THE SAME CORRUPT PEOPLE I WAS TALKING ABOUT. YOU ARE ALL SPIES!
AAH!A
JUST A MINUTE!
I WANT YOU TO KNOW YOU'VE THROWN AWAY THE ADVANTAGE EVERY ACCUSED MAN HAS AT SUCH A TRIBUNAL.
RIFFRAFF!
YOU KNOW WHAT YOU CAN DO WITH YOUR TRIBUNAL!
!

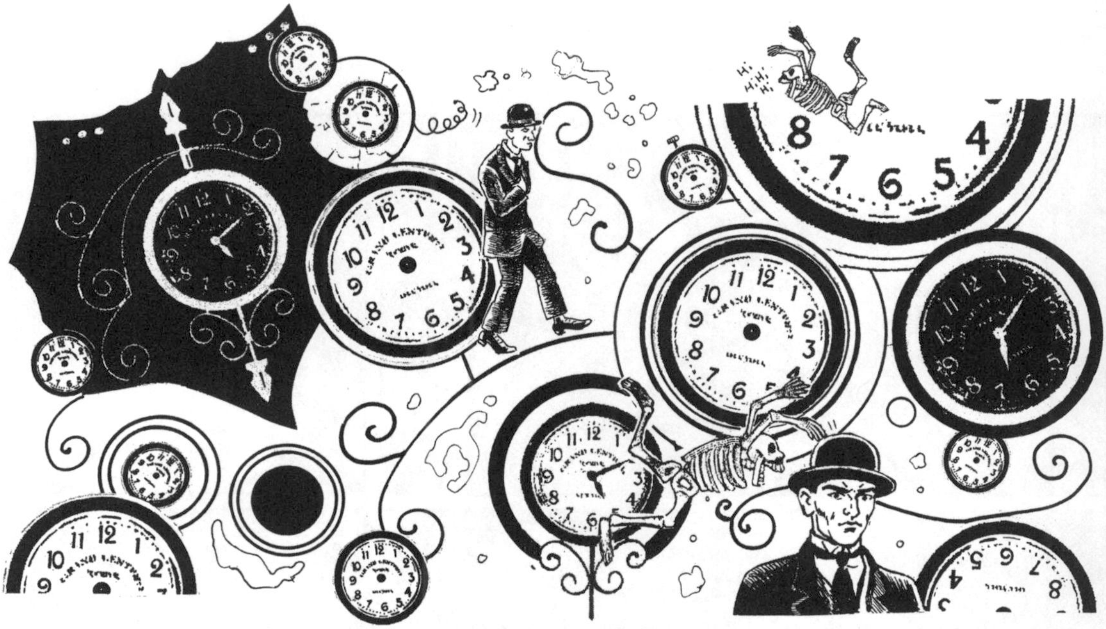

K WAITED FOR A NEW CONVOCATION ALL THE NEXT WEEK. WHEN IT HAD NOT COME BY SATURDAY EVENING, HE DECIDED TO GO AGAIN ON SUNDAY.

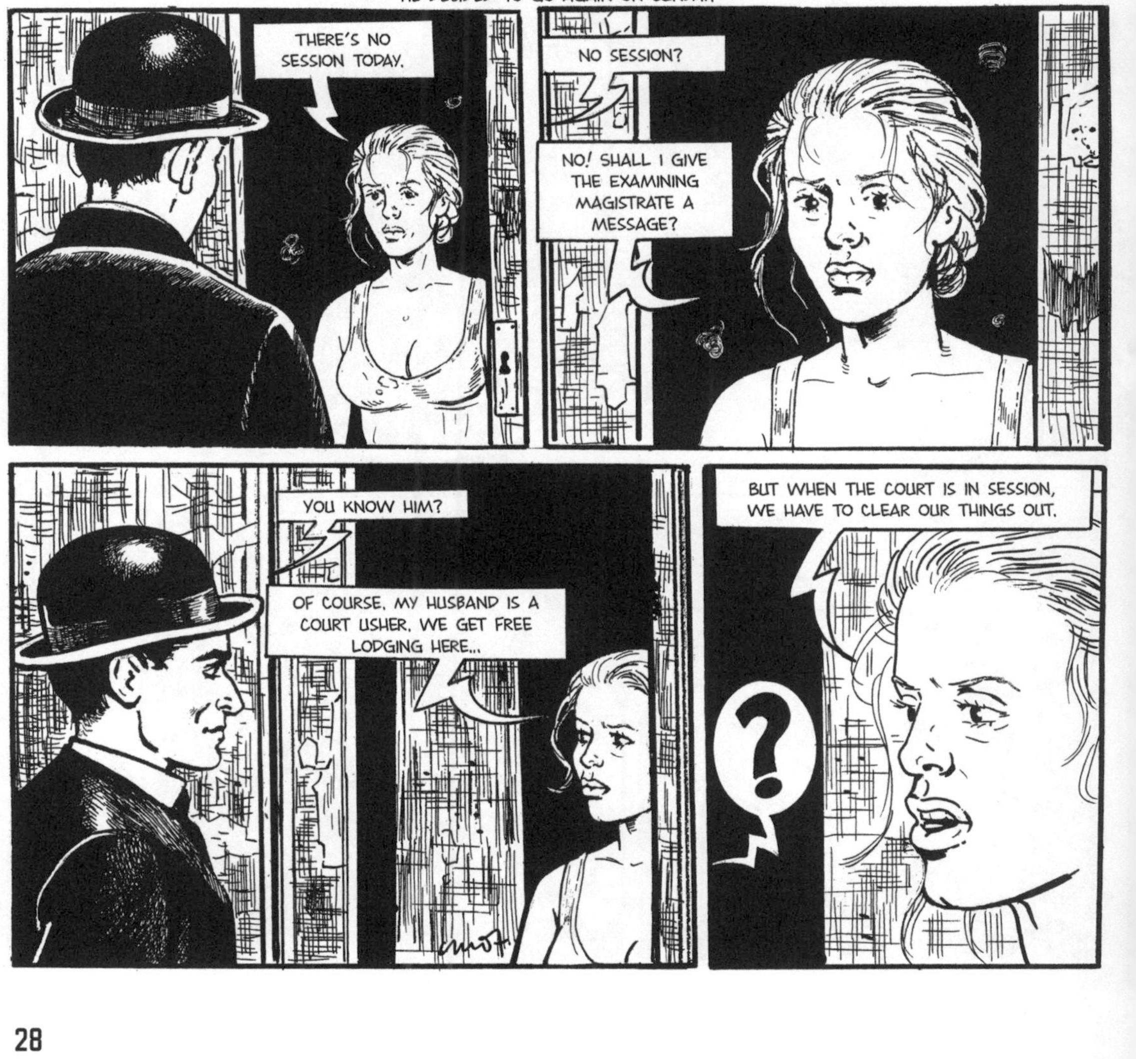
THERE'S NO SESSION TODAY.
NO SESSION?
NO! SHALL I GIVE THE EXAMINING MAGISTRATE A MESSAGE?
YOU KNOW HIM?
OF COURSE. MY HUSBAND IS A COURT USHER. WE GET FREE LODGING HERE...
BUT WHEN THE COURT IS IN SESSION, WE HAVE TO CLEAR OUR THINGS OUT.
?

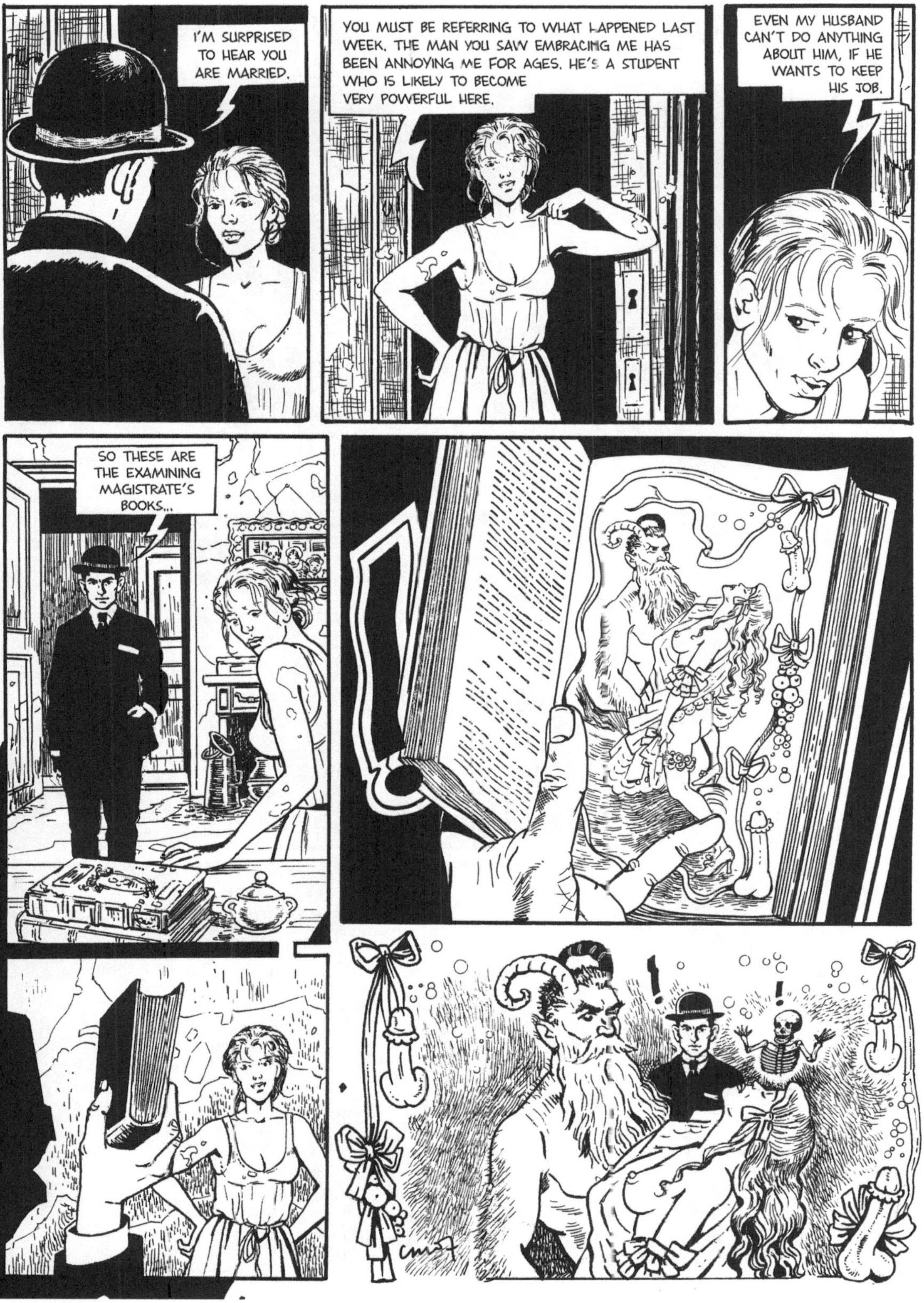

I'M SURPRISED TO HEAR YOU ARE MARRIED.
YOU MUST BE REFERRING TO WHAT HAPPENED LAST WEEK. THE MAN YOU SAW EMBRACING ME HAS BEEN ANNOYING ME FOR AGES. HE'S A STUDENT WHO IS LIKELY TO BECOME VERY POWERFUL HERE.
EVEN MY HUSBAND CAN'T DO ANYTHING ABOUT HIM, IF HE WANTS TO KEEP HIS JOB.
SO THESE ARE THE EXAMINING MAGISTRATE'S BOOKS...
!
!

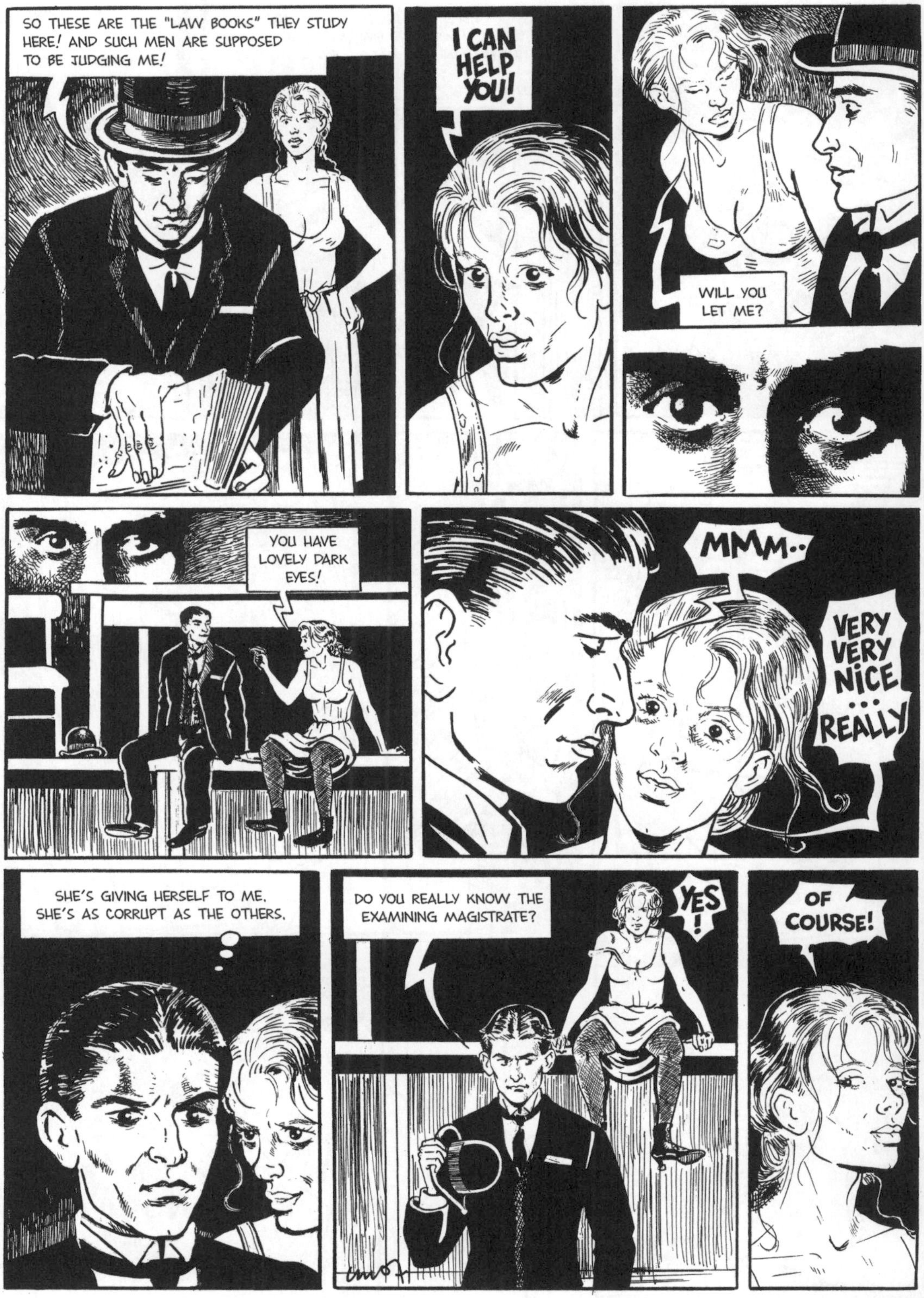
SO THESE ARE THE "LAW BOOKS" THEY STUDY HERE! AND SUCH MEN ARE SUPPOSED TO BE JUDGING ME!
I CAN HELP YOU!
WILL YOU LET ME?
YOU HAVE LOVELY DARK EYES!
MMM..
VERY VERY NICE ... REALLY
SHE'S GIVING HERSELF TO ME. SHE'S AS CORRUPT AS THE OTHERS.
DO YOU REALLY KNOW THE EXAMINING MAGISTRATE?
YES!
OF COURSE!

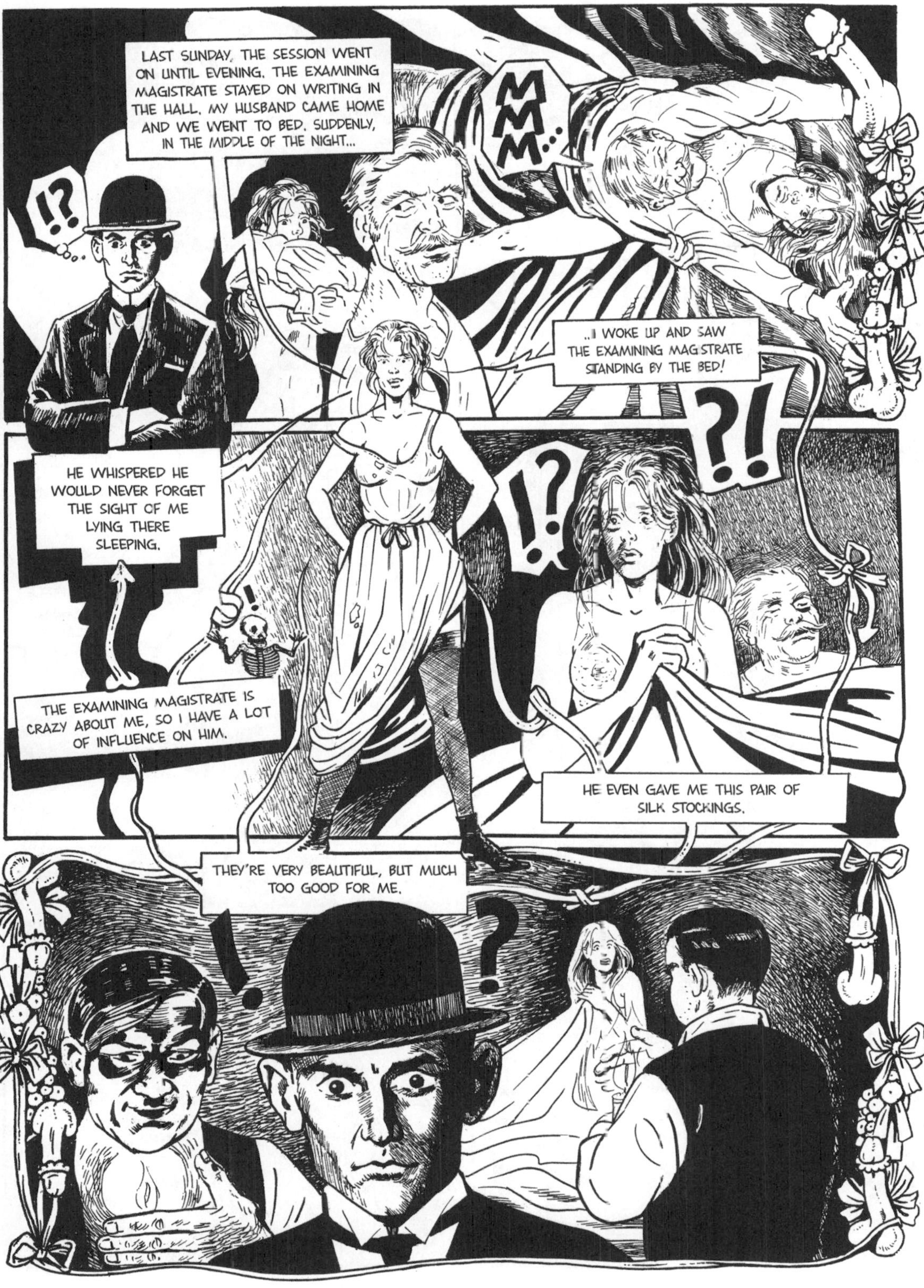
LAST SUNDAY, THE SESSION WENT ON UNTIL EVENING. THE EXAMINING MAGISTRATE STAYED ON WRITING IN THE HALL. MY HUSBAND CAME HOME AND WE WENT TO BED. SUDDENLY, IN THE MIDDLE OF THE NIGHT...
MMMM...
!?
...I WOKE UP AND SAW THE EXAMINING MAGISTRATE STANDING BY THE BED!
?!
!?
HE WHISPERED HE WOULD NEVER FORGET THE SIGHT OF ME LYING THERE SLEEPING.
!
THE EXAMINING MAGISTRATE IS CRAZY ABOUT ME, SO I HAVE A LOT OF INFLUENCE ON HIM.
HE EVEN GAVE ME THIS PAIR OF SILK STOCKINGS.
THEY'RE VERY BEAUTIFUL, BUT MUCH TOO GOOD FOR ME.
!
?

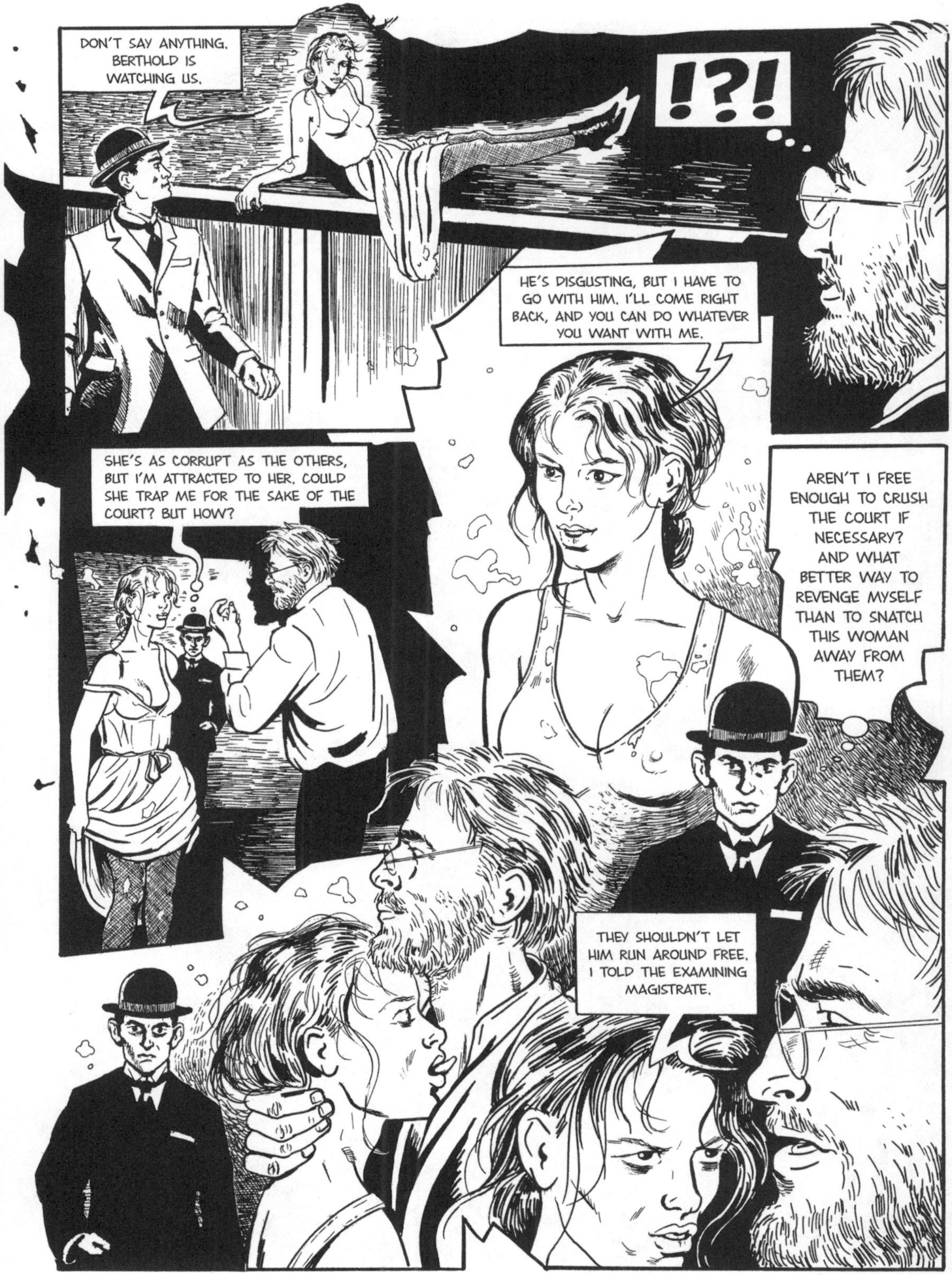
DON'T SAY ANYTHING. BERTHOLD IS WATCHING US.
!?!
HE'S DISGUSTING, BUT I HAVE TO GO WITH HIM. I'LL COME RIGHT BACK, AND YOU CAN DO WHATEVER YOU WANT WITH ME.
SHE'S AS CORRUPT AS THE OTHERS, BUT I'M ATTRACTED TO HER. COULD SHE TRAP ME FOR THE SAKE OF THE COURT? BUT HOW?
AREN'T I FREE ENOUGH TO CRUSH THE COURT IF NECESSARY? AND WHAT BETTER WAY TO REVENGE MYSELF THAN TO SNATCH THIS WOMAN AWAY FROM THEM?
THEY SHOULDN'T LET HIM RUN AROUND FREE. I TOLD THE EXAMINING MAGISTRATE.

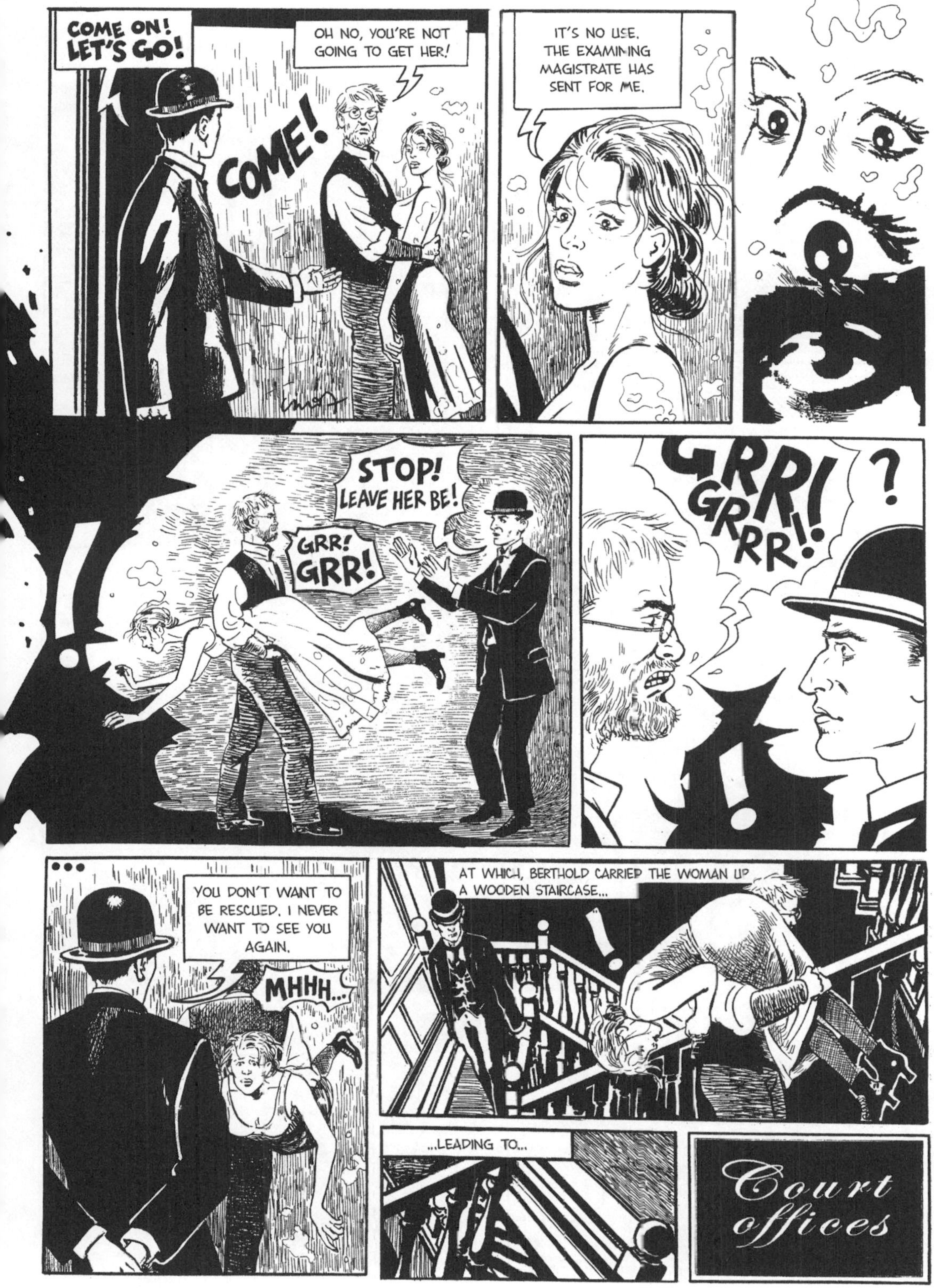
COME ON! LET'S GO!
OH NO, YOU'RE NOT GOING TO GET HER!
COME!
IT'S NO USE. THE EXAMINING MAGISTRATE HAS SENT FOR ME.
STOP! LEAVE HER BE!
GRR! GRR!
GRR! GRRRR!!
?
YOU DON'T WANT TO BE RESCUED. I NEVER WANT TO SEE YOU AGAIN.
MHHH...
AT WHICH, BERTHOLD CARRIED THE WOMAN UP A WOODEN STAIRCASE...
...LEADING TO...
Court offices

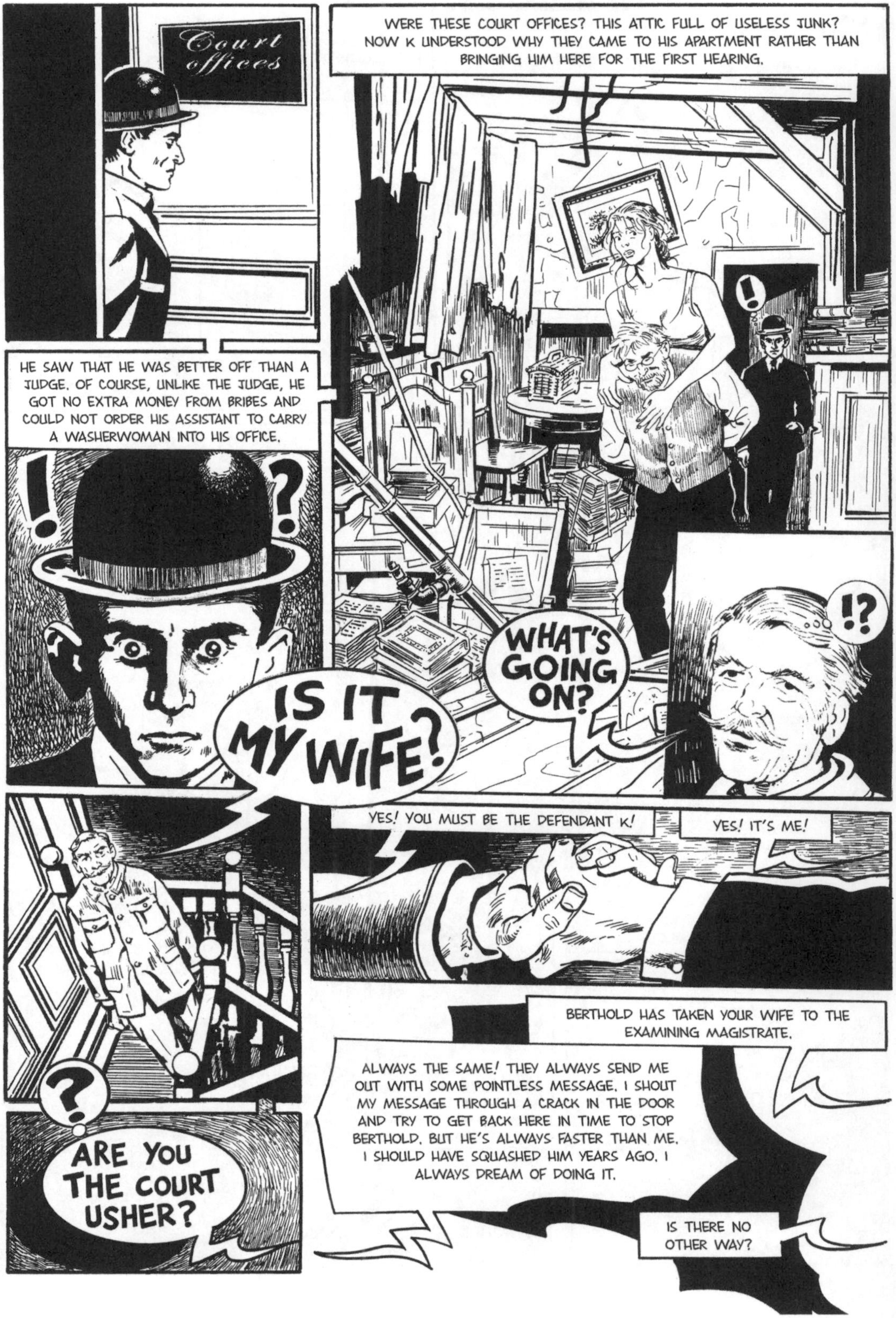
Court offices
WERE THESE COURT OFFICES? THIS ATTIC FULL OF USELESS JUNK? NOW K UNDERSTOOD WHY THEY CAME TO HIS APARTMENT RATHER THAN BRINGING HIM HERE FOR THE FIRST HEARING.
HE SAW THAT HE WAS BETTER OFF THAN A JUDGE. OF COURSE, UNLIKE THE JUDGE, HE GOT NO EXTRA MONEY FROM BRIBES AND COULD NOT ORDER HIS ASSISTANT TO CARRY A WASHERWOMAN INTO HIS OFFICE.
!
!?
WHAT'S GOING ON?
!?
IS IT MY WIFE?
YES! YOU MUST BE THE DEFENDANT K!
YES! IT'S ME!
?
ARE YOU THE COURT USHER?
BERTHOLD HAS TAKEN YOUR WIFE TO THE EXAMINING MAGISTRATE.
ALWAYS THE SAME! THEY ALWAYS SEND ME OUT WITH SOME POINTLESS MESSAGE. I SHOUT MY MESSAGE THROUGH A CRACK IN THE DOOR AND TRY TO GET BACK HERE IN TIME TO STOP BERTHOLD, BUT HE'S ALWAYS FASTER THAN ME. I SHOULD HAVE SQUASHED HIM YEARS AGO. I ALWAYS DREAM OF DOING IT.
IS THERE NO OTHER WAY?

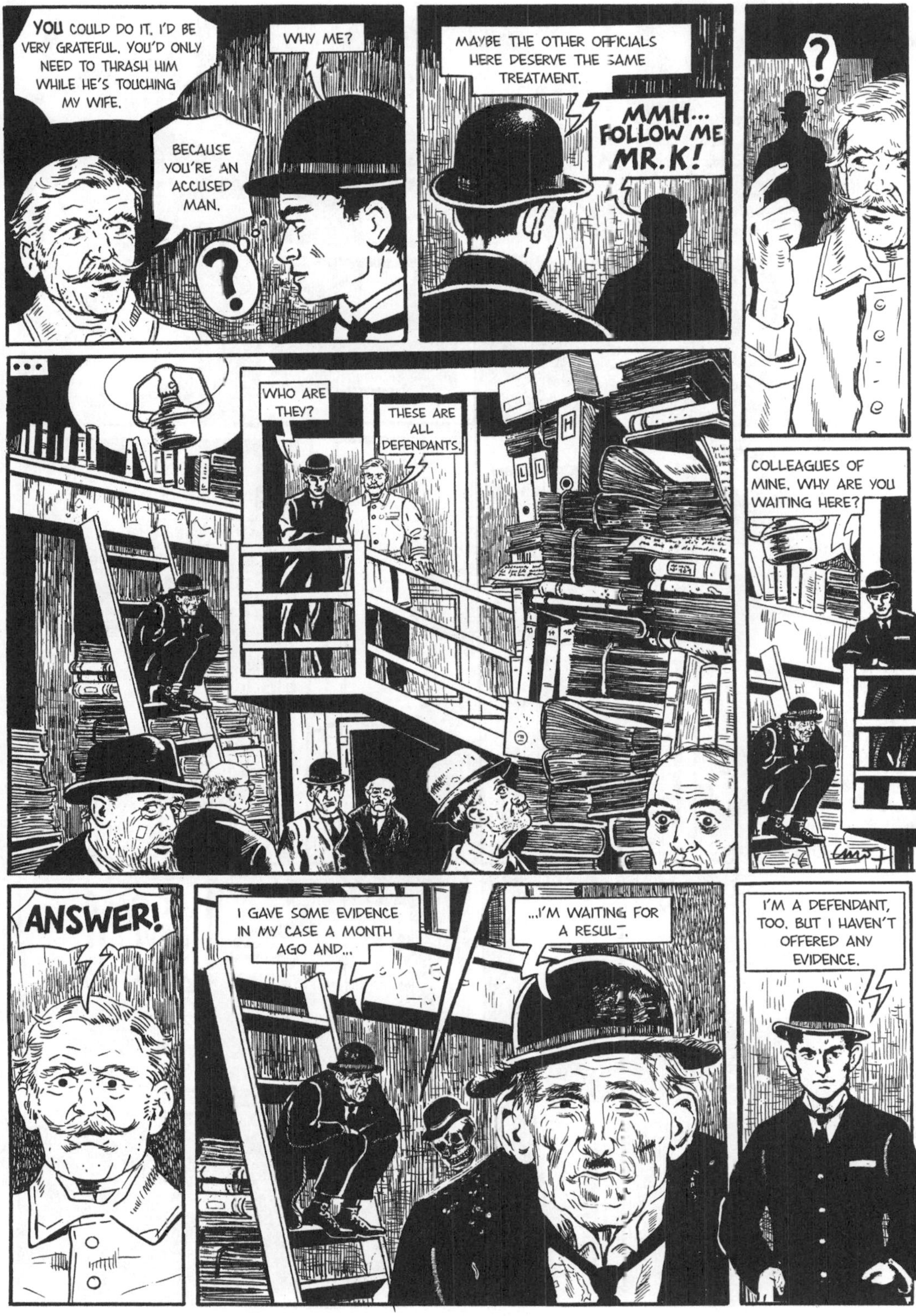
YOU COULD DO IT. I'D BE VERY GRATEFUL. YOU'D ONLY NEED TO THRASH HIM WHILE HE'S TOUCHING MY WIFE.
WHY ME?
BECAUSE YOU'RE AN ACCUSED MAN.
?
MAYBE THE OTHER OFFICIALS HERE DESERVE THE SAME TREATMENT.
MMH... FOLLOW ME MR. K!
?
...
WHO ARE THEY?
THESE ARE ALL DEFENDANTS.
COLLEAGUES OF MINE. WHY ARE YOU WAITING HERE?
ANSWER!
I GAVE SOME EVIDENCE IN MY CASE A MONTH AGO AND...
...I'M WAITING FOR A RESULT.
I'M A DEFENDANT, TOO. BUT I HAVEN'T OFFERED ANY EVIDENCE.

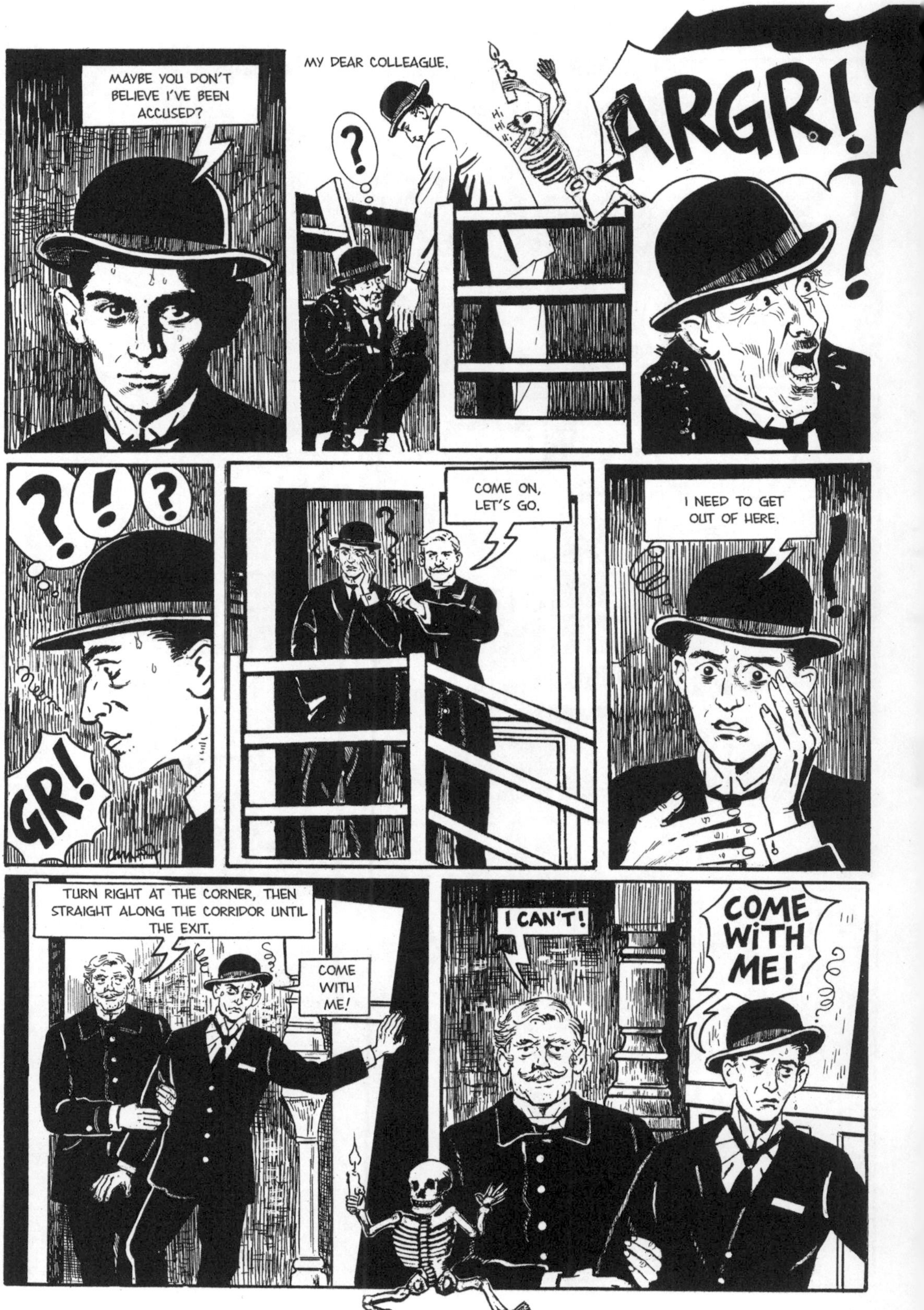
MAYBE YOU DON'T BELIEVE I'VE BEEN ACCUSED?
MY DEAR COLLEAGUE.
?
Hi Hi Hi
ARGR!
?!?
GR!
COME ON, LET'S GO.
I NEED TO GET OUT OF HERE.
!
TURN RIGHT AT THE CORNER, THEN STRAIGHT ALONG THE CORRIDOR UNTIL THE EXIT.
COME WITH ME!
I CAN'T!
COME WITH ME!

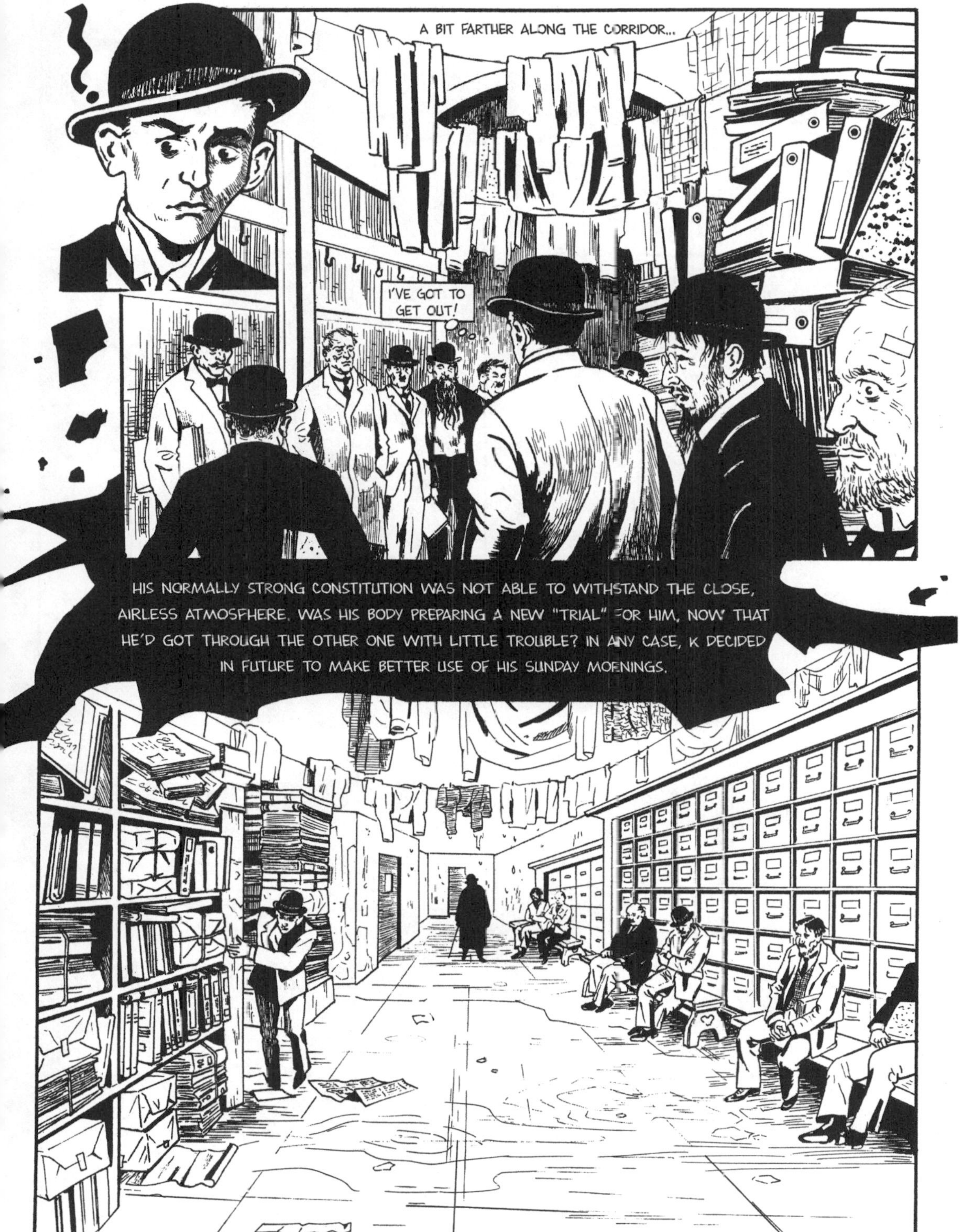
A BIT FARTHER ALONG THE CORRIDOR...
I'VE GOT TO GET OUT!
HIS NORMALLY STRONG CONSTITUTION WAS NOT ABLE TO WITHSTAND THE CLOSE, AIRLESS ATMOSPHERE. WAS HIS BODY PREPARING A NEW "TRIAL" FOR HIM, NOW THAT HE'D GOT THROUGH THE OTHER ONE WITH LITTLE TROUBLE? IN ANY CASE, K DECIDED IN FUTURE TO MAKE BETTER USE OF HIS SUNDAY MORNINGS.

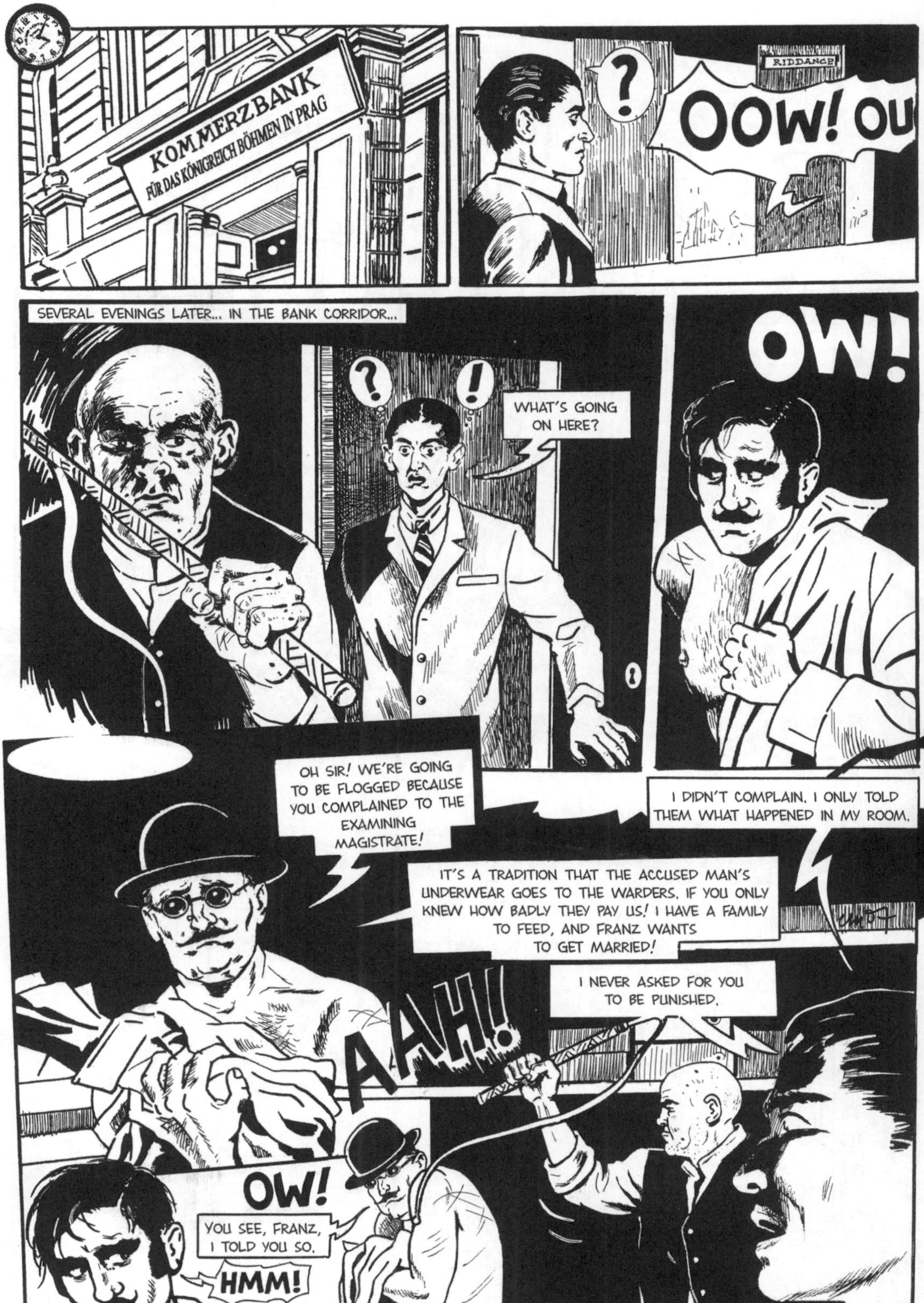
KOMMERZBANK
FÜR DAS KÖNIGREICH BÖHMEN IN PRAG
?
RIDDANCE
OOW! OU
SEVERAL EVENINGS LATER... IN THE BANK CORRIDOR...
?
!
WHAT'S GOING ON HERE?
OW!
OH SIR! WE'RE GOING TO BE FLOGGED BECAUSE YOU COMPLAINED TO THE EXAMINING MAGISTRATE!
I DIDN'T COMPLAIN. I ONLY TOLD THEM WHAT HAPPENED IN MY ROOM.
IT'S A TRADITION THAT THE ACCUSED MAN'S UNDERWEAR GOES TO THE WARDERS. IF YOU ONLY KNEW HOW BADLY THEY PAY US! I HAVE A FAMILY TO FEED, AND FRANZ WANTS TO GET MARRIED!
I NEVER ASKED FOR YOU TO BE PUNISHED.
AAH!
OW!
YOU SEE, FRANZ, I TOLD YOU SO.
HMM!

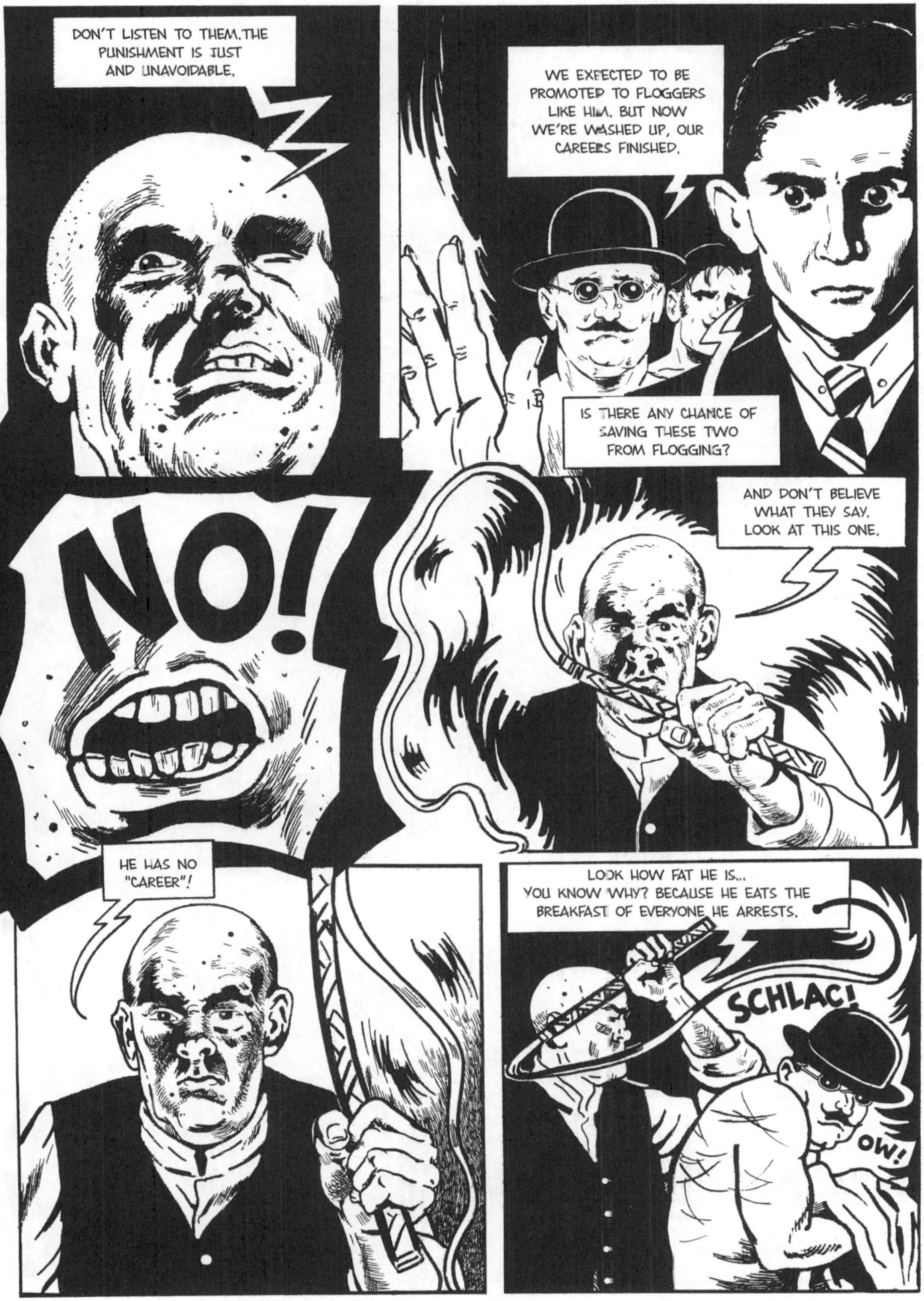
DON'T LISTEN TO THEM.THE PUNISHMENT IS JUST AND UNAVOIDABLE.
WE EXPECTED TO BE PROMOTED TO FLOGGERS LIKE HIM. BUT NOW WE'RE WASHED UP, OUR CAREERS FINISHED.
IS THERE ANY CHANCE OF SAVING THESE TWO FROM FLOGGING?
NO!
AND DON'T BELIEVE WHAT THEY SAY. LOOK AT THIS ONE.
HE HAS NO "CAREER"!
LOOK HOW FAT HE IS... YOU KNOW WHY? BECAUSE HE EATS THE BREAKFAST OF EVERYONE HE ARRESTS.
SCHLAC!
OW!

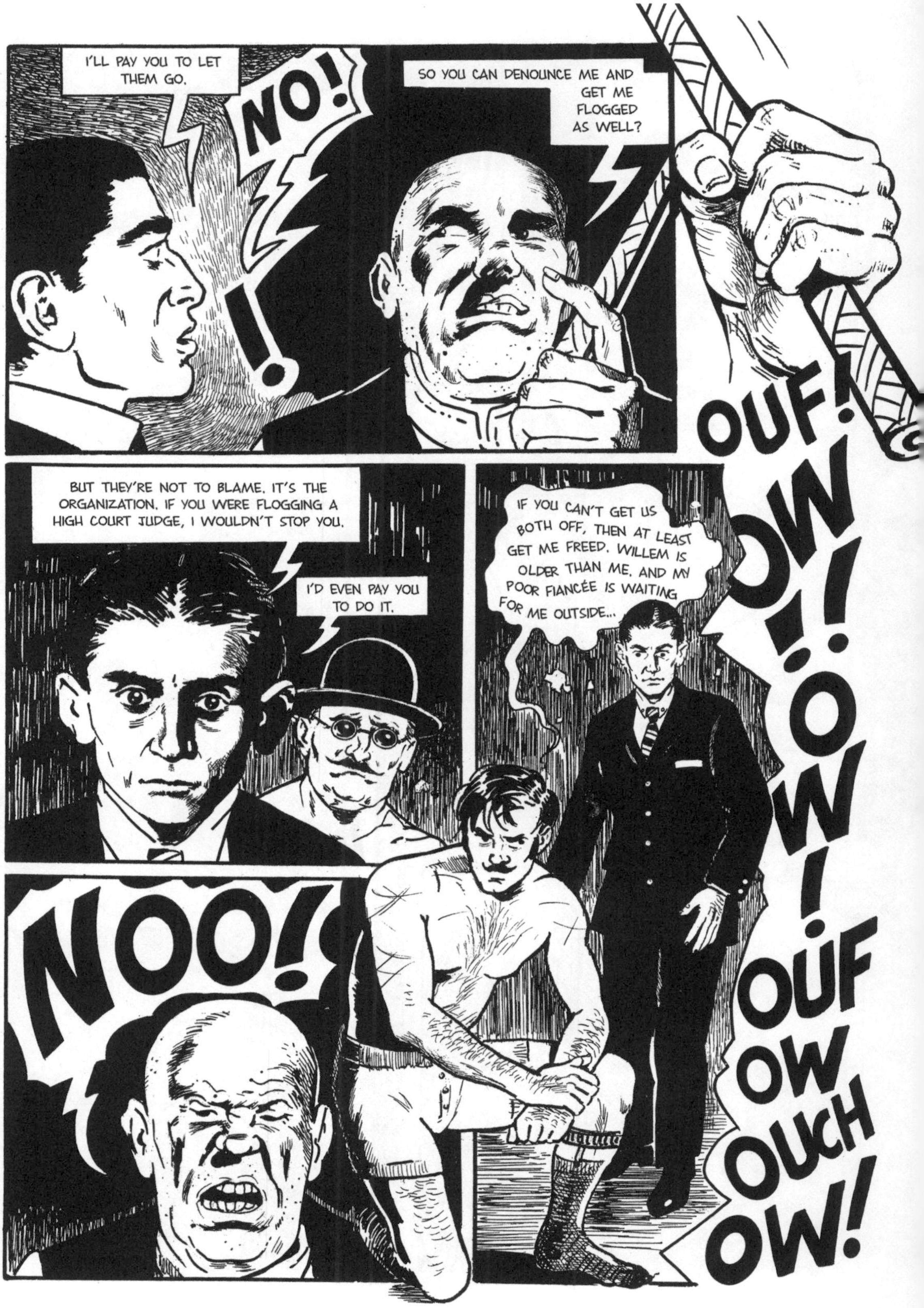
I'LL PAY YOU TO LET THEM GO.
NO!
SO YOU CAN DENOUNCE ME AND GET ME FLOGGED AS WELL?
BUT THEY'RE NOT TO BLAME. IT'S THE ORGANIZATION. IF YOU WERE FLOGGING A HIGH COURT JUDGE, I WOULDN'T STOP YOU.
I'D EVEN PAY YOU TO DO IT.
IF YOU CAN'T GET US BOTH OFF, THEN AT LEAST GET ME FREED. WILLEM IS OLDER THAN ME, AND MY POOR FIANCÉE IS WAITING FOR ME OUTSIDE...
NOO!
OUF!
OW!
OW!
OW!
OUF
OW
OUCH
OW!

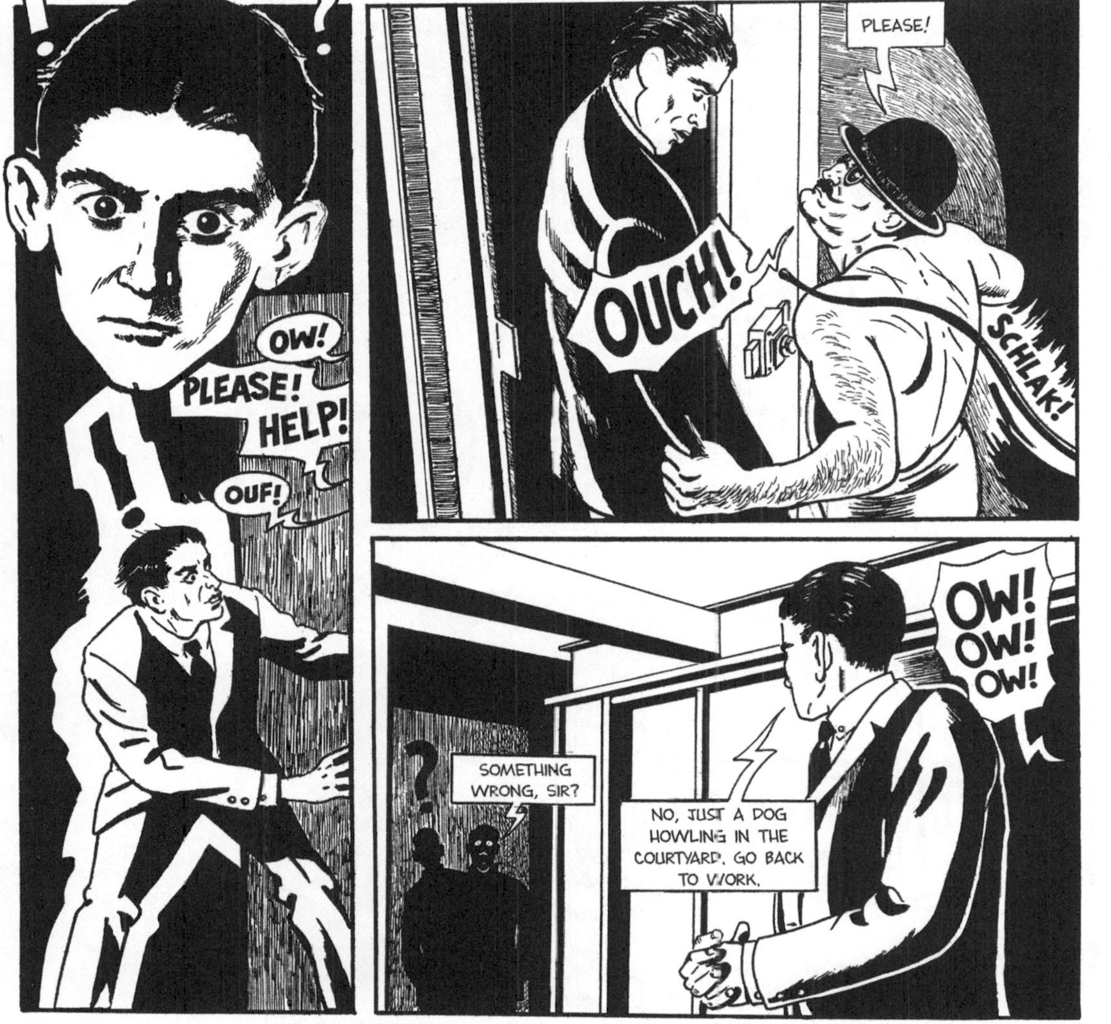
!
?
OW!
PLEASE!
HELP!
OUF!
!
PLEASE!
OUCH!
SCHLAK!
OW!
OW!
OW!
?
SOMETHING WRONG, SIR?
NO, JUST A DOG HOWLING IN THE COURTYARD. GO BACK TO WORK.

CHAPTER 3

IT WAS VERY IMPORTANT FOR K TO FREE THE WARDERS. HE HAD TO FIGHT AGAINST THIS CORRUPT LEGAL SYSTEM. HE THOUGHT OF OFFERING HIMSELF TO BE FLOGGED INSTEAD, BUT THE FLOGGER WOULD NOT HAVE AGREED TO THIS. HE COULD BE OF NO FURTHER HELP AT THE MOMENT, BUT HE VOWED TO DO EVERYTHING IN HIS POWER TO SEE THAT THE HIGH COURT OFFICIALS WERE PUNISHED.

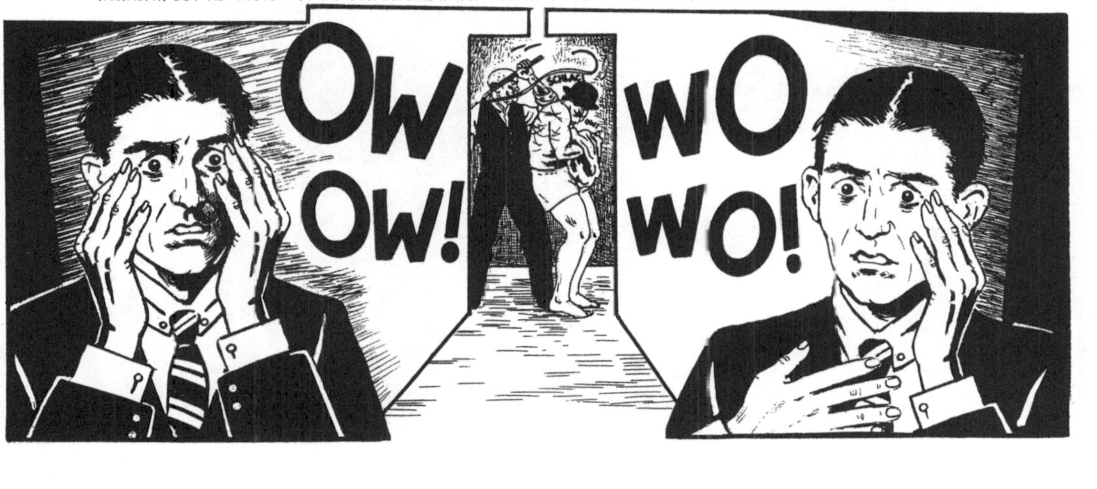
OW
OW!
WO
WO!

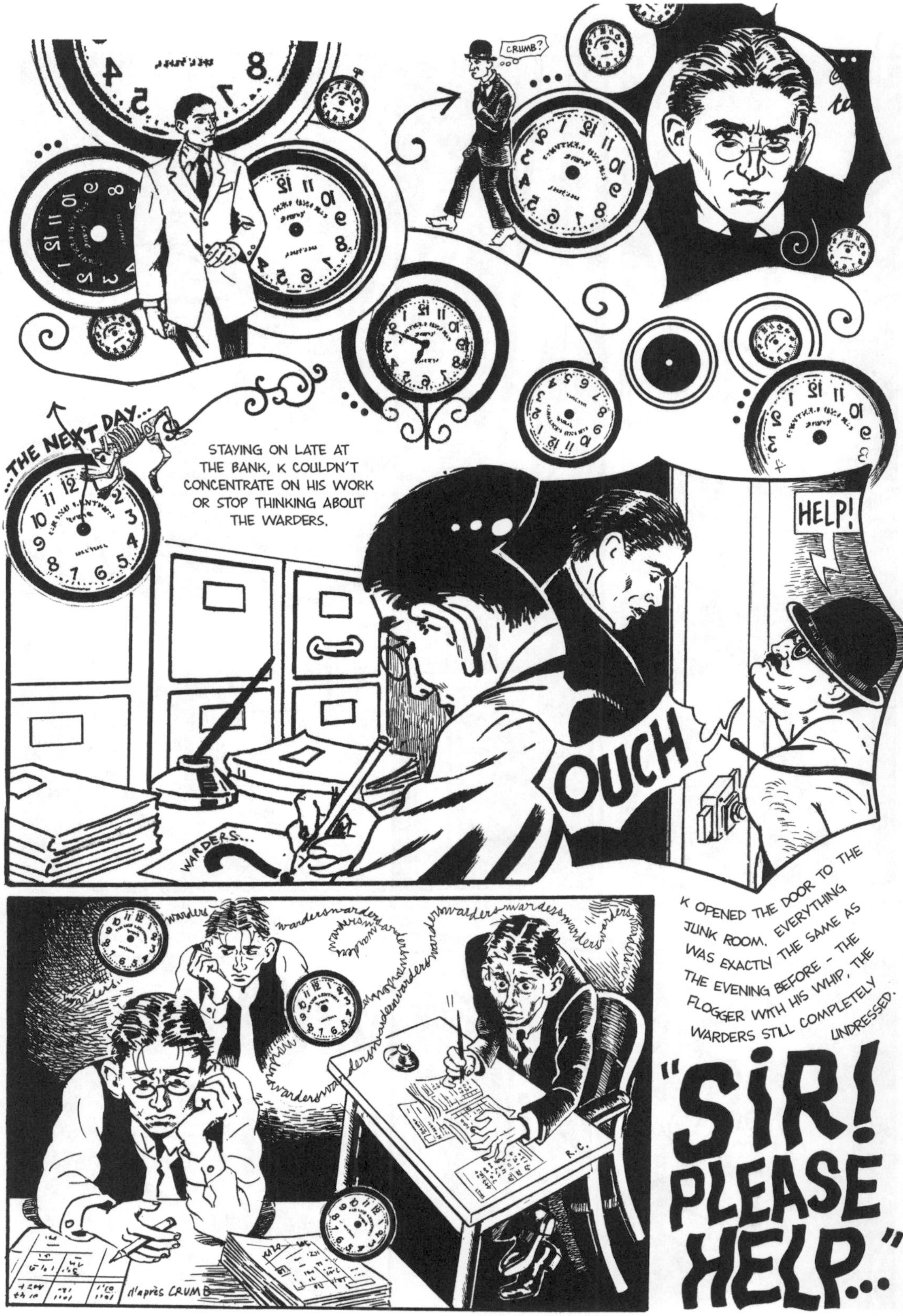
CRUMB?
...THE NEXT DAY...
STAYING ON LATE AT THE BANK, K COULDN'T CONCENTRATE ON HIS WORK OR STOP THINKING ABOUT THE WARDERS.
HELP!
OUCH
WARDERS...
K OPENED THE DOOR TO THE JUNK ROOM. EVERYTHING WAS EXACTLY THE SAME AS THE EVENING BEFORE - THE FLOGGER WITH HIS WHIP, THE WARDERS STILL COMPLETELY UNDRESSED.
"SIR! PLEASE HELP..."
d'après CRUMB
R.C.

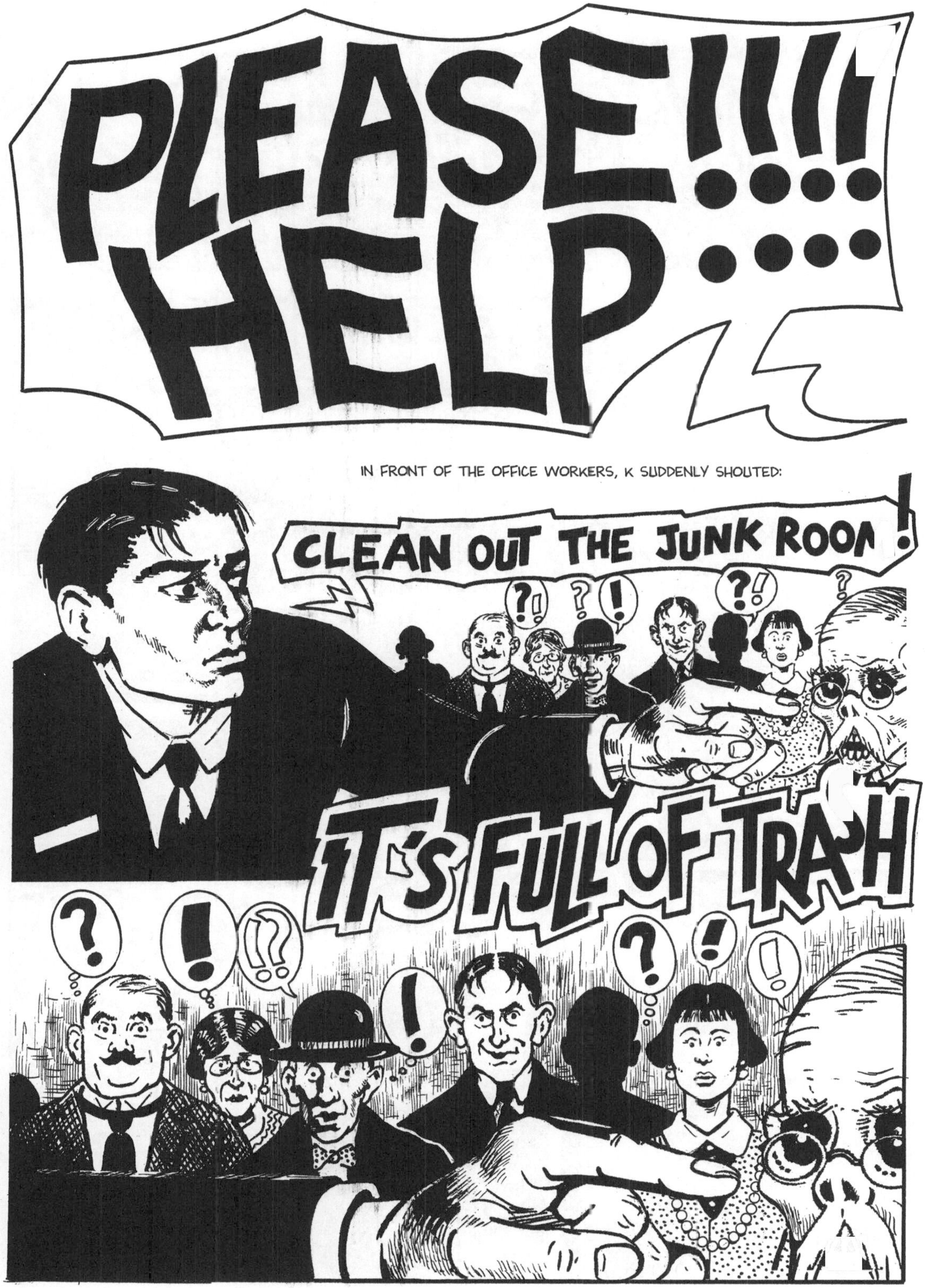
PLEASE!!!! HELP....
IN FRONT OF THE OFFICE WORKERS, K SUDDENLY SHOUTED:
CLEAN OUT THE JUNK ROOM!
IT'S FULL OF TRASH

UNCLE KARL!

the specter from the countryside...

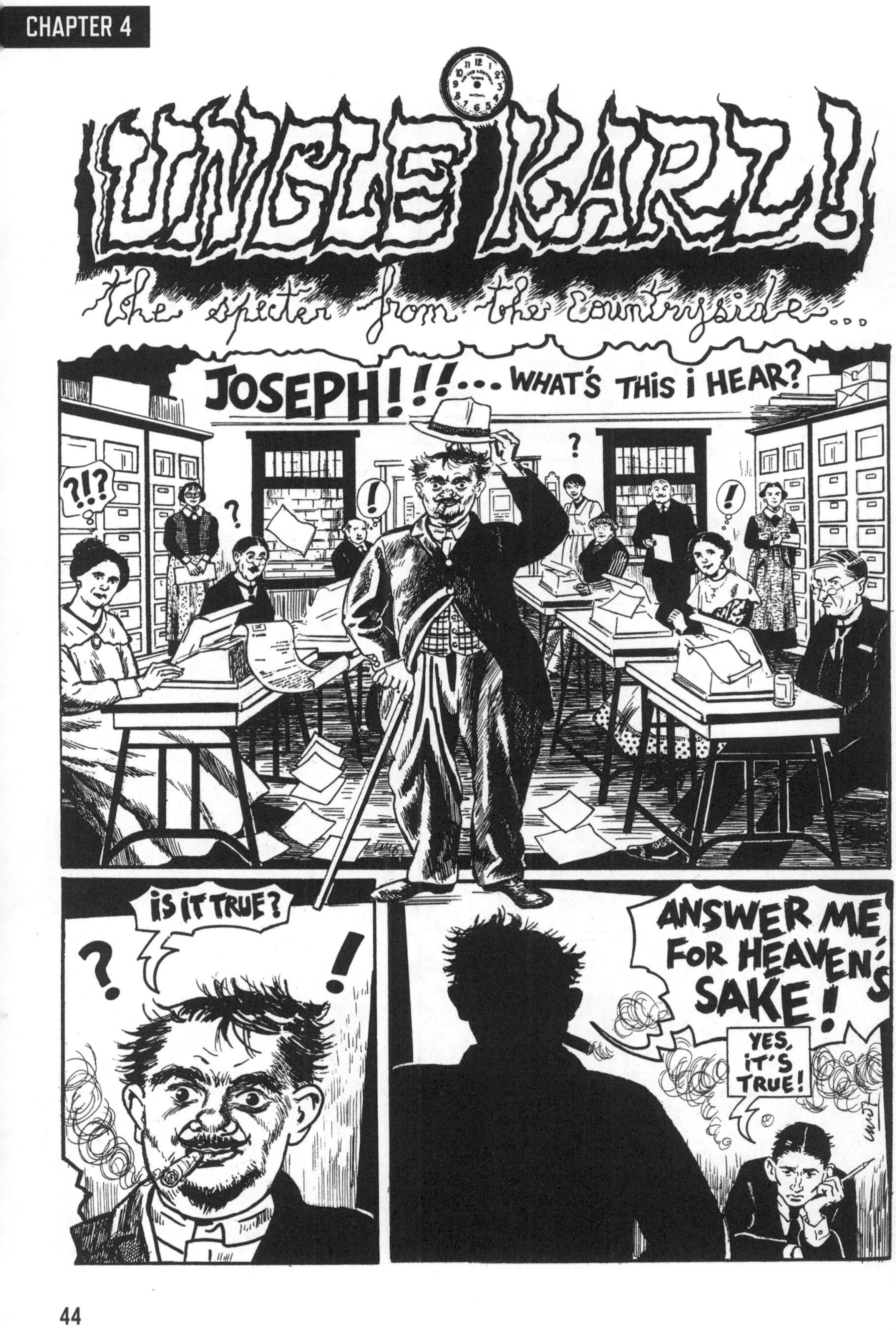
JOSEPH!!!... WHAT'S THIS I HEAR?
?!?
?
!
?
!
IS IT TRUE?
?
!
ANSWER ME FOR HEAVEN'S SAKE!
YES, IT'S TRUE!

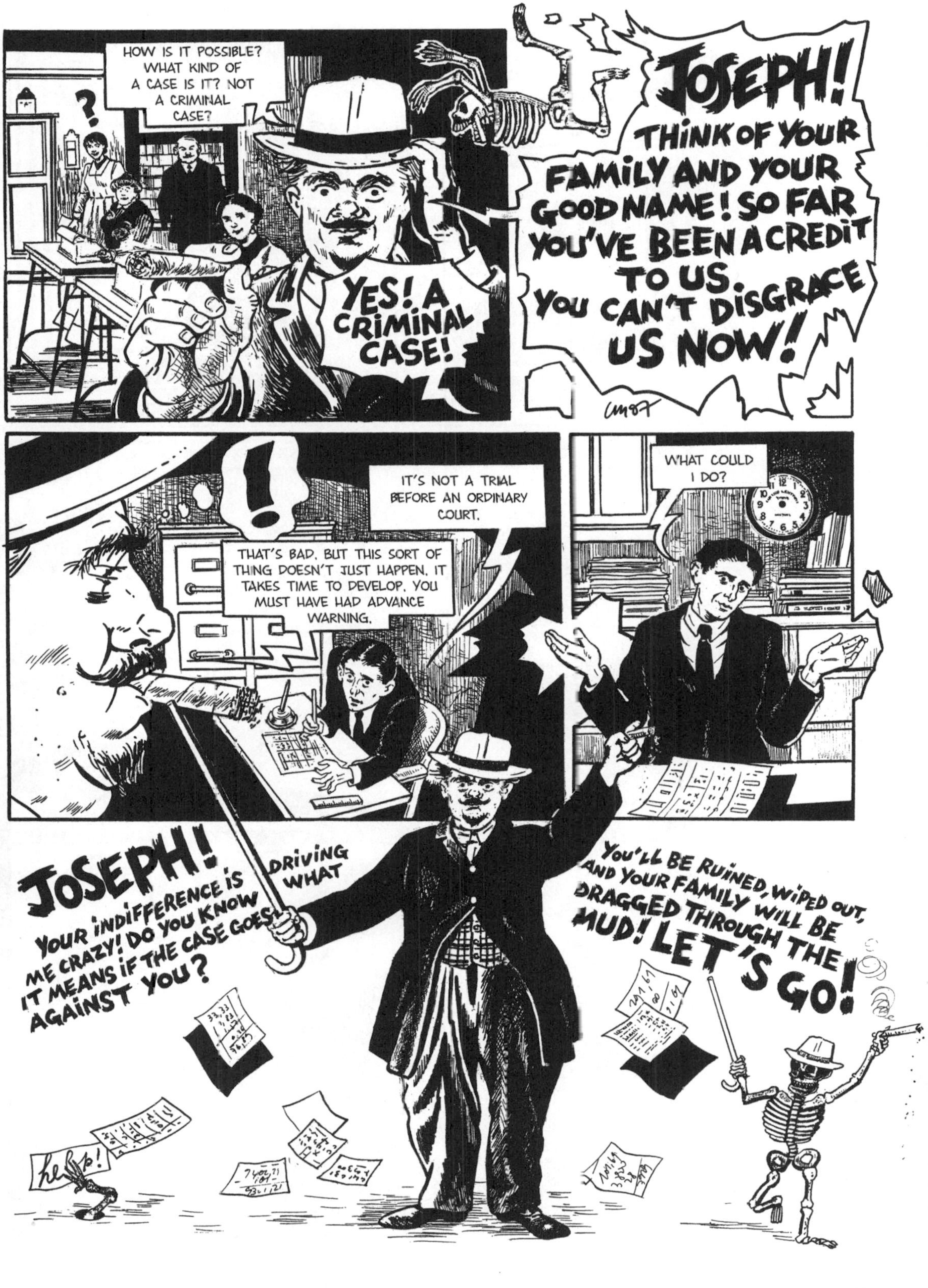
HOW IS IT POSSIBLE? WHAT KIND OF A CASE IS IT? NOT A CRIMINAL CASE?
YES! A CRIMINAL CASE!
JOSEPH! THINK OF YOUR FAMILY AND YOUR GOOD NAME! SO FAR YOU'VE BEEN A CREDIT TO US. YOU CAN'T DISGRACE US NOW!
cm87
IT'S NOT A TRIAL BEFORE AN ORDINARY COURT.
THAT'S BAD, BUT THIS SORT OF THING DOESN'T JUST HAPPEN. IT TAKES TIME TO DEVELOP. YOU MUST HAVE HAD ADVANCE WARNING.
WHAT COULD I DO?
JOSEPH!
YOUR INDIFFERENCE IS
DRIVING
ME CRAZY! DO YOU KNOW
WHAT
IT MEANS IF THE CASE GOES AGAINST YOU?
YOU'LL BE RUINED, WIPED OUT, AND YOUR FAMILY WILL BE DRAGGED THROUGH THE MUD! LET'S GO!
help!

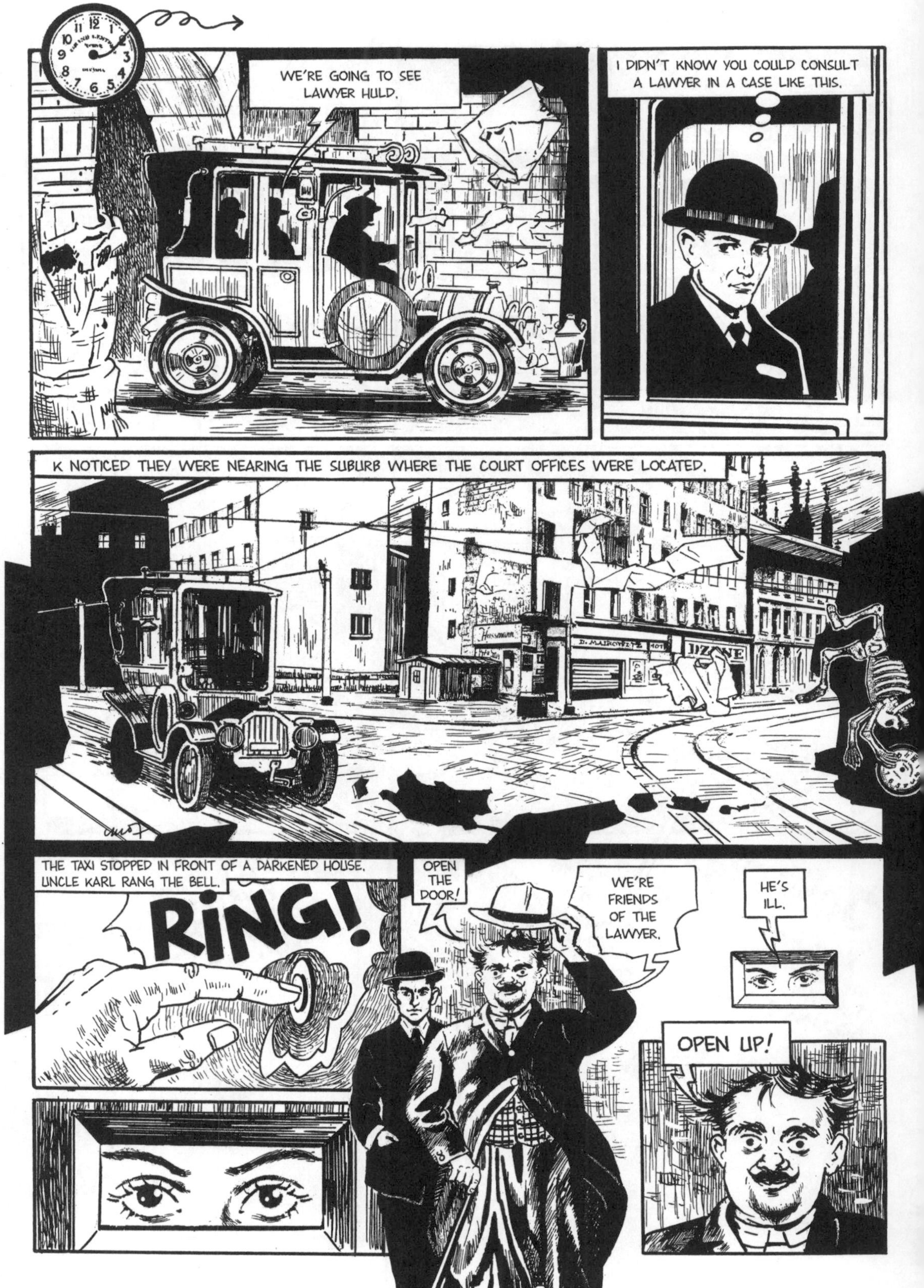

WE'RE GOING TO SEE LAWYER HULD.
I DIDN'T KNOW YOU COULD CONSULT A LAWYER IN A CASE LIKE THIS.
K NOTICED THEY WERE NEARING THE SUBURB WHERE THE COURT OFFICES WERE LOCATED.
THE TAXI STOPPED IN FRONT OF A DARKENED HOUSE. UNCLE KARL RANG THE BELL.
RING!
OPEN THE DOOR!
WE'RE FRIENDS OF THE LAWYER.
HE'S ILL.
OPEN UP!

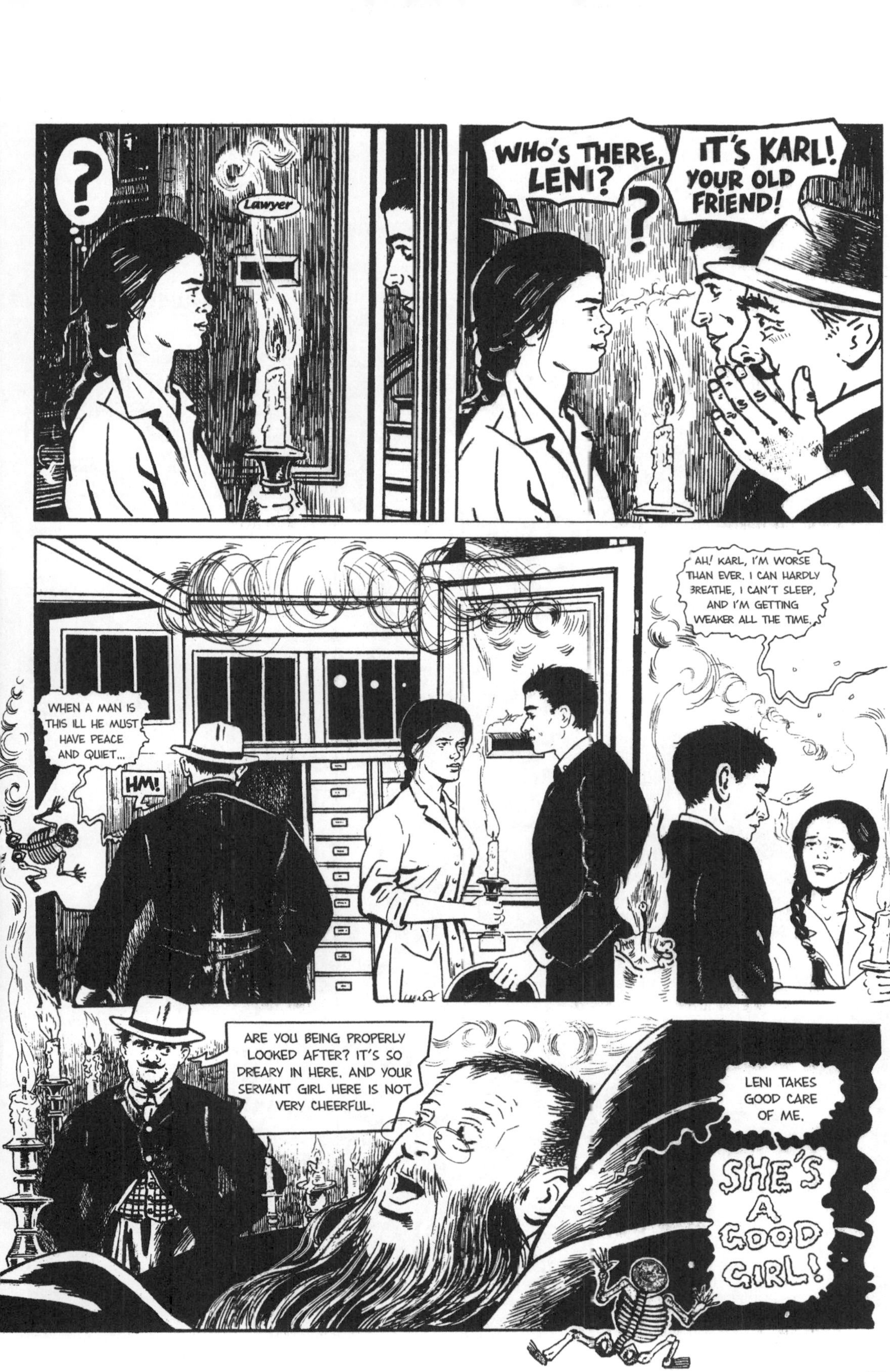
?
Lawyer
WHO'S THERE, LENI?
?
IT'S KARL! YOUR OLD FRIEND!
AH! KARL, I'M WORSE THAN EVER. I CAN HARDLY BREATHE, I CAN'T SLEEP, AND I'M GETTING WEAKER ALL THE TIME.
WHEN A MAN IS THIS ILL HE MUST HAVE PEACE AND QUIET...
HM!
ARE YOU BEING PROPERLY LOOKED AFTER? IT'S SO DREARY IN HERE. AND YOUR SERVANT GIRL HERE IS NOT VERY CHEERFUL.
LENI TAKES GOOD CARE OF ME.
SHE'S A GOOD GIRL!

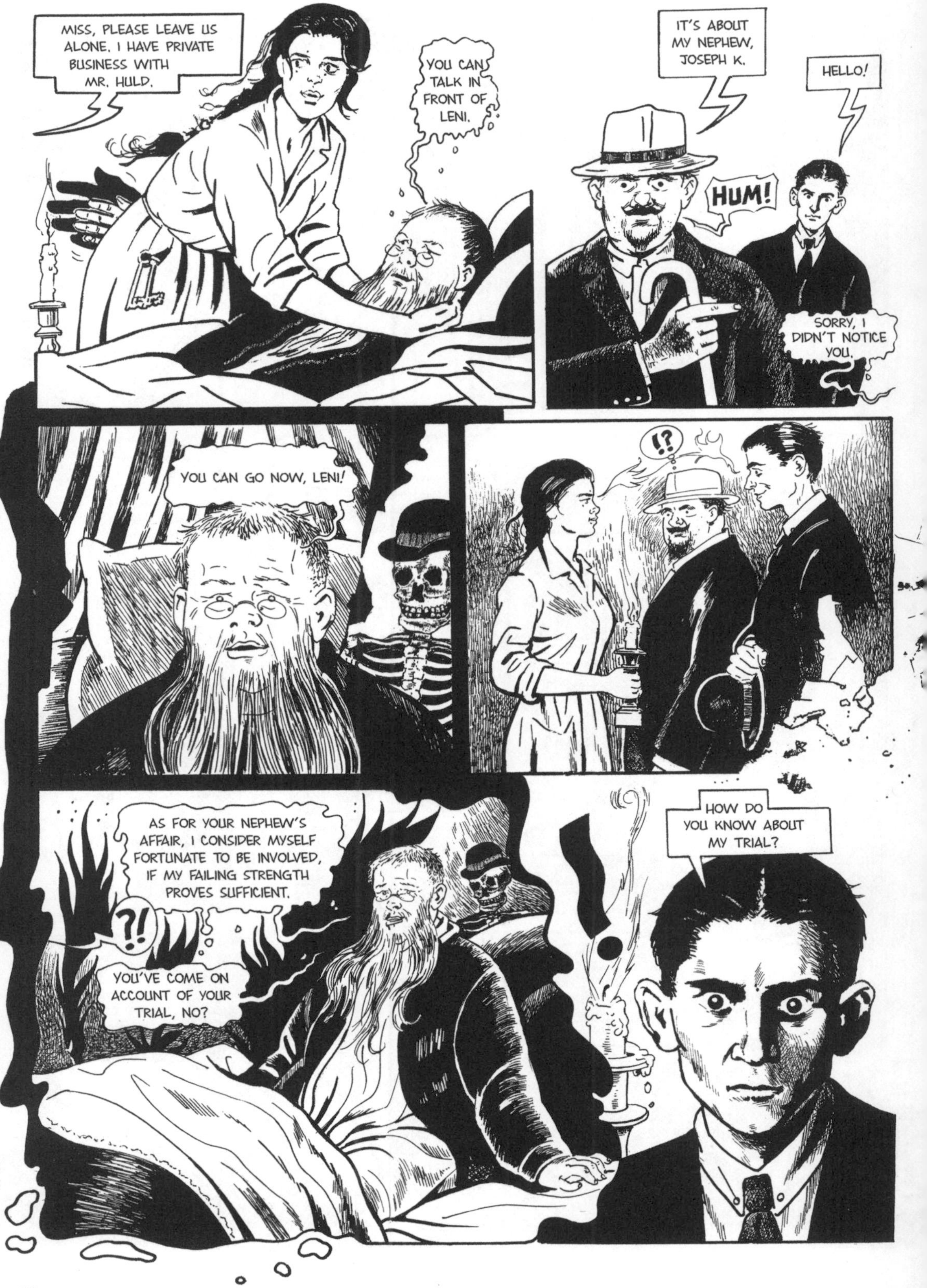
MISS, PLEASE LEAVE US ALONE. I HAVE PRIVATE BUSINESS WITH MR. HULD.
YOU CAN TALK IN FRONT OF LENI.
IT'S ABOUT MY NEPHEW, JOSEPH K.
HELLO!
HUM!
SORRY, I DIDN'T NOTICE YOU.
YOU CAN GO NOW, LENI!
!?
AS FOR YOUR NEPHEW'S AFFAIR, I CONSIDER MYSELF FORTUNATE TO BE INVOLVED, IF MY FAILING STRENGTH PROVES SUFFICIENT.
?!
YOU'VE COME ON ACCOUNT OF YOUR TRIAL, NO?
!
HOW DO YOU KNOW ABOUT MY TRIAL?

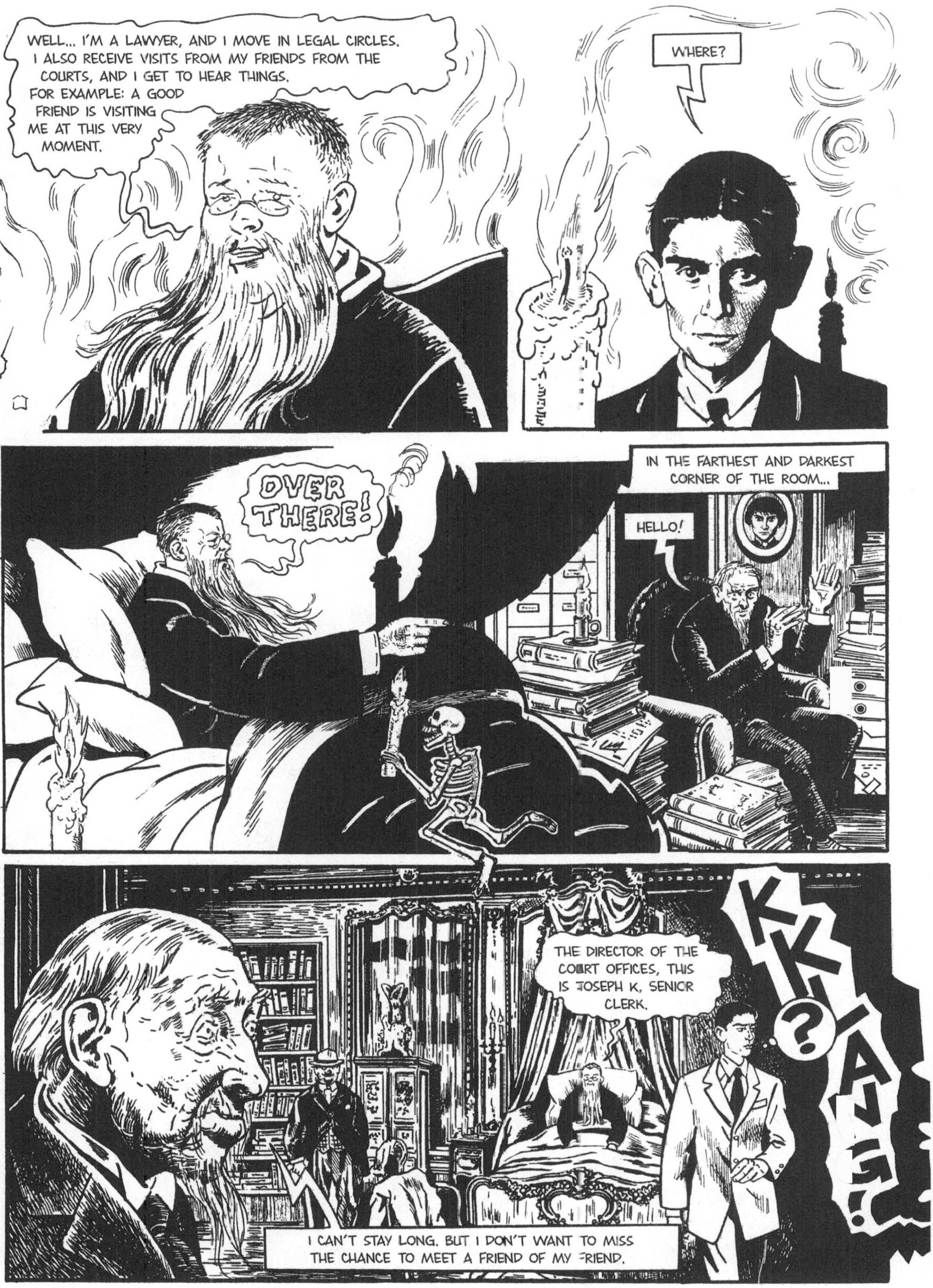
WELL... I'M A LAWYER, AND I MOVE IN LEGAL CIRCLES. I ALSO RECEIVE VISITS FROM MY FRIENDS FROM THE COURTS, AND I GET TO HEAR THINGS. FOR EXAMPLE: A GOOD FRIEND IS VISITING ME AT THIS VERY MOMENT.
WHERE?
OVER THERE!
IN THE FARTHEST AND DARKEST CORNER OF THE ROOM...
HELLO!
THE DIRECTOR OF THE COURT OFFICES, THIS IS JOSEPH K, SENIOR CLERK.
KLANG!
?
I CAN'T STAY LONG, BUT I DON'T WANT TO MISS THE CHANCE TO MEET A FRIEND OF MY FRIEND.

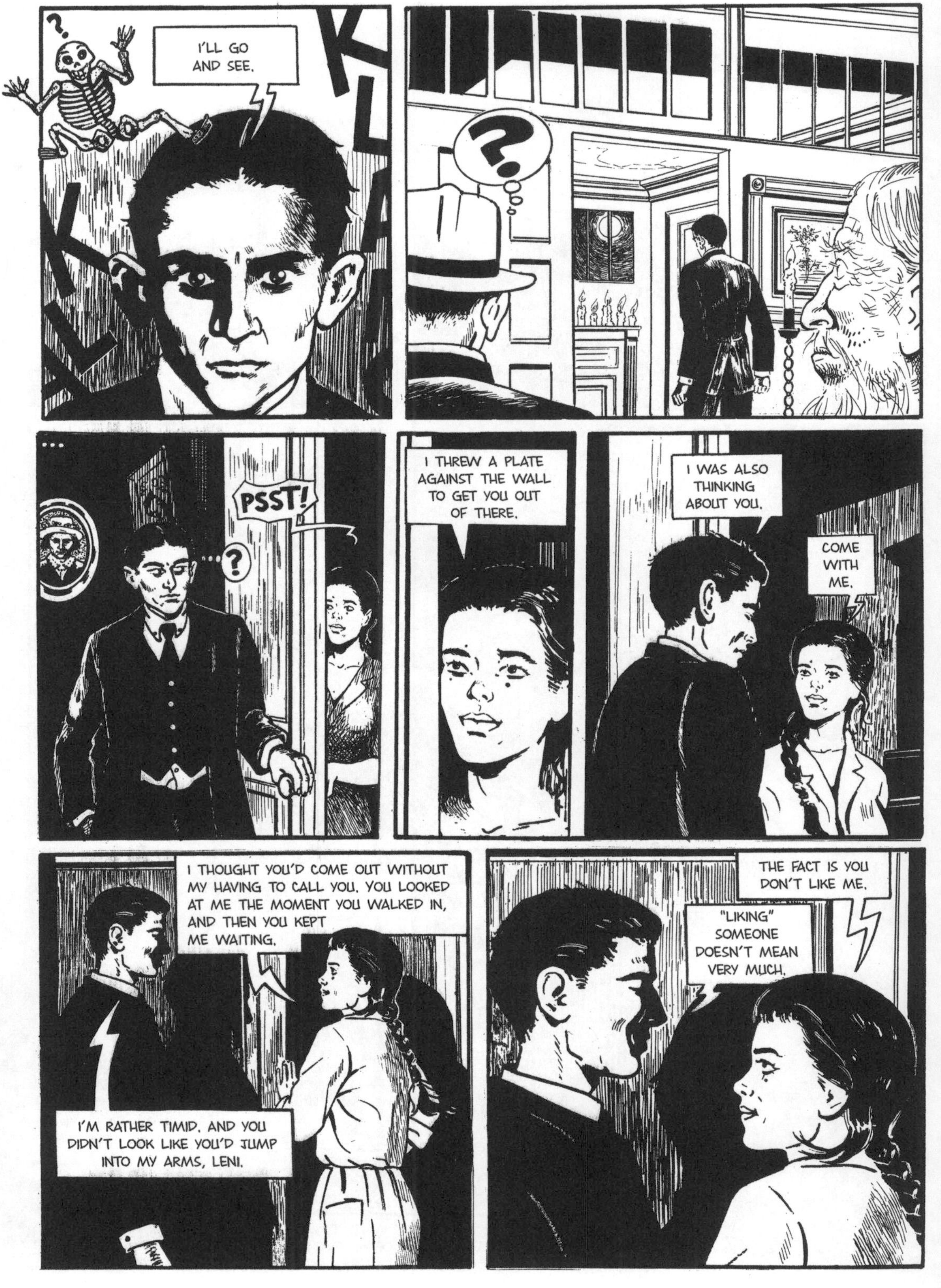
?
I'LL GO AND SEE.
KLAKLAK
?
PSST!
?
I THREW A PLATE AGAINST THE WALL TO GET YOU OUT OF THERE.
I WAS ALSO THINKING ABOUT YOU.
COME WITH ME.
I THOUGHT YOU'D COME OUT WITHOUT MY HAVING TO CALL YOU. YOU LOOKED AT ME THE MOMENT YOU WALKED IN, AND THEN YOU KEPT ME WAITING.
I'M RATHER TIMID. AND YOU DIDN'T LOOK LIKE YOU'D JUMP INTO MY ARMS, LENI.
THE FACT IS YOU DON'T LIKE ME.
"LIKING" SOMEONE DOESN'T MEAN VERY MUCH.

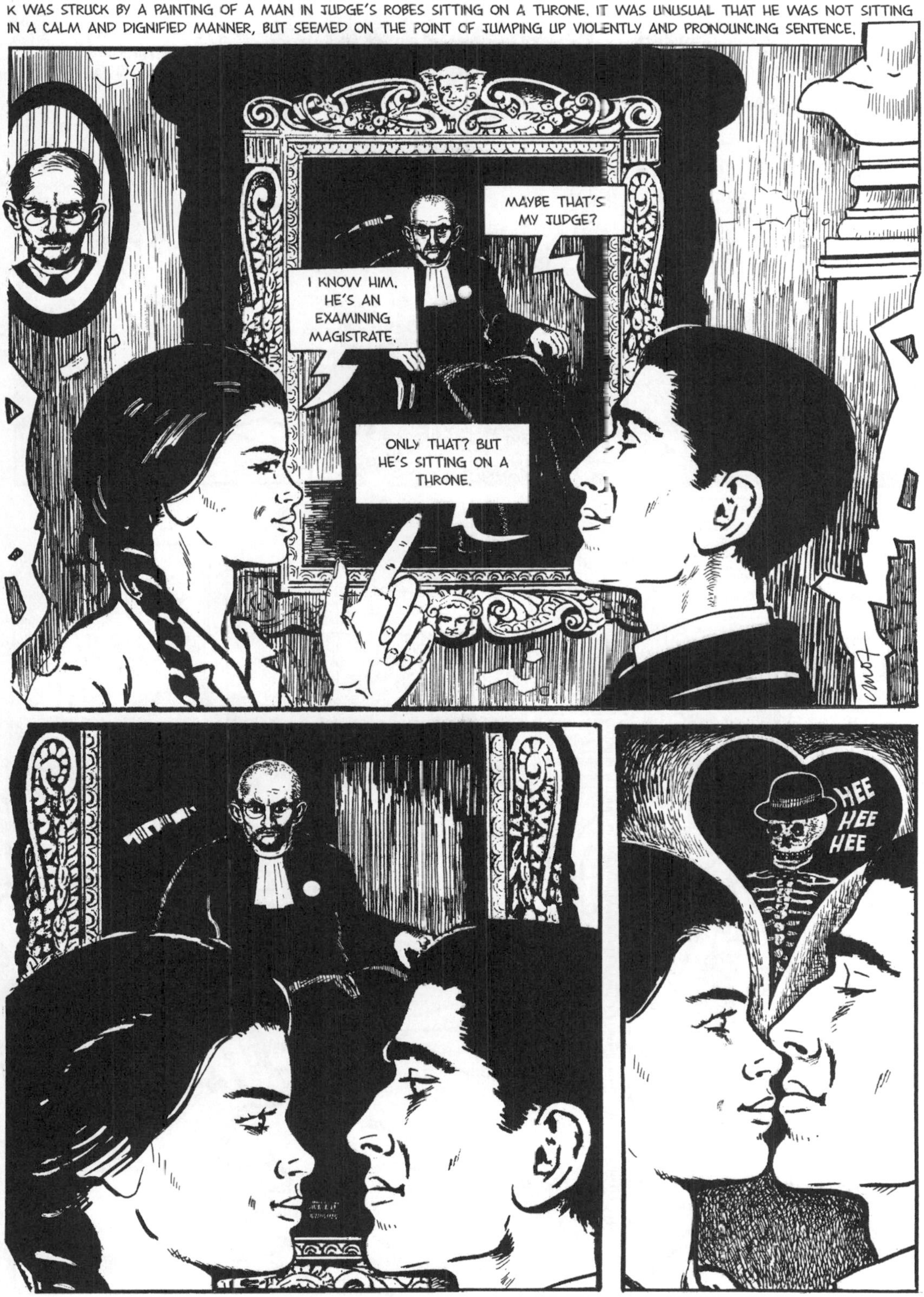
K WAS STRUCK BY A PAINTING OF A MAN IN JUDGE'S ROBES SITTING ON A THRONE. IT WAS UNUSUAL THAT HE WAS NOT SITTING IN A CALM AND DIGNIFIED MANNER, BUT SEEMED ON THE POINT OF JUMPING UP VIOLENTLY AND PRONOUNCING SENTENCE.
MAYBE THAT'S MY JUDGE?
I KNOW HIM. HE'S AN EXAMINING MAGISTRATE.
ONLY THAT? BUT HE'S SITTING ON A THRONE.
HEE HEE HEE

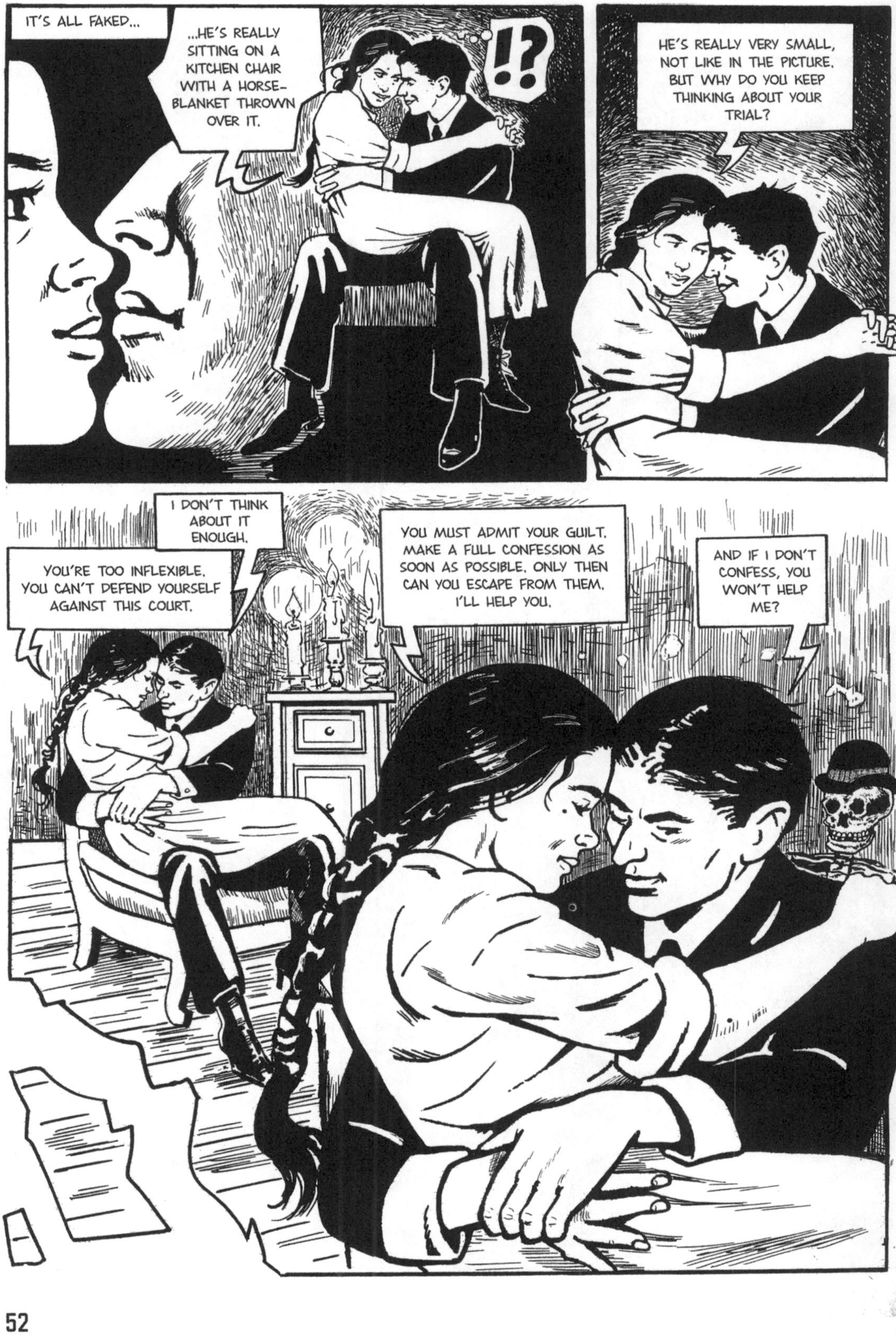
IT'S ALL FAKED...
...HE'S REALLY SITTING ON A KITCHEN CHAIR WITH A HORSE-BLANKET THROWN OVER IT.
!?
HE'S REALLY VERY SMALL, NOT LIKE IN THE PICTURE. BUT WHY DO YOU KEEP THINKING ABOUT YOUR TRIAL?
I DON'T THINK ABOUT IT ENOUGH.
YOU'RE TOO INFLEXIBLE. YOU CAN'T DEFEND YOURSELF AGAINST THIS COURT.
YOU MUST ADMIT YOUR GUILT. MAKE A FULL CONFESSION AS SOON AS POSSIBLE. ONLY THEN CAN YOU ESCAPE FROM THEM. I'LL HELP YOU.
AND IF I DON'T CONFESS, YOU WON'T HELP ME?

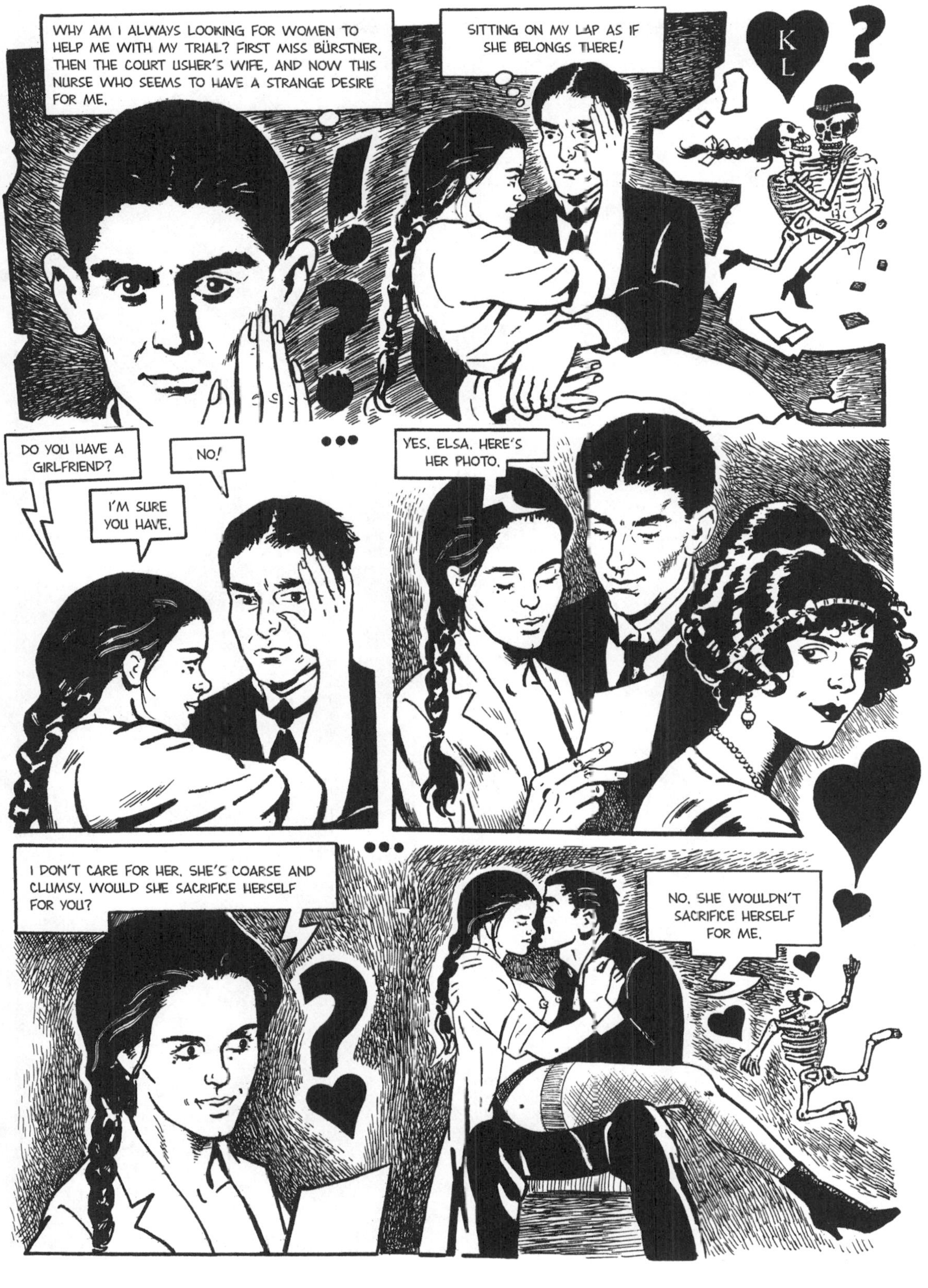
WHY AM I ALWAYS LOOKING FOR WOMEN TO HELP ME WITH MY TRIAL? FIRST MISS BÜRSTNER, THEN THE COURT USHER'S WIFE, AND NOW THIS NURSE WHO SEEMS TO HAVE A STRANGE DESIRE FOR ME.
SITTING ON MY LAP AS IF SHE BELONGS THERE!
K
L
DO YOU HAVE A GIRLFRIEND?
I'M SURE YOU HAVE.
NO!
YES. ELSA. HERE'S HER PHOTO.
I DON'T CARE FOR HER. SHE'S COARSE AND CLUMSY. WOULD SHE SACRIFICE HERSELF FOR YOU?
NO. SHE WOULDN'T SACRIFICE HERSELF FOR ME.

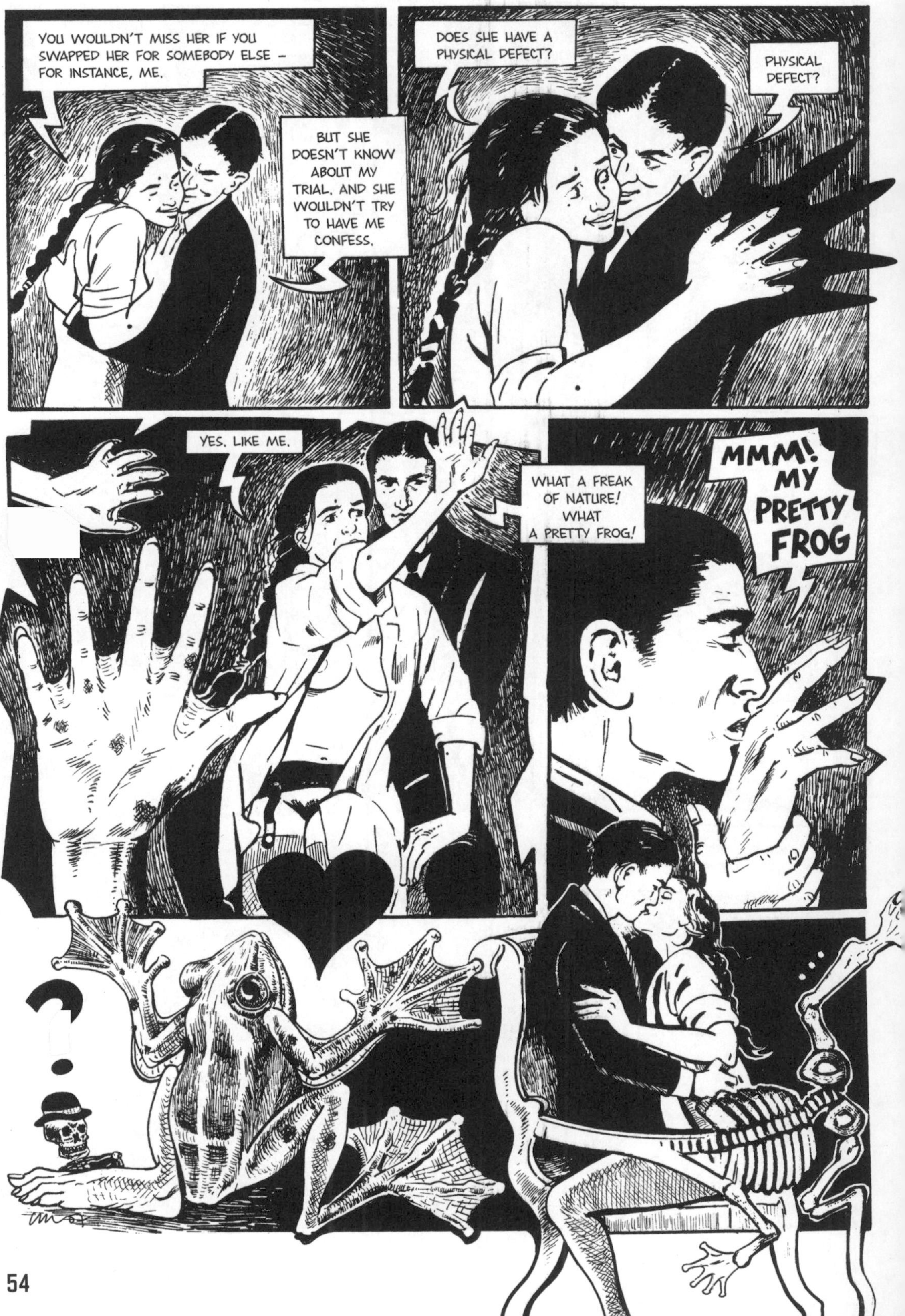

YOU WOULDN'T MISS HER IF YOU SWAPPED HER FOR SOMEBODY ELSE – FOR INSTANCE, ME.
BUT SHE DOESN'T KNOW ABOUT MY TRIAL, AND SHE WOULDN'T TRY TO HAVE ME CONFESS.
DOES SHE HAVE A PHYSICAL DEFECT?
PHYSICAL DEFECT?
YES, LIKE ME.
WHAT A FREAK OF NATURE! WHAT A PRETTY FROG!
MMM! MY PRETTY FROG

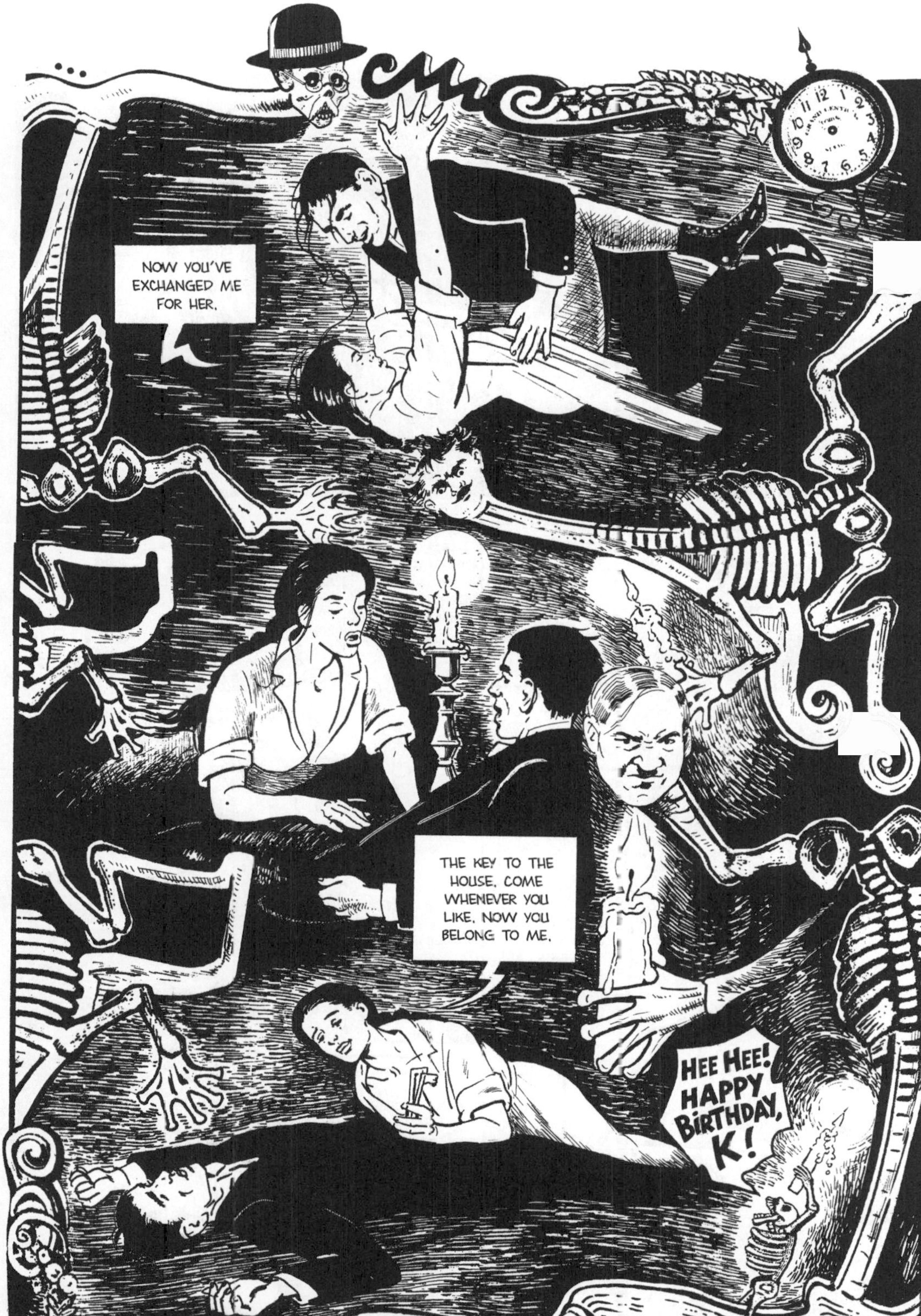
NOW YOU'VE EXCHANGED ME FOR HER.
THE KEY TO THE HOUSE. COME WHENEVER YOU LIKE. NOW YOU BELONG TO ME.
HEE HEE! HAPPY BIRTHDAY, K!

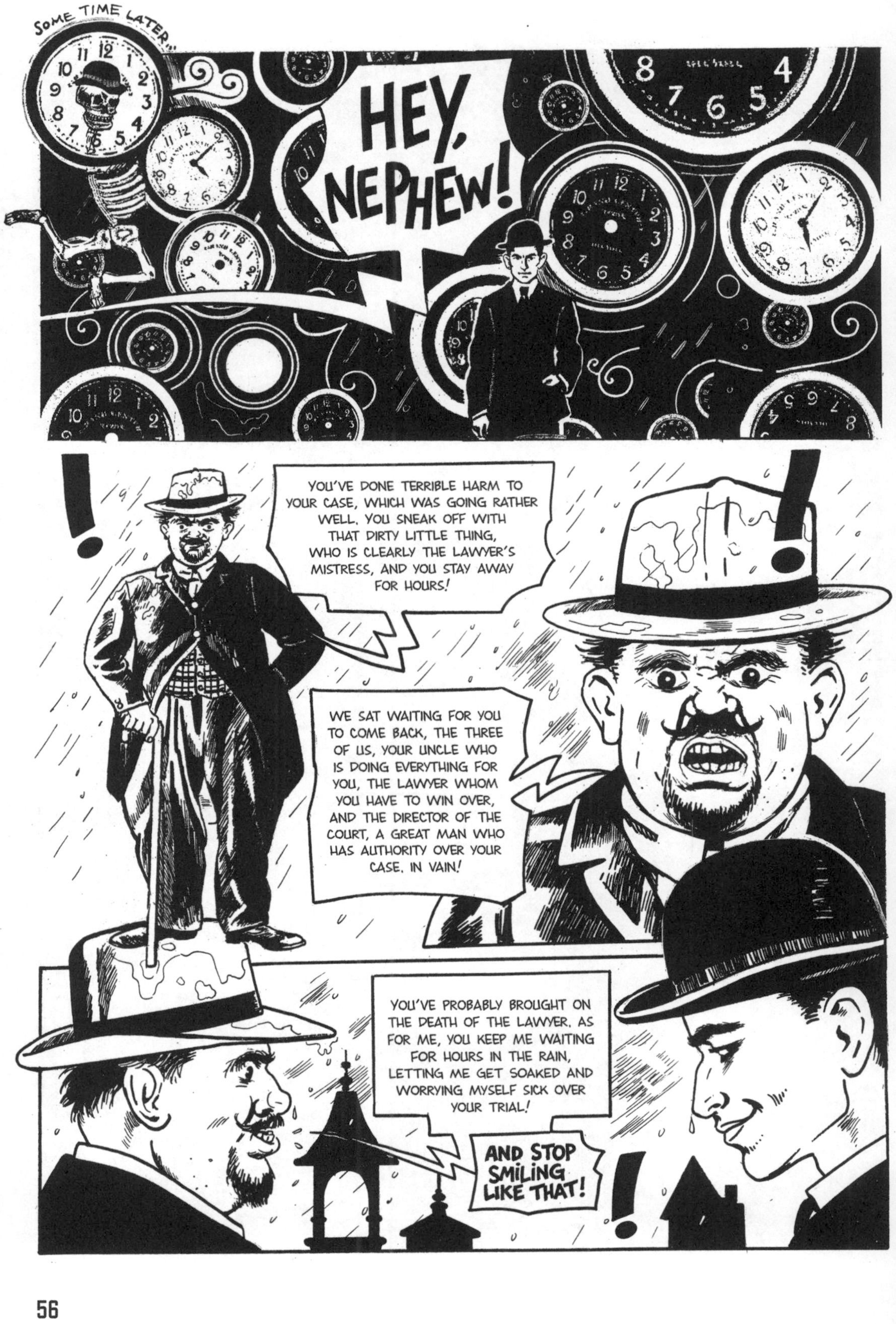
SOME TIME LATER...
HEY, NEPHEW!
YOU'VE DONE TERRIBLE HARM TO YOUR CASE, WHICH WAS GOING RATHER WELL. YOU SNEAK OFF WITH THAT DIRTY LITTLE THING, WHO IS CLEARLY THE LAWYER'S MISTRESS, AND YOU STAY AWAY FOR HOURS!
WE SAT WAITING FOR YOU TO COME BACK, THE THREE OF US, YOUR UNCLE WHO IS DOING EVERYTHING FOR YOU, THE LAWYER WHOM YOU HAVE TO WIN OVER, AND THE DIRECTOR OF THE COURT, A GREAT MAN WHO HAS AUTHORITY OVER YOUR CASE. IN VAIN!
YOU'VE PROBABLY BROUGHT ON THE DEATH OF THE LAWYER. AS FOR ME, YOU KEEP ME WAITING FOR HOURS IN THE RAIN, LETTING ME GET SOAKED AND WORRYING MYSELF SICK OVER YOUR TRIAL!
AND STOP SMILING LIKE THAT!

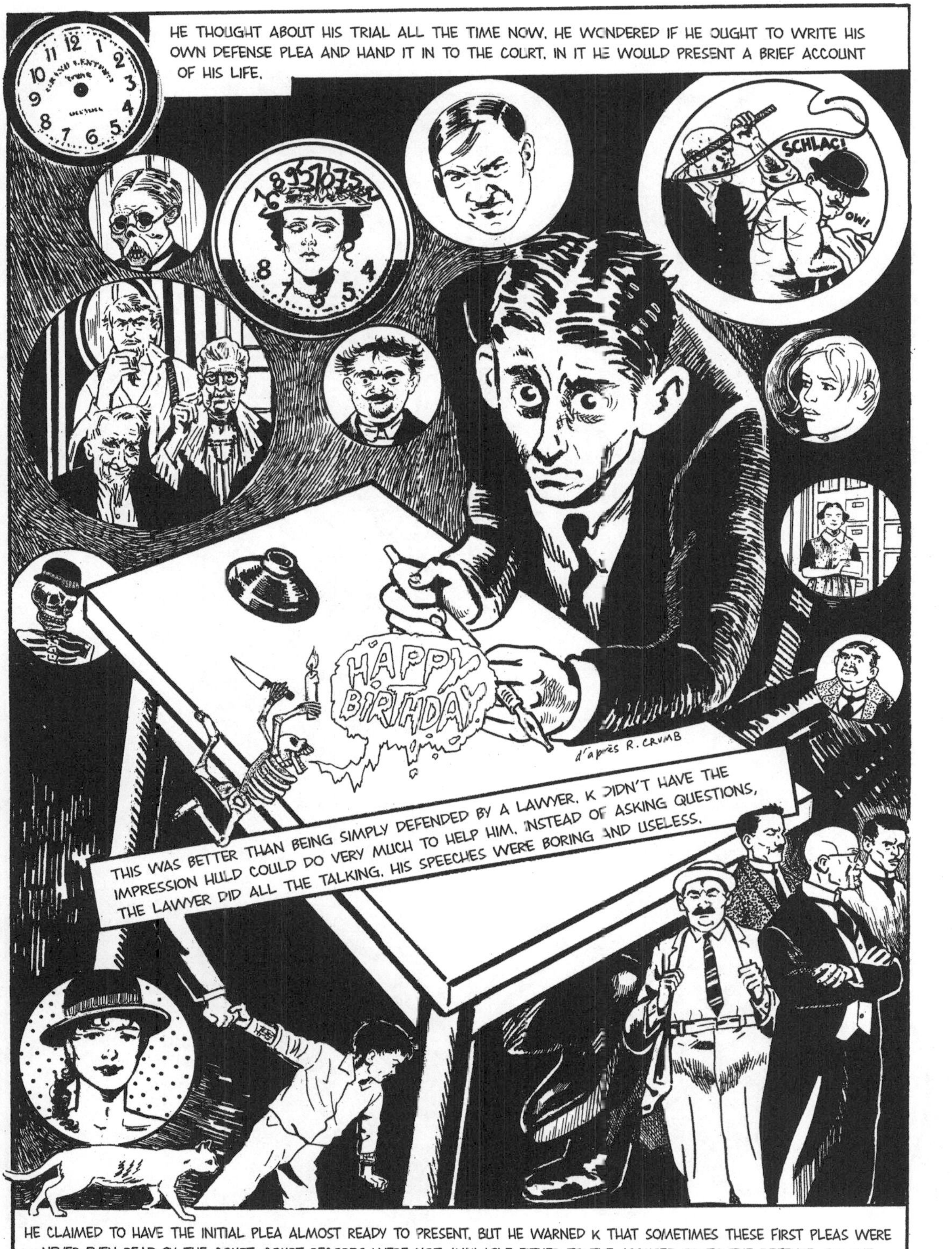
HE THOUGHT ABOUT HIS TRIAL ALL THE TIME NOW. HE WONDERED IF HE OUGHT TO WRITE HIS OWN DEFENSE PLEA AND HAND IT IN TO THE COURT. IN IT HE WOULD PRESENT A BRIEF ACCOUNT OF HIS LIFE.
SCHLAG!
OW!
HAPPY BIRTHDAY
d'après R. CRUMB
THIS WAS BETTER THAN BEING SIMPLY DEFENDED BY A LAWYER. K DIDN'T HAVE THE IMPRESSION HULD COULD DO VERY MUCH TO HELP HIM. INSTEAD OF ASKING QUESTIONS, THE LAWYER DID ALL THE TALKING. HIS SPEECHES WERE BORING AND USELESS.
HE CLAIMED TO HAVE THE INITIAL PLEA ALMOST READY TO PRESENT, BUT HE WARNED K THAT SOMETIMES THESE FIRST PLEAS WERE NEVER EVEN READ BY THE COURT. COURT RECORDS WERE NOT AVAILABLE EITHER TO THE ACCUSED OR TO THE DEFENSE, SO ONE DIDN'T KNOW THE ARGUMENT OF THE INITIAL PLEA OR WHETHER IT CONTAINED ANYTHING IMPORTANT FOR THE CASE.

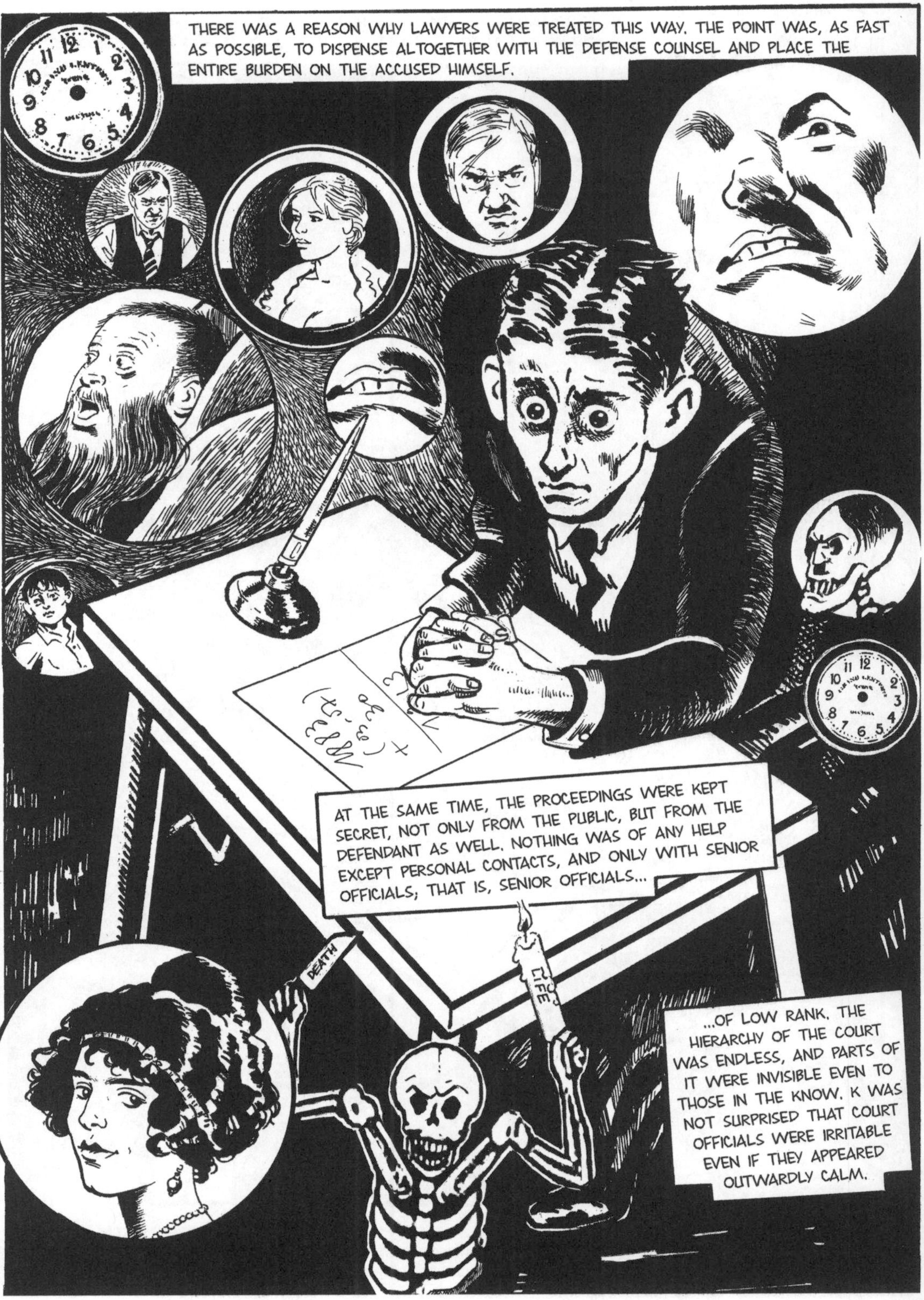
THERE WAS A REASON WHY LAWYERS WERE TREATED THIS WAY. THE POINT WAS, AS FAST AS POSSIBLE, TO DISPENSE ALTOGETHER WITH THE DEFENSE COUNSEL AND PLACE THE ENTIRE BURDEN ON THE ACCUSED HIMSELF.
AT THE SAME TIME, THE PROCEEDINGS WERE KEPT SECRET, NOT ONLY FROM THE PUBLIC, BUT FROM THE DEFENDANT AS WELL. NOTHING WAS OF ANY HELP EXCEPT PERSONAL CONTACTS, AND ONLY WITH SENIOR OFFICIALS; THAT IS, SENIOR OFFICIALS...
DEATH
LIFE
...OF LOW RANK. THE HIERARCHY OF THE COURT WAS ENDLESS, AND PARTS OF IT WERE INVISIBLE EVEN TO THOSE IN THE KNOW. K WAS NOT SURPRISED THAT COURT OFFICIALS WERE IRRITABLE EVEN IF THEY APPEARED OUTWARDLY CALM.

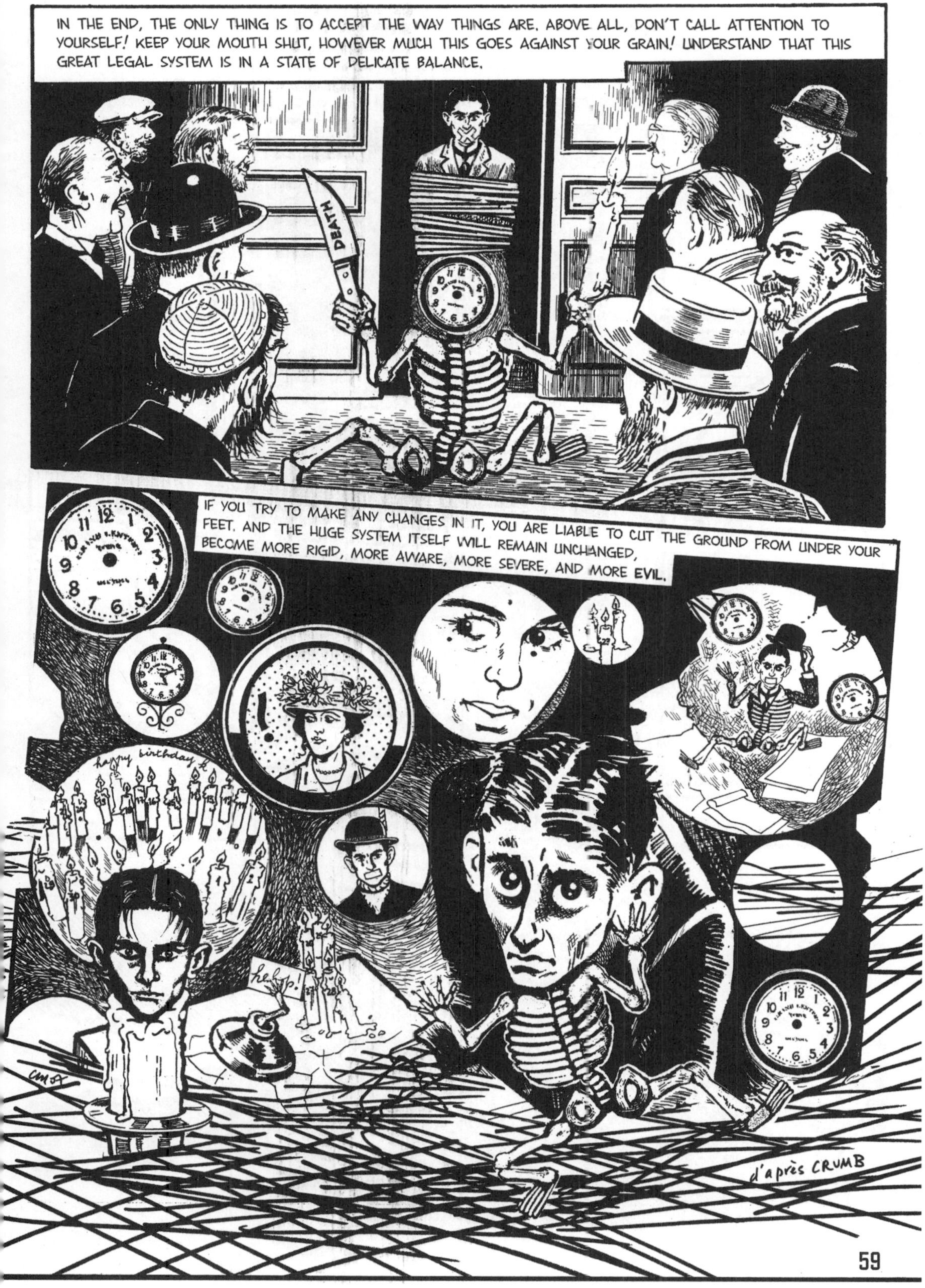
IN THE END, THE ONLY THING IS TO ACCEPT THE WAY THINGS ARE. ABOVE ALL, DON'T CALL ATTENTION TO YOURSELF! KEEP YOUR MOUTH SHUT, HOWEVER MUCH THIS GOES AGAINST YOUR GRAIN! UNDERSTAND THAT THIS GREAT LEGAL SYSTEM IS IN A STATE OF DELICATE BALANCE.
DEATH
IF YOU TRY TO MAKE ANY CHANGES IN IT, YOU ARE LIABLE TO CUT THE GROUND FROM UNDER YOUR FEET, AND THE HUGE SYSTEM ITSELF WILL REMAIN UNCHANGED, BECOME MORE RIGID, MORE AWARE, MORE SEVERE, AND MORE EVIL.
happy birthday
help!
d'après CRUMB

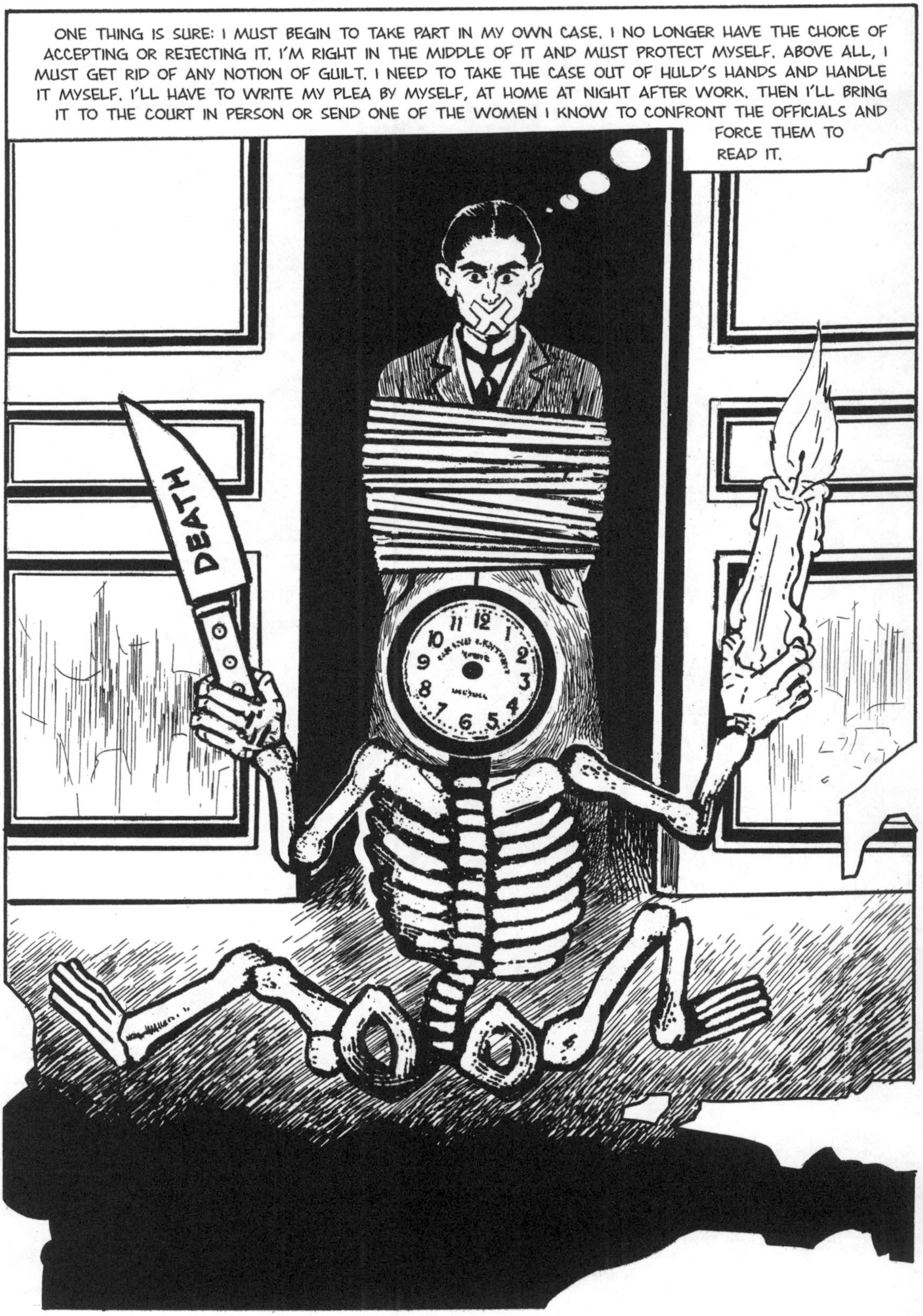
ONE THING IS SURE: I MUST BEGIN TO TAKE PART IN MY OWN CASE. I NO LONGER HAVE THE CHOICE OF ACCEPTING OR REJECTING IT. I'M RIGHT IN THE MIDDLE OF IT AND MUST PROTECT MYSELF. ABOVE ALL, I MUST GET RID OF ANY NOTION OF GUILT. I NEED TO TAKE THE CASE OUT OF HULD'S HANDS AND HANDLE IT MYSELF. I'LL HAVE TO WRITE MY PLEA BY MYSELF, AT HOME AT NIGHT AFTER WORK. THEN I'LL BRING IT TO THE COURT IN PERSON OR SEND ONE OF THE WOMEN I KNOW TO CONFRONT THE OFFICIALS AND FORCE THEM TO READ IT.
DEATH

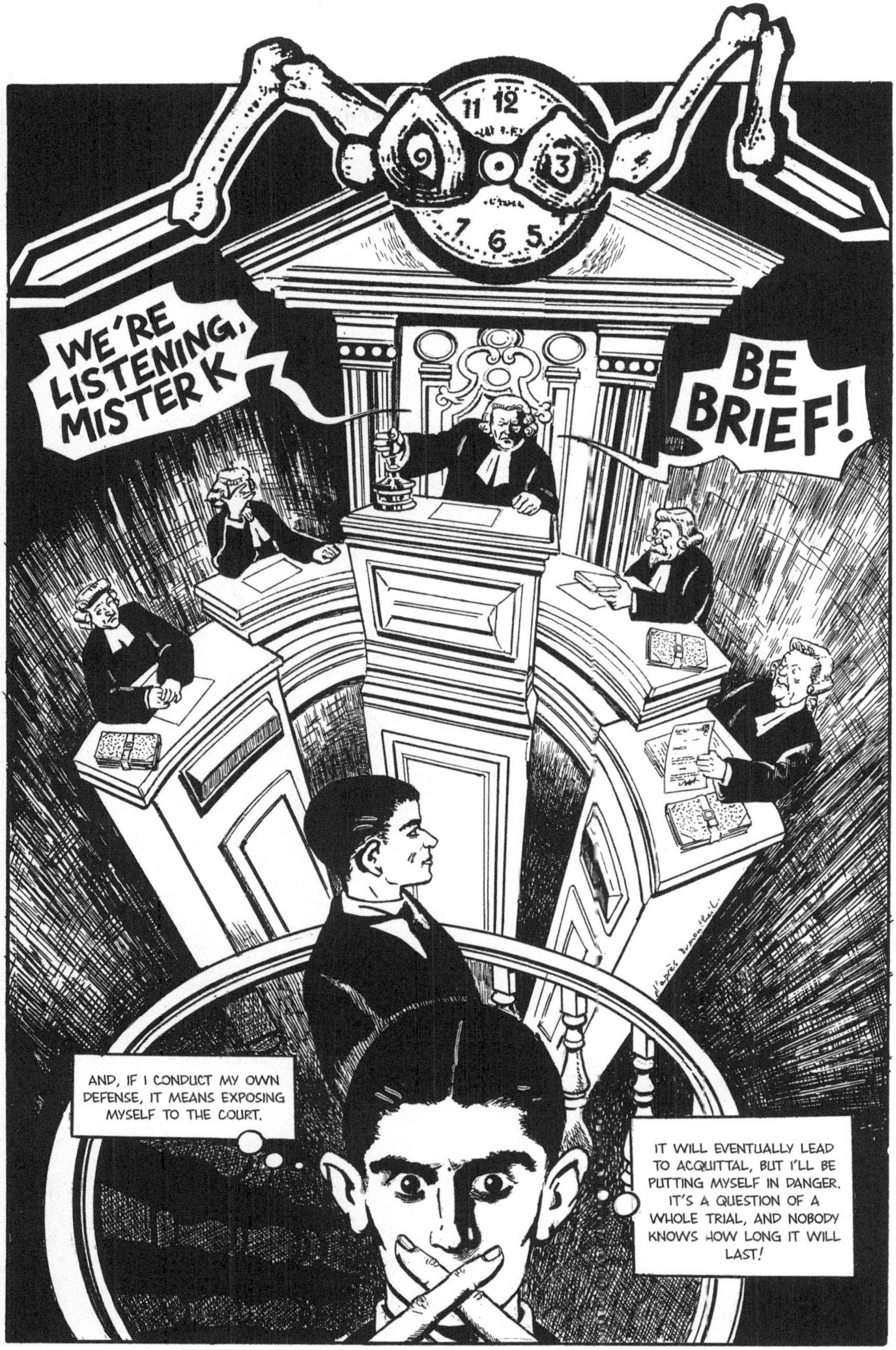
WE'RE LISTENING, MISTER K
BE BRIEF!
AND, IF I CONDUCT MY OWN DEFENSE, IT MEANS EXPOSING MYSELF TO THE COURT.
IT WILL EVENTUALLY LEAD TO ACQUITTAL, BUT I'LL BE PUTTING MYSELF IN DANGER. IT'S A QUESTION OF A WHOLE TRIAL, AND NOBODY KNOWS HOW LONG IT WILL LAST!

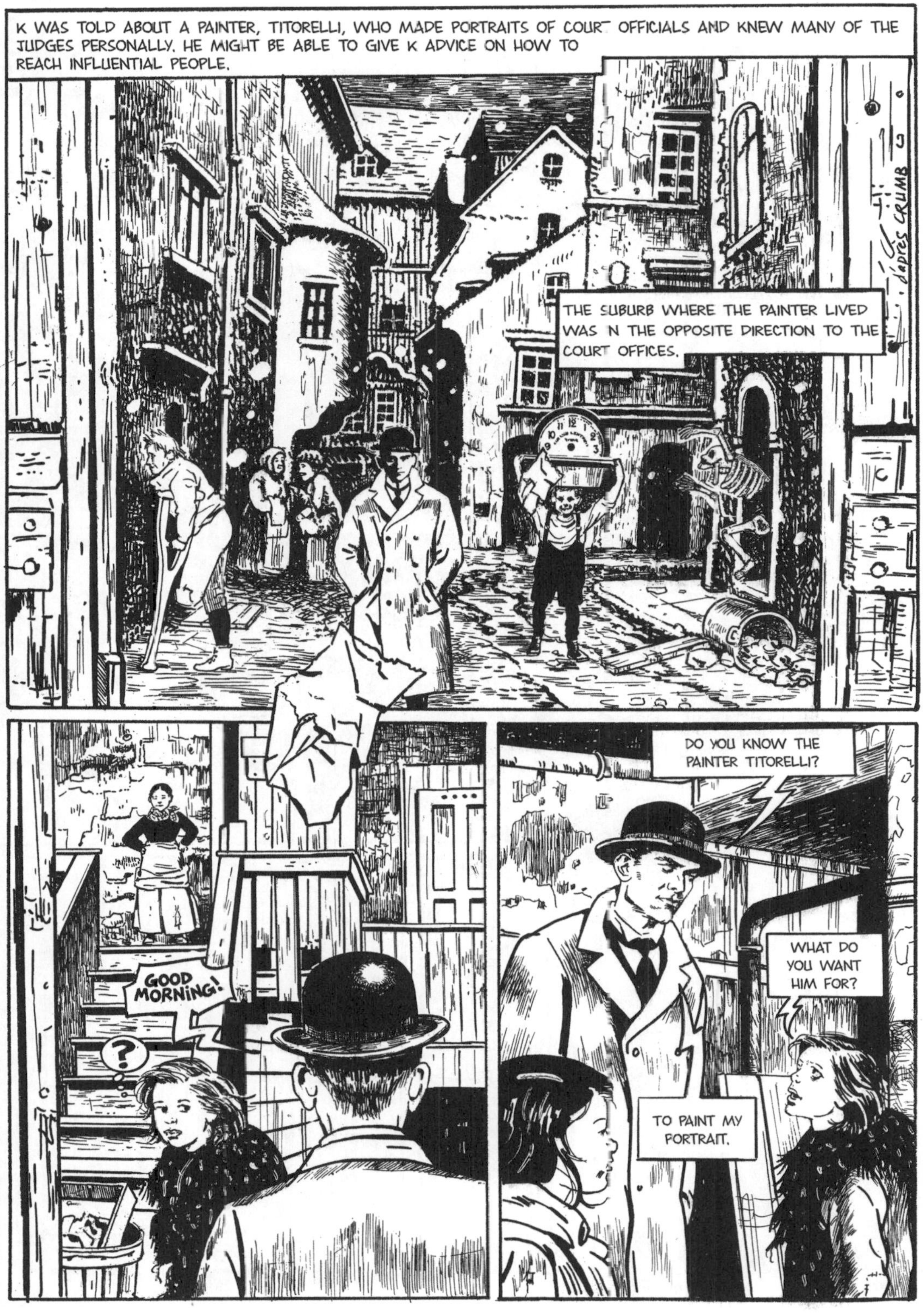
K WAS TOLD ABOUT A PAINTER, TITORELLI, WHO MADE PORTRAITS OF COURT OFFICIALS AND KNEW MANY OF THE JUDGES PERSONALLY. HE MIGHT BE ABLE TO GIVE K ADVICE ON HOW TO REACH INFLUENTIAL PEOPLE.
d'après CRUMB
THE SUBURB WHERE THE PAINTER LIVED WAS IN THE OPPOSITE DIRECTION TO THE COURT OFFICES.
GOOD MORNING!
?
DO YOU KNOW THE PAINTER TITORELLI?
WHAT DO YOU WANT HIM FOR?
TO PAINT MY PORTRAIT.

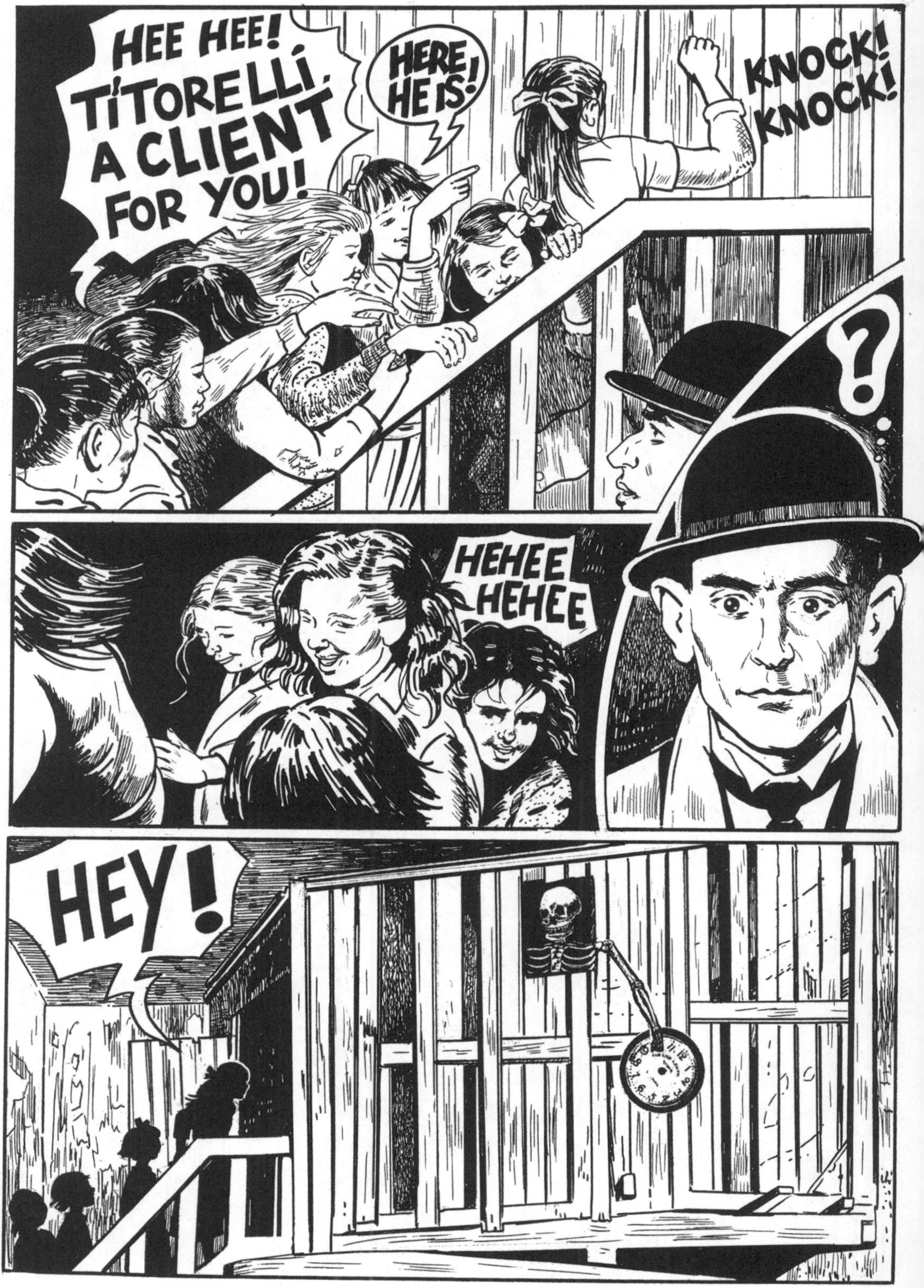
HEE HEE! TITORELLI, A CLIENT FOR YOU!
HERE HE IS!
KNOCK! KNOCK!
?
HEHEE HEHEE
HEY!

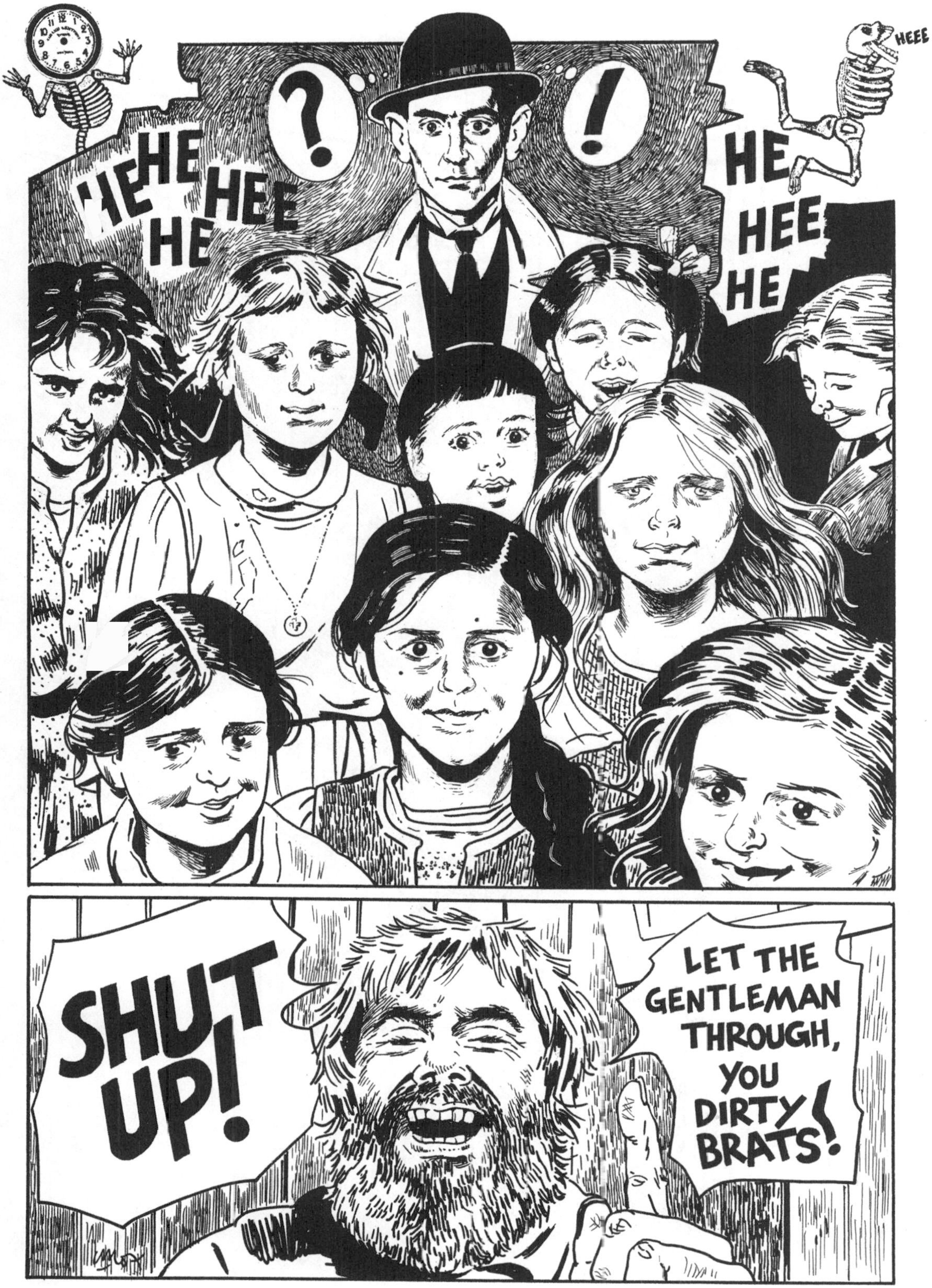
HE HE HE HEE
HE
?
!
HEEE
HE HEE HE
SHUT UP!
LET THE GENTLEMAN THROUGH, YOU DIRTY BRATS!

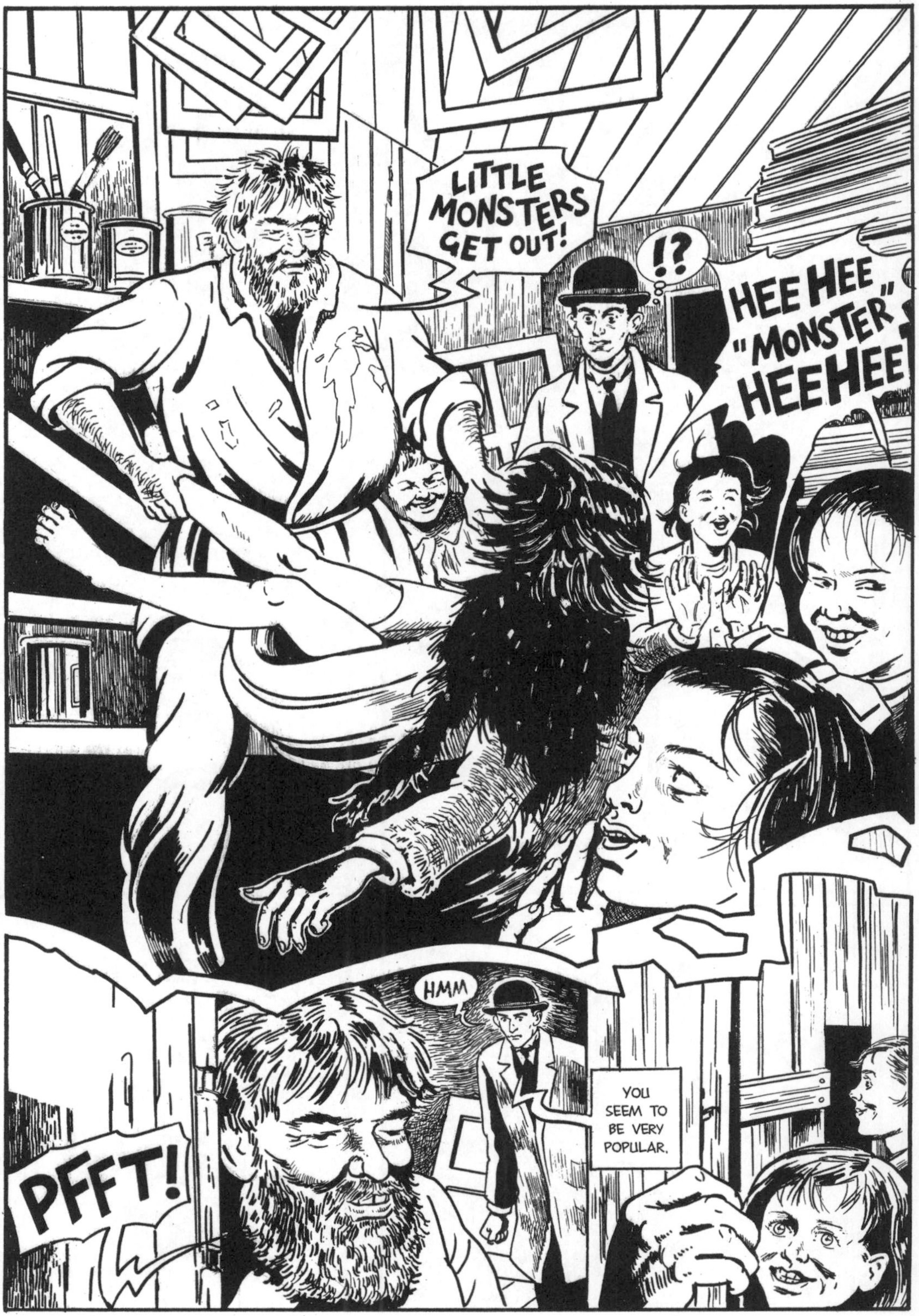
LITTLE MONSTERS GET OUT!
!?
HEE HEE "MONSTER" HEE HEE
HMM
YOU SEEM TO BE VERY POPULAR.
PFFT!

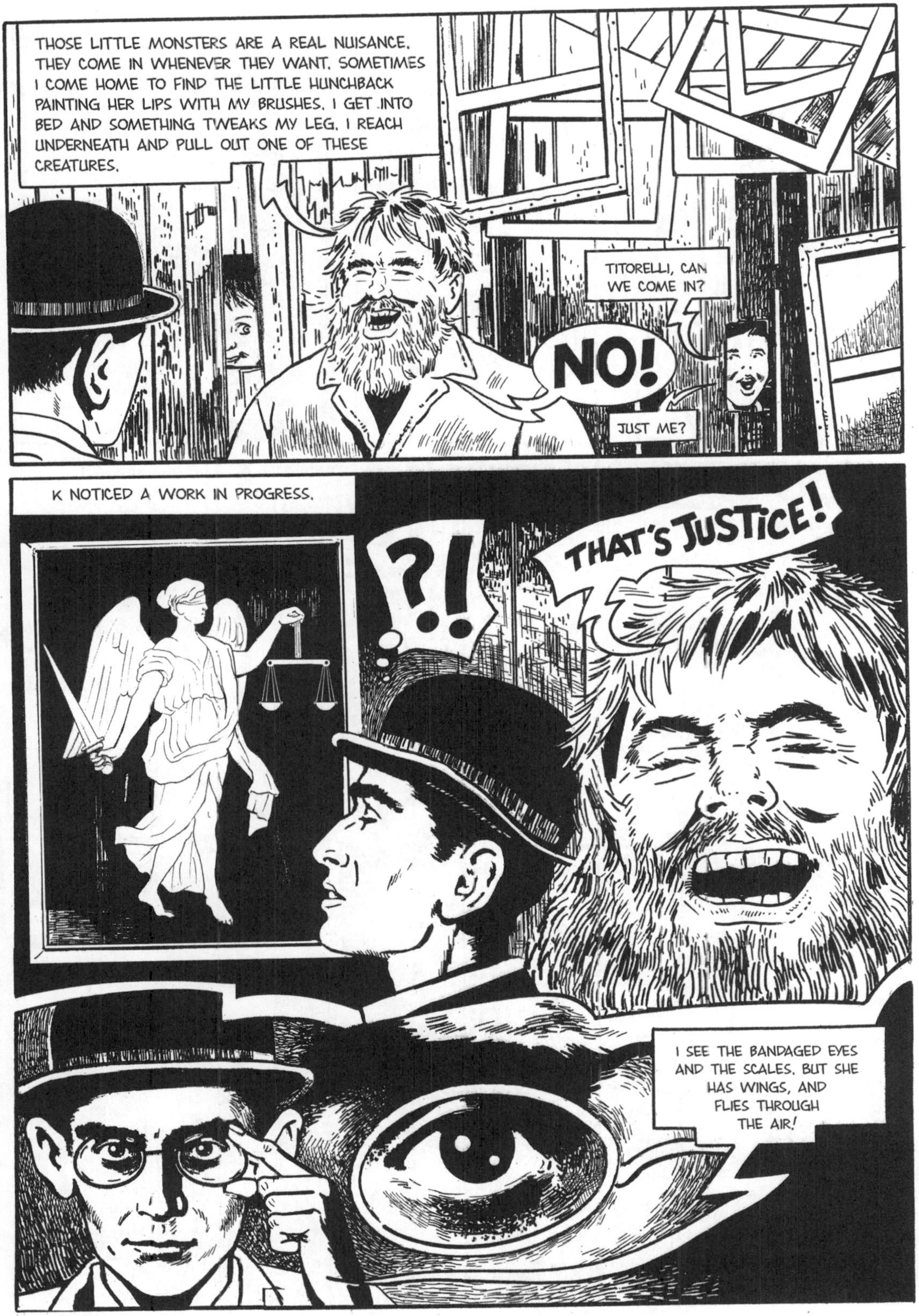
THOSE LITTLE MONSTERS ARE A REAL NUISANCE. THEY COME IN WHENEVER THEY WANT. SOMETIMES I COME HOME TO FIND THE LITTLE HUNCHBACK PAINTING HER LIPS WITH MY BRUSHES. I GET INTO BED AND SOMETHING TWEAKS MY LEG. I REACH UNDERNEATH AND PULL OUT ONE OF THESE CREATURES.
TITORELLI, CAN WE COME IN?
NO!
JUST ME?
K NOTICED A WORK IN PROGRESS.
?!
THAT'S JUSTICE!
I SEE THE BANDAGED EYES AND THE SCALES. BUT SHE HAS WINGS, AND FLIES THROUGH THE AIR!

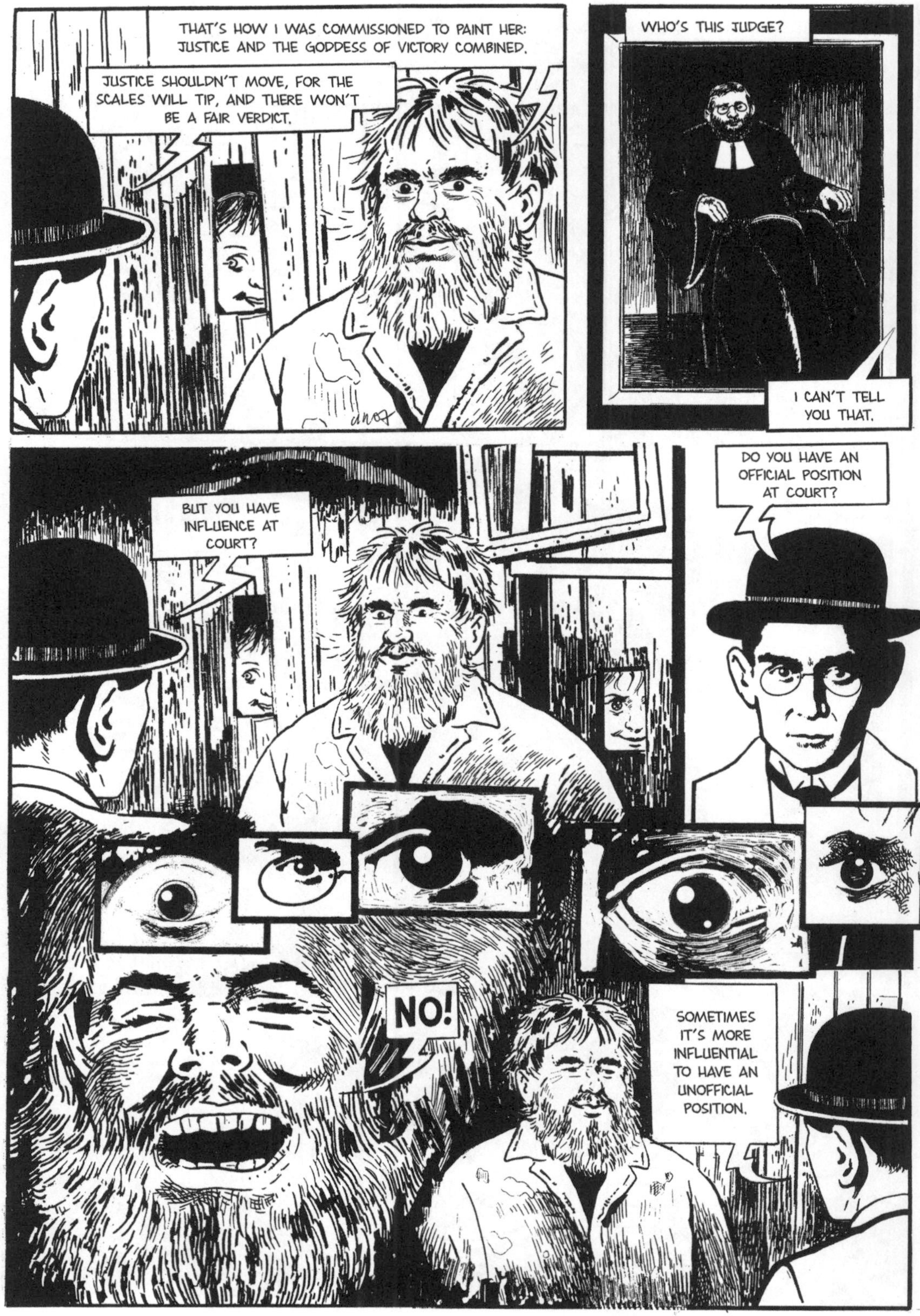
THAT'S HOW I WAS COMMISSIONED TO PAINT HER: JUSTICE AND THE GODDESS OF VICTORY COMBINED.
JUSTICE SHOULDN'T MOVE, FOR THE SCALES WILL TIP, AND THERE WON'T BE A FAIR VERDICT.
WHO'S THIS JUDGE?
I CAN'T TELL YOU THAT.
BUT YOU HAVE INFLUENCE AT COURT?
DO YOU HAVE AN OFFICIAL POSITION AT COURT?
NO!
SOMETIMES IT'S MORE INFLUENTIAL TO HAVE AN UNOFFICIAL POSITION.

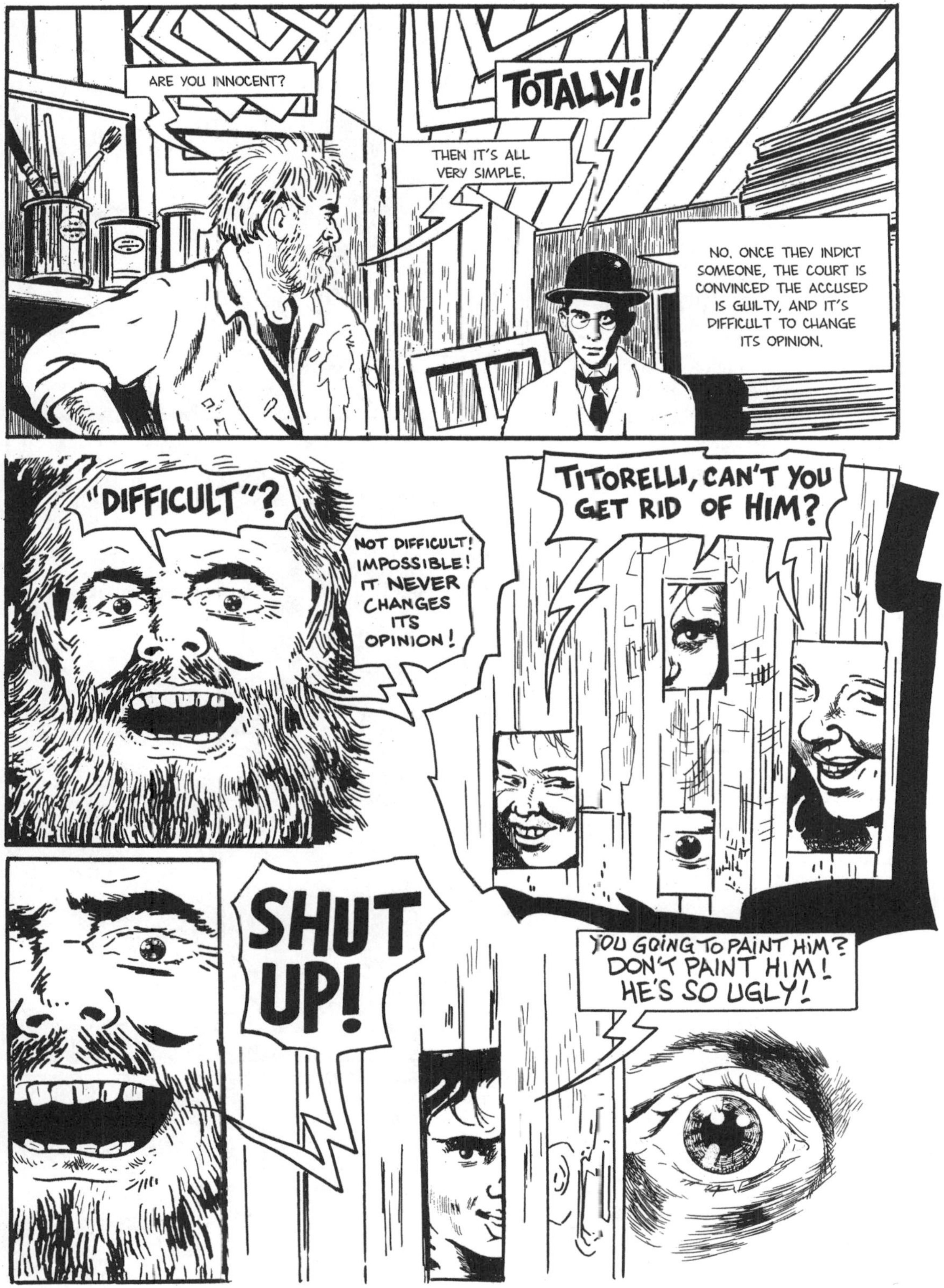
ARE YOU INNOCENT?
TOTALLY!
THEN IT'S ALL VERY SIMPLE.
NO. ONCE THEY INDICT SOMEONE, THE COURT IS CONVINCED THE ACCUSED IS GUILTY, AND IT'S DIFFICULT TO CHANGE ITS OPINION.
"DIFFICULT"?
NOT DIFFICULT! IMPOSSIBLE! IT NEVER CHANGES ITS OPINION!
TITORELLI, CAN'T YOU GET RID OF HIM?
SHUT UP!
YOU GOING TO PAINT HIM? DON'T PAINT HIM! HE'S SO UGLY!

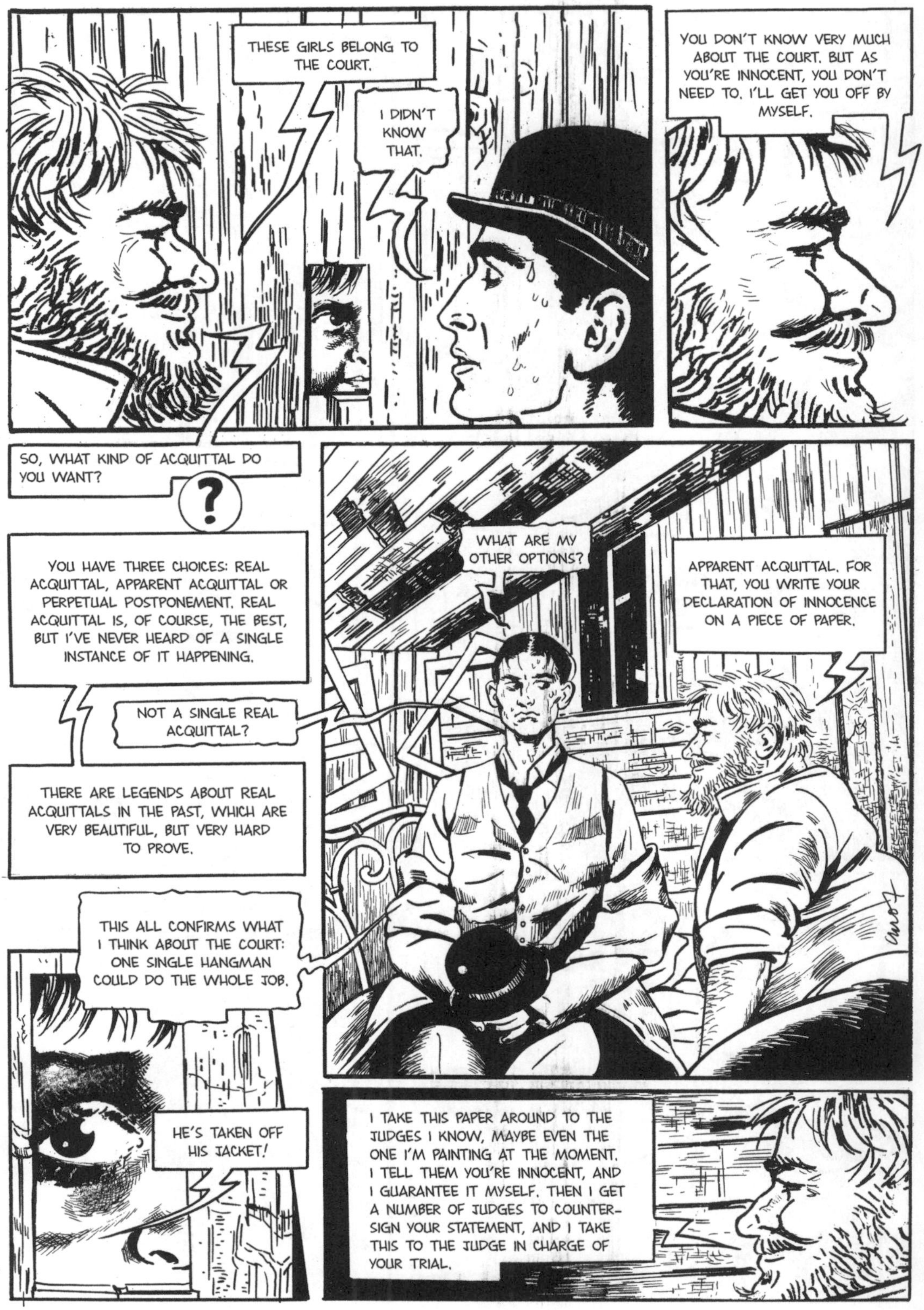
THESE GIRLS BELONG TO THE COURT.
I DIDN'T KNOW THAT.
YOU DON'T KNOW VERY MUCH ABOUT THE COURT. BUT AS YOU'RE INNOCENT, YOU DON'T NEED TO. I'LL GET YOU OFF BY MYSELF.
SO, WHAT KIND OF ACQUITTAL DO YOU WANT?
?
YOU HAVE THREE CHOICES: REAL ACQUITTAL, APPARENT ACQUITTAL OR PERPETUAL POSTPONEMENT. REAL ACQUITTAL IS, OF COURSE, THE BEST, BUT I'VE NEVER HEARD OF A SINGLE INSTANCE OF IT HAPPENING.
NOT A SINGLE REAL ACQUITTAL?
THERE ARE LEGENDS ABOUT REAL ACQUITTALS IN THE PAST, WHICH ARE VERY BEAUTIFUL, BUT VERY HARD TO PROVE.
THIS ALL CONFIRMS WHAT I THINK ABOUT THE COURT: ONE SINGLE HANGMAN COULD DO THE WHOLE JOB.
WHAT ARE MY OTHER OPTIONS?
APPARENT ACQUITTAL. FOR THAT, YOU WRITE YOUR DECLARATION OF INNOCENCE ON A PIECE OF PAPER.
HE'S TAKEN OFF HIS JACKET!
I TAKE THIS PAPER AROUND TO THE JUDGES I KNOW, MAYBE EVEN THE ONE I'M PAINTING AT THE MOMENT. I TELL THEM YOU'RE INNOCENT, AND I GUARANTEE IT MYSELF. THEN I GET A NUMBER OF JUDGES TO COUNTER-SIGN YOUR STATEMENT, AND I TAKE THIS TO THE JUDGE IN CHARGE OF YOUR TRIAL.

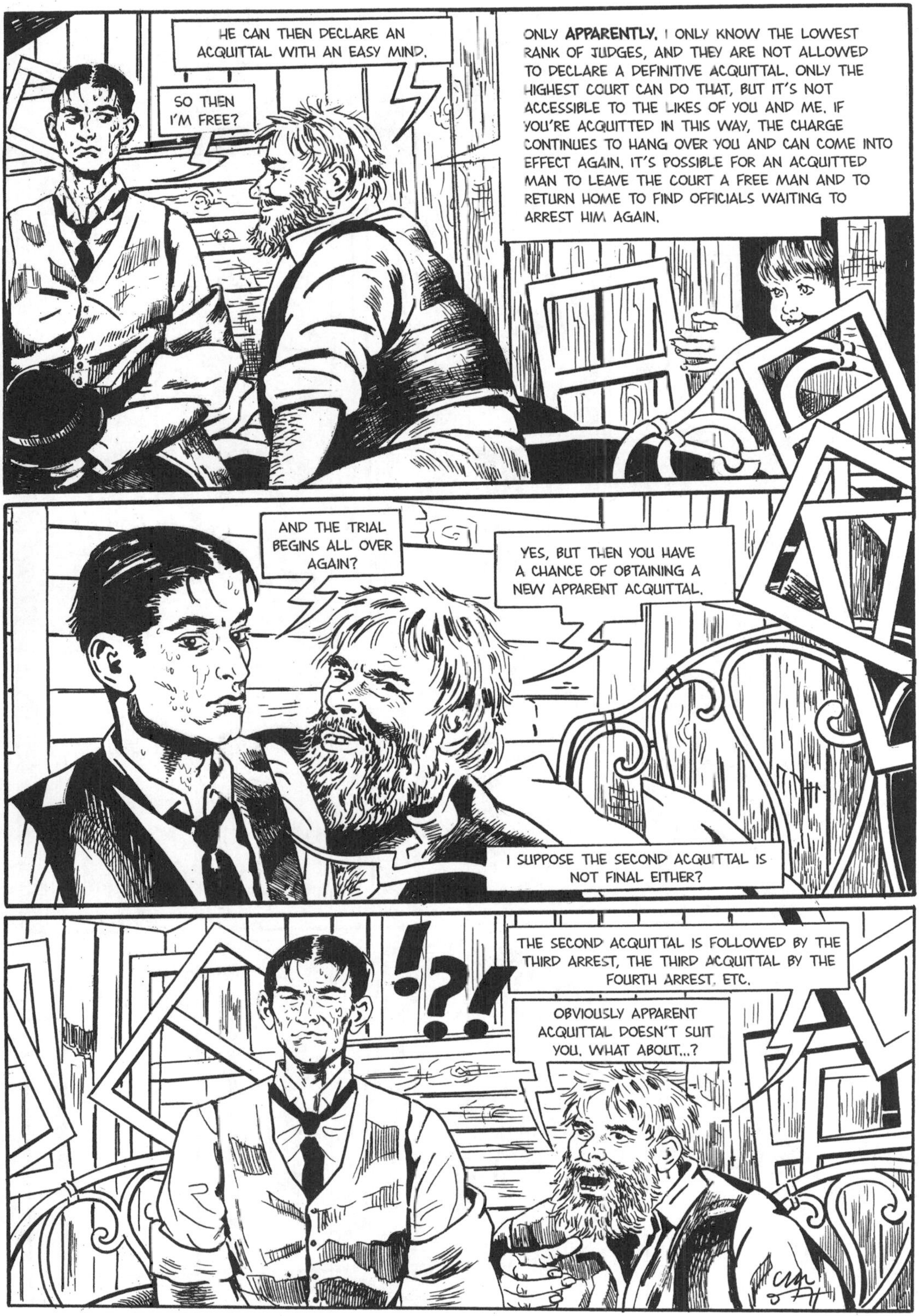
HE CAN THEN DECLARE AN ACQUITTAL WITH AN EASY MIND.
SO THEN I'M FREE?
ONLY **APPARENTLY**. I ONLY KNOW THE LOWEST RANK OF JUDGES, AND THEY ARE NOT ALLOWED TO DECLARE A DEFINITIVE ACQUITTAL. ONLY THE HIGHEST COURT CAN DO THAT, BUT IT'S NOT ACCESSIBLE TO THE LIKES OF YOU AND ME. IF YOU'RE ACQUITTED IN THIS WAY, THE CHARGE CONTINUES TO HANG OVER YOU AND CAN COME INTO EFFECT AGAIN. IT'S POSSIBLE FOR AN ACQUITTED MAN TO LEAVE THE COURT A FREE MAN AND TO RETURN HOME TO FIND OFFICIALS WAITING TO ARREST HIM AGAIN.
AND THE TRIAL BEGINS ALL OVER AGAIN?
YES, BUT THEN YOU HAVE A CHANCE OF OBTAINING A NEW APPARENT ACQUITTAL.
I SUPPOSE THE SECOND ACQUITTAL IS NOT FINAL EITHER?
!?!
THE SECOND ACQUITTAL IS FOLLOWED BY THE THIRD ARREST, THE THIRD ACQUITTAL BY THE FOURTH ARREST, ETC.
OBVIOUSLY APPARENT ACQUITTAL DOESN'T SUIT YOU. WHAT ABOUT...?

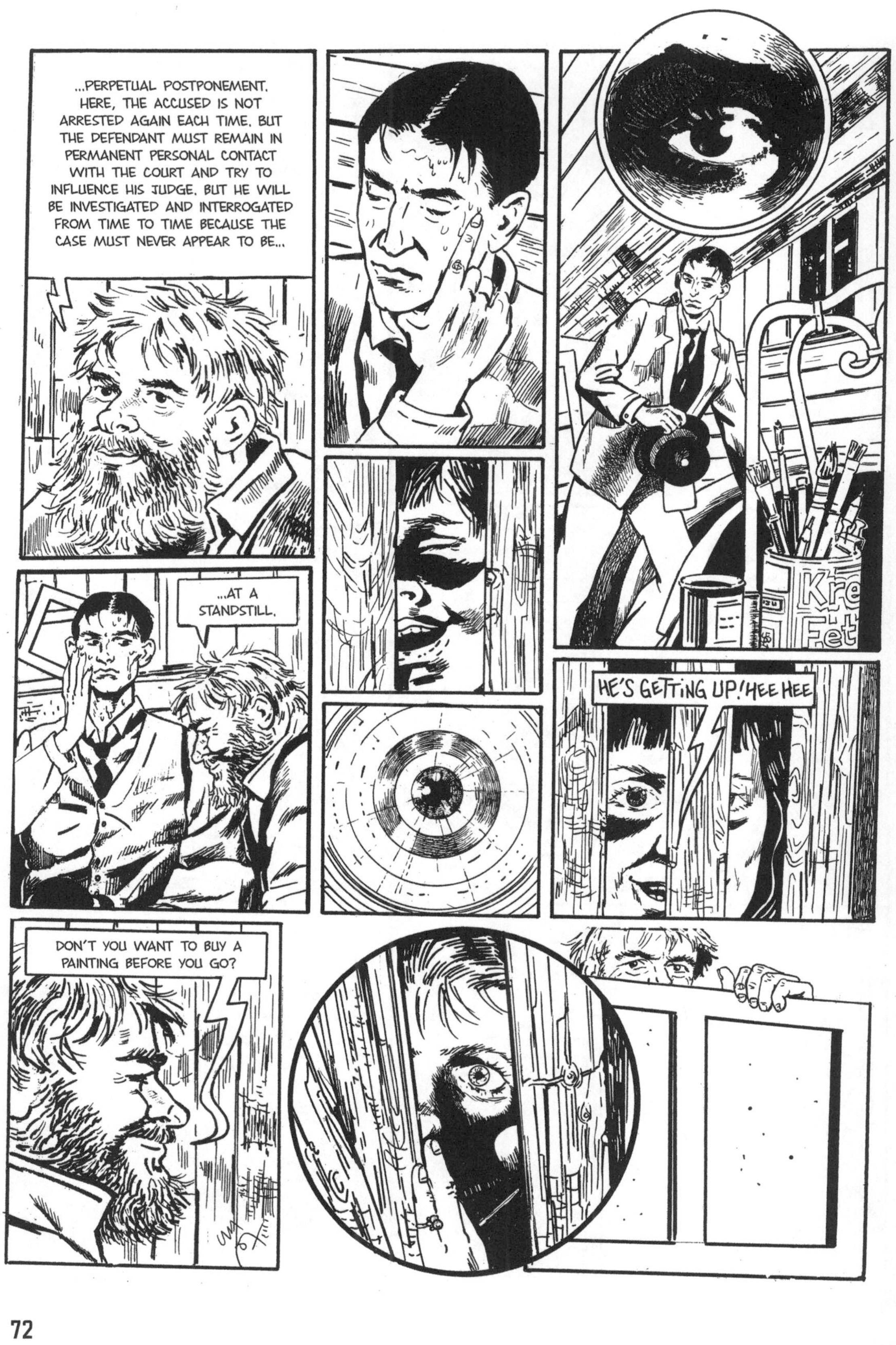
...PERPETUAL POSTPONEMENT. HERE, THE ACCUSED IS NOT ARRESTED AGAIN EACH TIME, BUT THE DEFENDANT MUST REMAIN IN PERMANENT PERSONAL CONTACT WITH THE COURT AND TRY TO INFLUENCE HIS JUDGE. BUT HE WILL BE INVESTIGATED AND INTERROGATED FROM TIME TO TIME BECAUSE THE CASE MUST NEVER APPEAR TO BE...
...AT A STANDSTILL.
HE'S GETTING UP! HEE HEE
DON'T YOU WANT TO BUY A PAINTING BEFORE YOU GO?

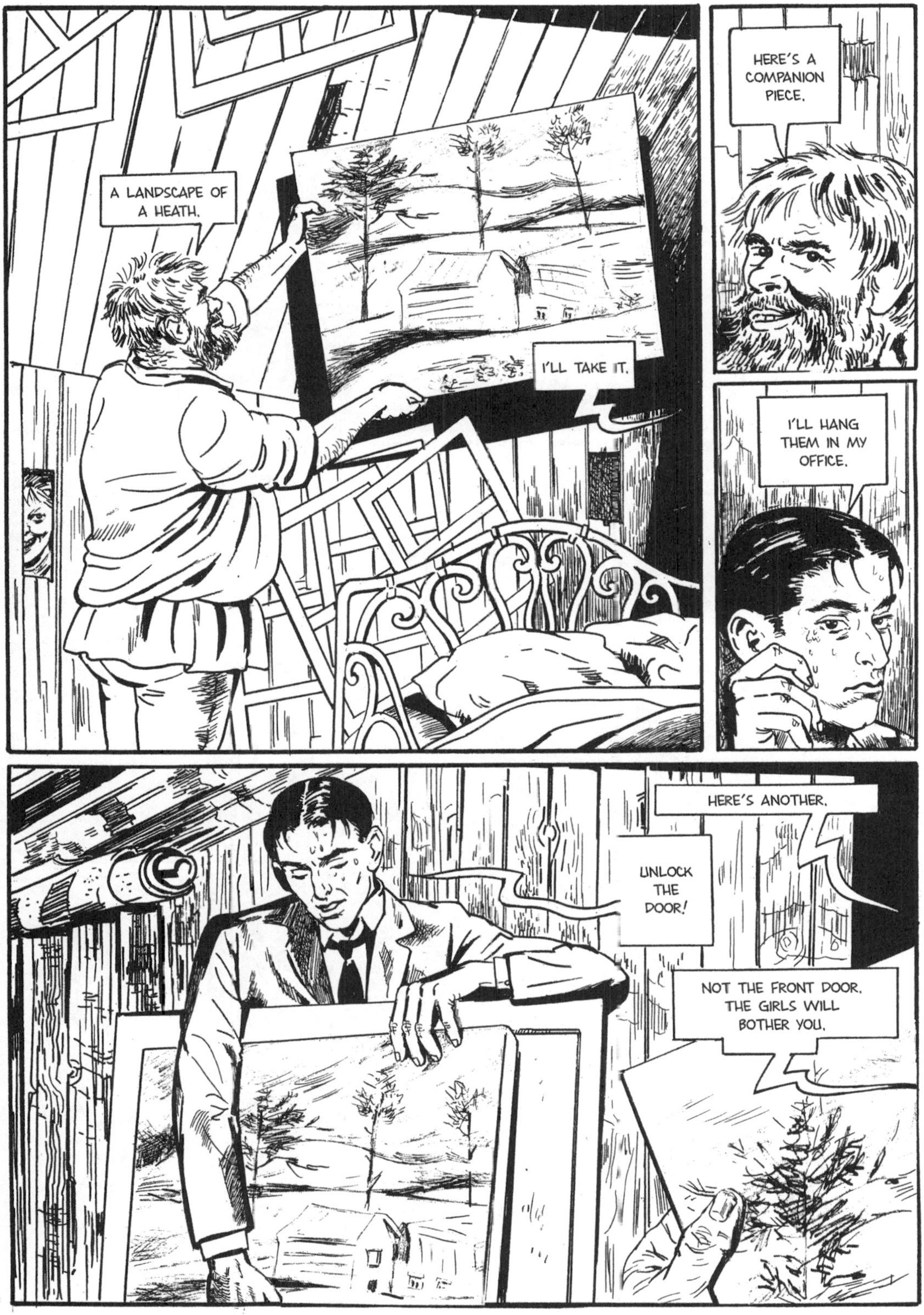
A LANDSCAPE OF A HEATH.
I'LL TAKE IT.
HERE'S A COMPANION PIECE.
I'LL HANG THEM IN MY OFFICE.
HERE'S ANOTHER.
UNLOCK THE DOOR!
NOT THE FRONT DOOR. THE GIRLS WILL BOTHER YOU.

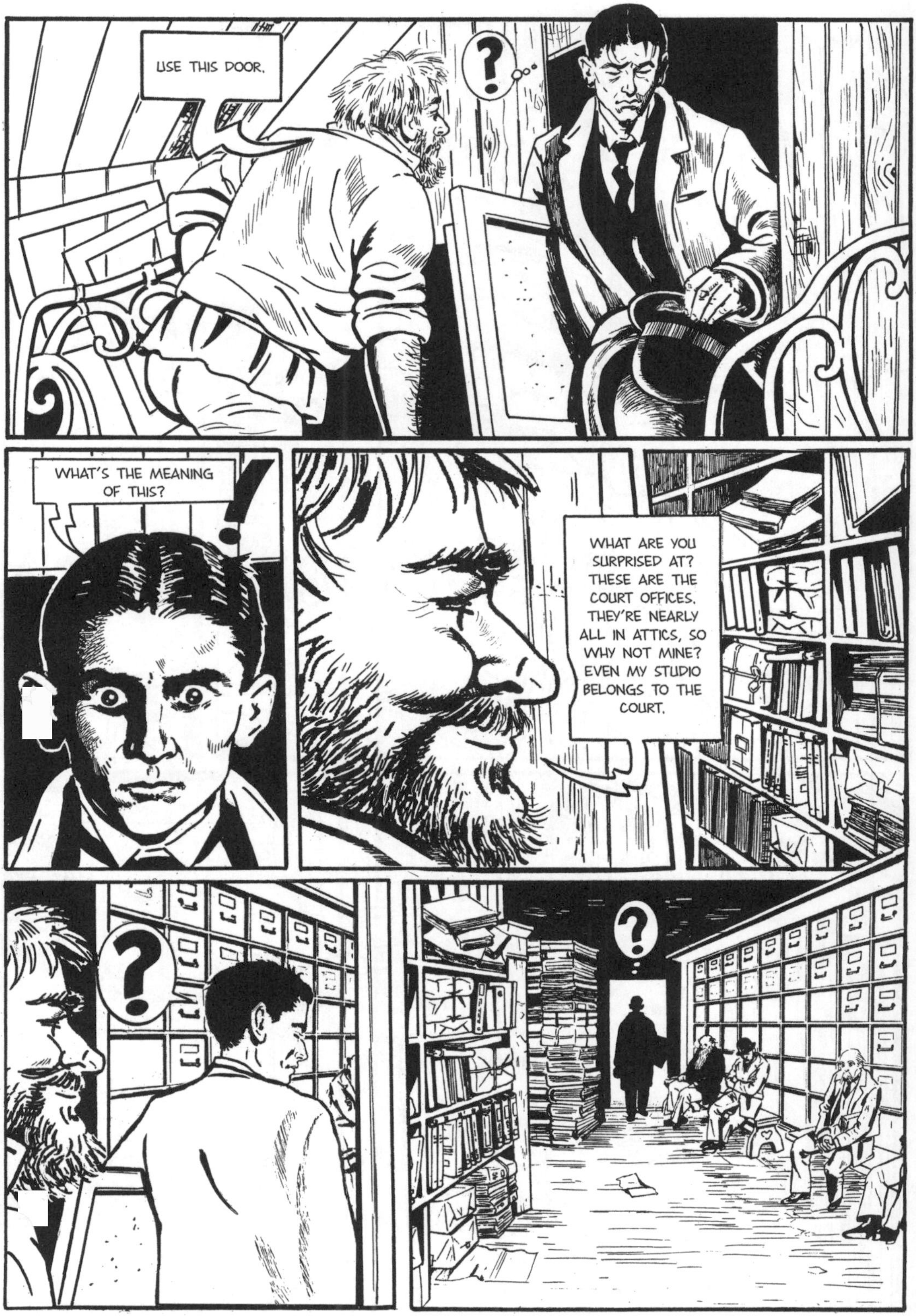
USE THIS DOOR.
?
WHAT'S THE MEANING OF THIS?
!
WHAT ARE YOU SURPRISED AT? THESE ARE THE COURT OFFICES. THEY'RE NEARLY ALL IN ATTICS, SO WHY NOT MINE? EVEN MY STUDIO BELONGS TO THE COURT.
?
?

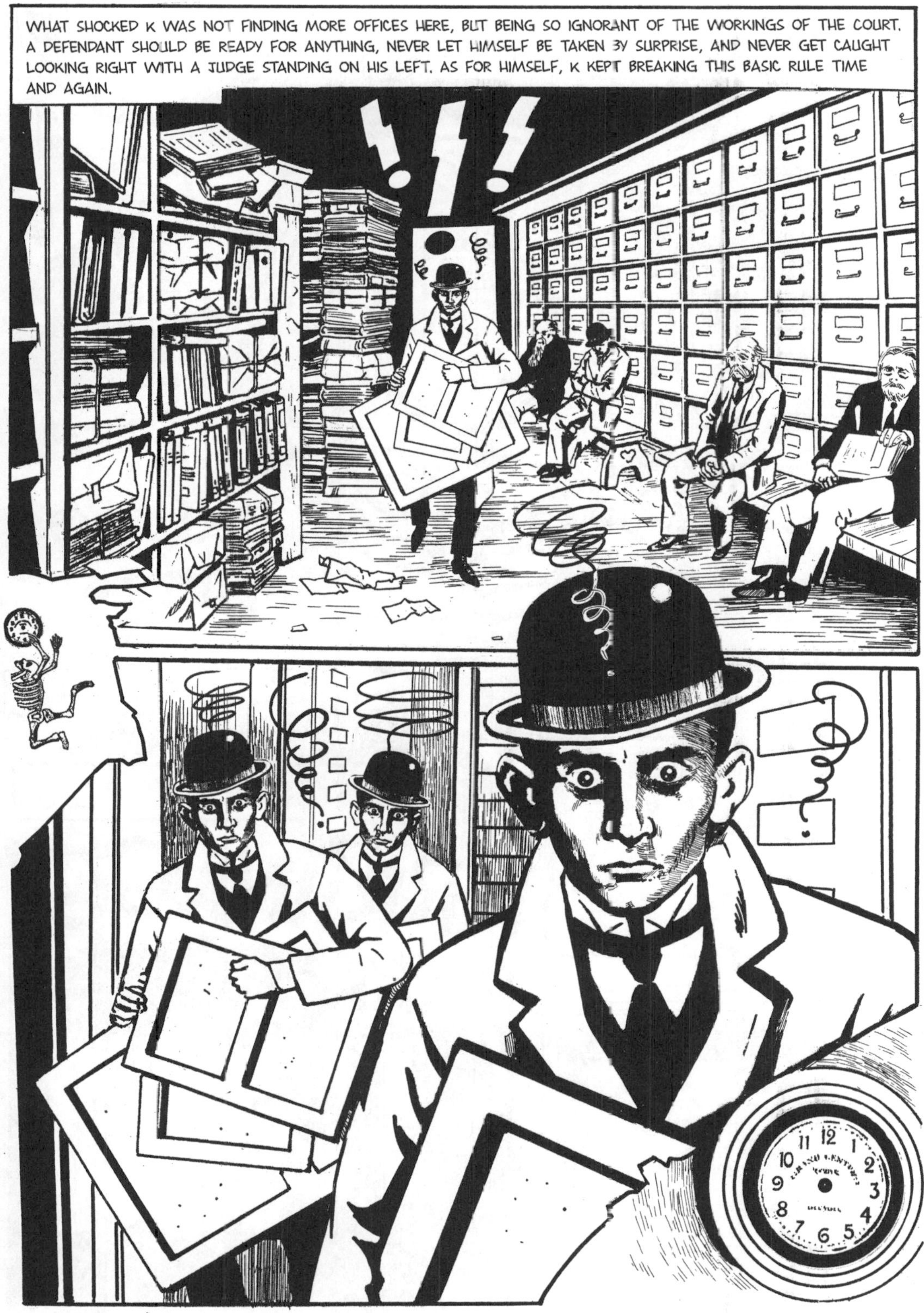
WHAT SHOCKED K WAS NOT FINDING MORE OFFICES HERE, BUT BEING SO IGNORANT OF THE WORKINGS OF THE COURT. A DEFENDANT SHOULD BE READY FOR ANYTHING, NEVER LET HIMSELF BE TAKEN BY SURPRISE, AND NEVER GET CAUGHT LOOKING RIGHT WITH A JUDGE STANDING ON HIS LEFT. AS FOR HIMSELF, K KEPT BREAKING THIS BASIC RULE TIME AND AGAIN.

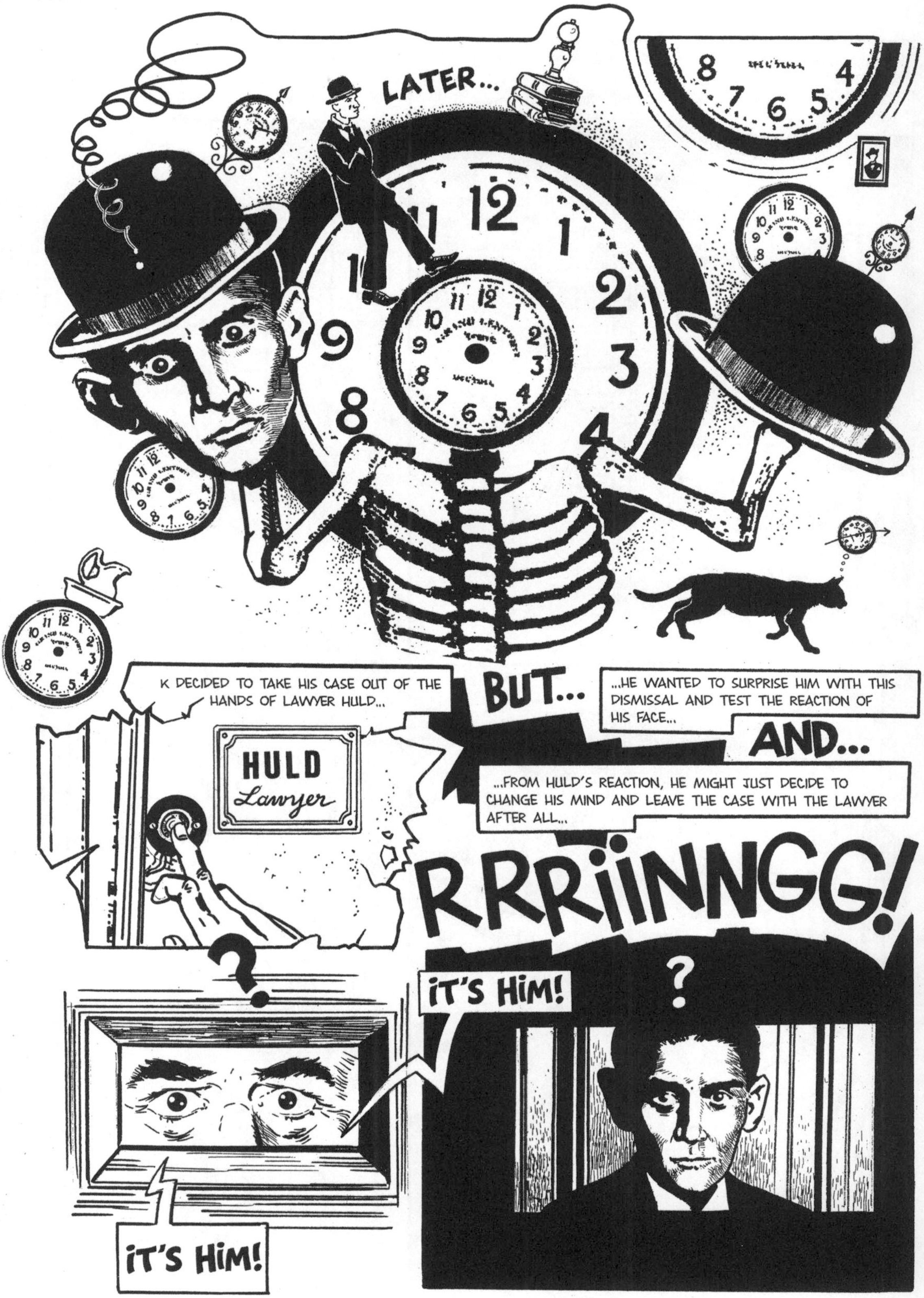
LATER...
K DECIDED TO TAKE HIS CASE OUT OF THE HANDS OF LAWYER HULD...
BUT...
...HE WANTED TO SURPRISE HIM WITH THIS DISMISSAL AND TEST THE REACTION OF HIS FACE...
AND...
...FROM HULD'S REACTION, HE MIGHT JUST DECIDE TO CHANGE HIS MIND AND LEAVE THE CASE WITH THE LAWYER AFTER ALL...
HULD
Lawyer
RRRIINNGG!
?
IT'S HIM!
?
IT'S HIM!

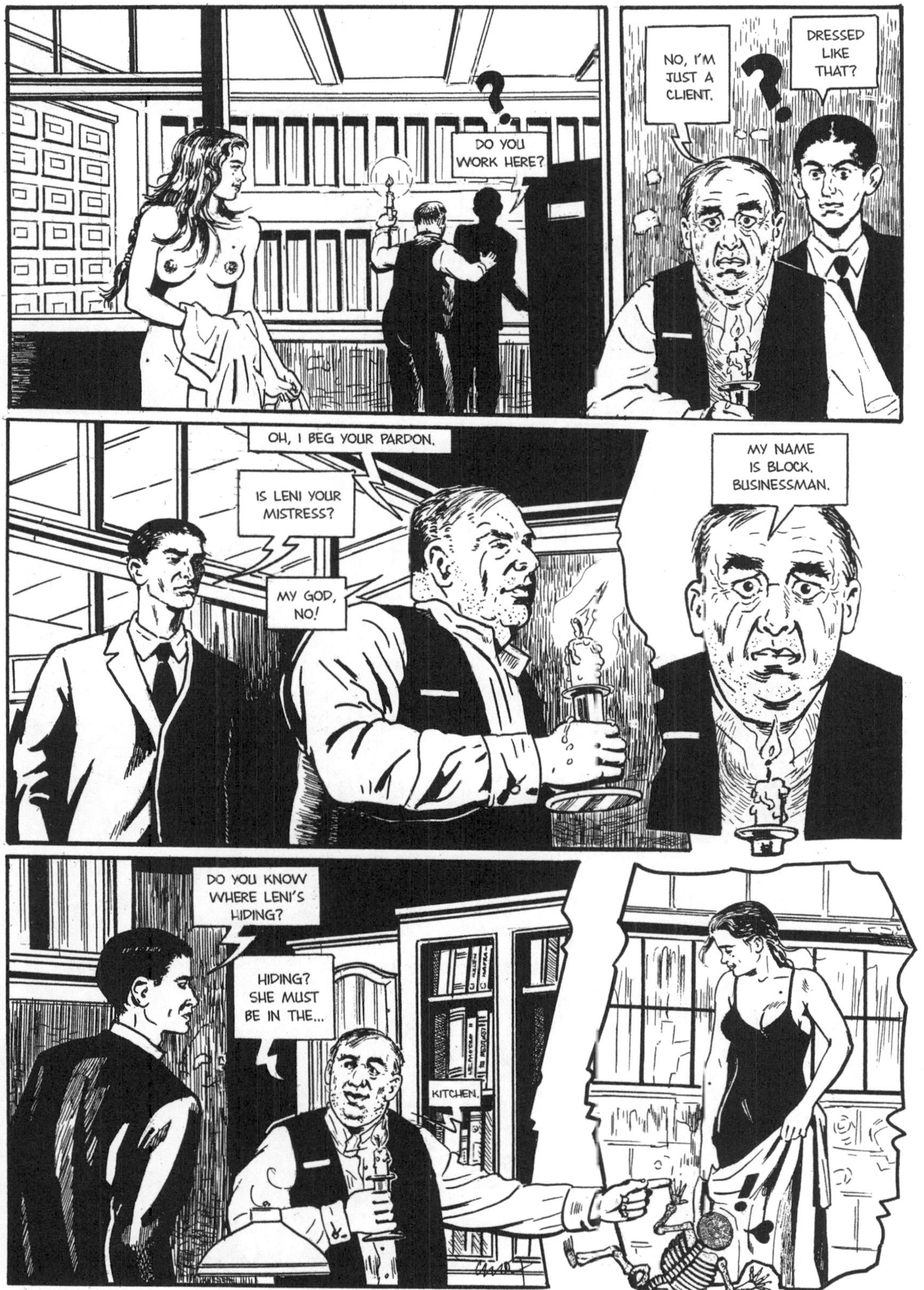
DO YOU WORK HERE?
NO, I'M JUST A CLIENT.
DRESSED LIKE THAT?
OH, I BEG YOUR PARDON.
IS LENI YOUR MISTRESS?
MY GOD, NO!
MY NAME IS BLOCK. BUSINESSMAN.
DO YOU KNOW WHERE LENI'S HIDING?
HIDING? SHE MUST BE IN THE...
KITCHEN.

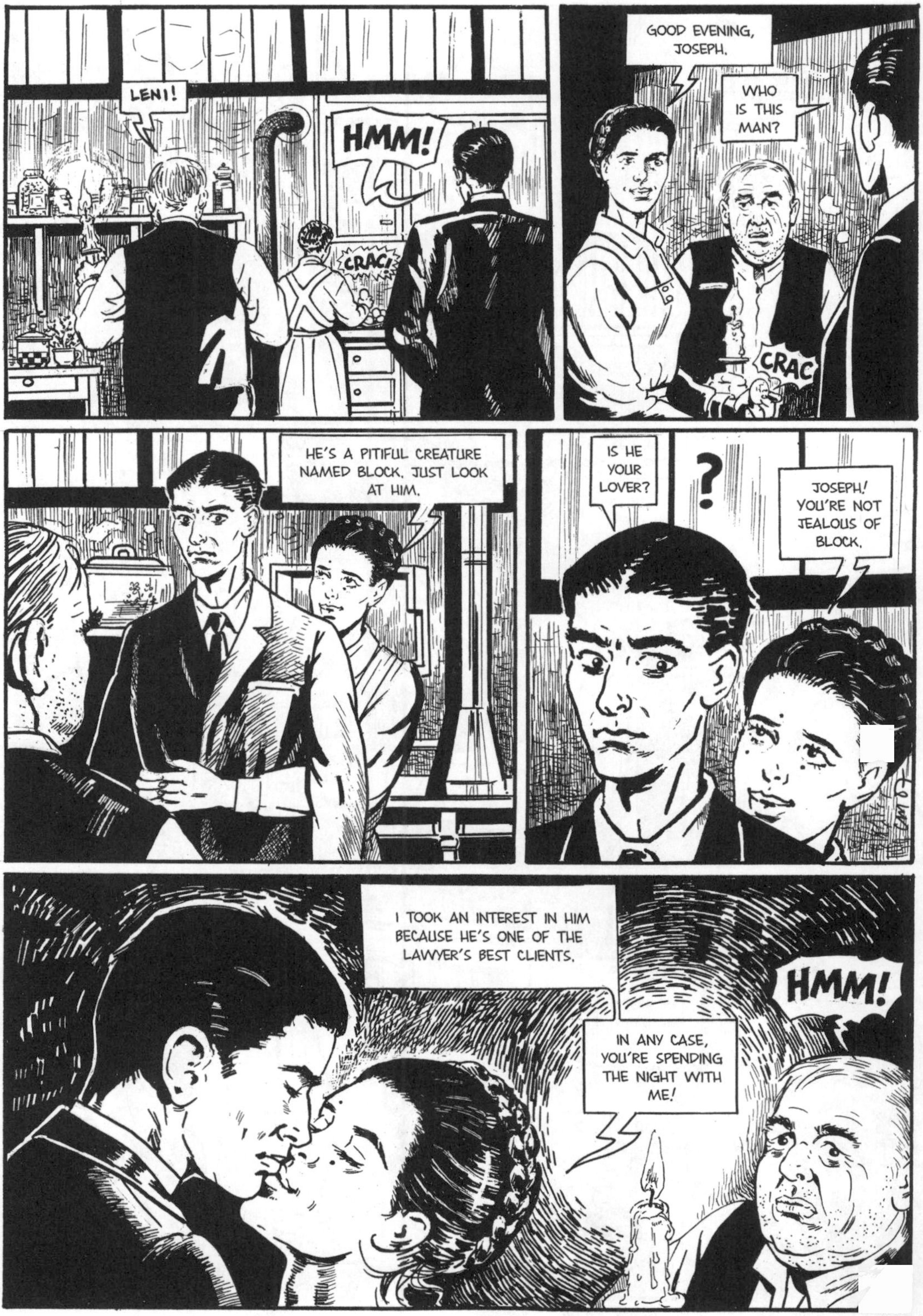
LENI!
HMM!
CRAC!
GOOD EVENING, JOSEPH.
WHO IS THIS MAN?
CRAC
HE'S A PITIFUL CREATURE NAMED BLOCK. JUST LOOK AT HIM.
IS HE YOUR LOVER?
?
JOSEPH! YOU'RE NOT JEALOUS OF BLOCK.
I TOOK AN INTEREST IN HIM BECAUSE HE'S ONE OF THE LAWYER'S BEST CLIENTS.
IN ANY CASE, YOU'RE SPENDING THE NIGHT WITH ME!
HMM!

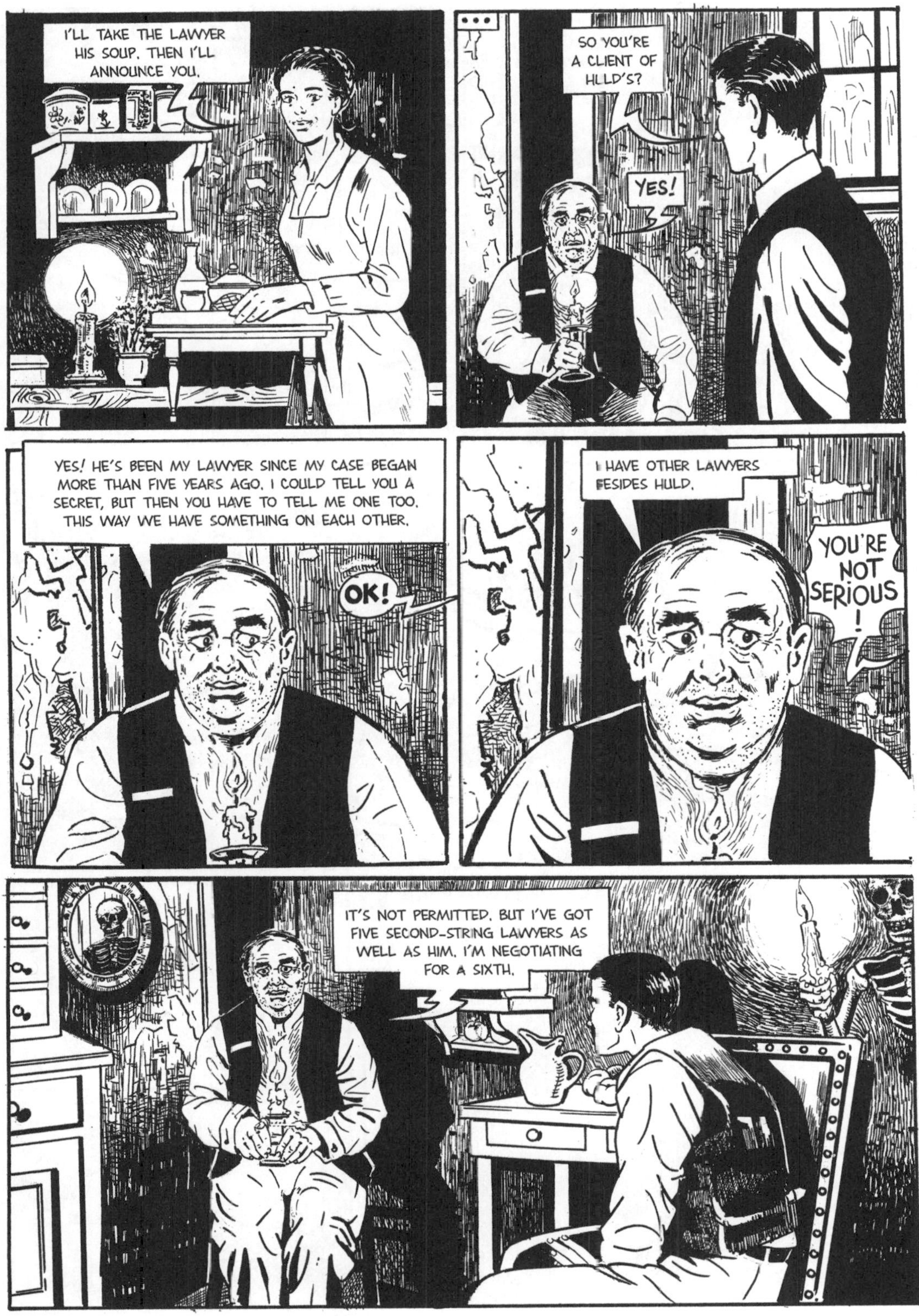
I'LL TAKE THE LAWYER HIS SOUP. THEN I'LL ANNOUNCE YOU.
SO YOU'RE A CLIENT OF HULD'S?
YES!
YES! HE'S BEEN MY LAWYER SINCE MY CASE BEGAN MORE THAN FIVE YEARS AGO. I COULD TELL YOU A SECRET, BUT THEN YOU HAVE TO TELL ME ONE TOO. THIS WAY WE HAVE SOMETHING ON EACH OTHER.
OK!
I HAVE OTHER LAWYERS BESIDES HULD.
YOU'RE NOT SERIOUS!
IT'S NOT PERMITTED. BUT I'VE GOT FIVE SECOND-STRING LAWYERS AS WELL AS HIM. I'M NEGOTIATING FOR A SIXTH.

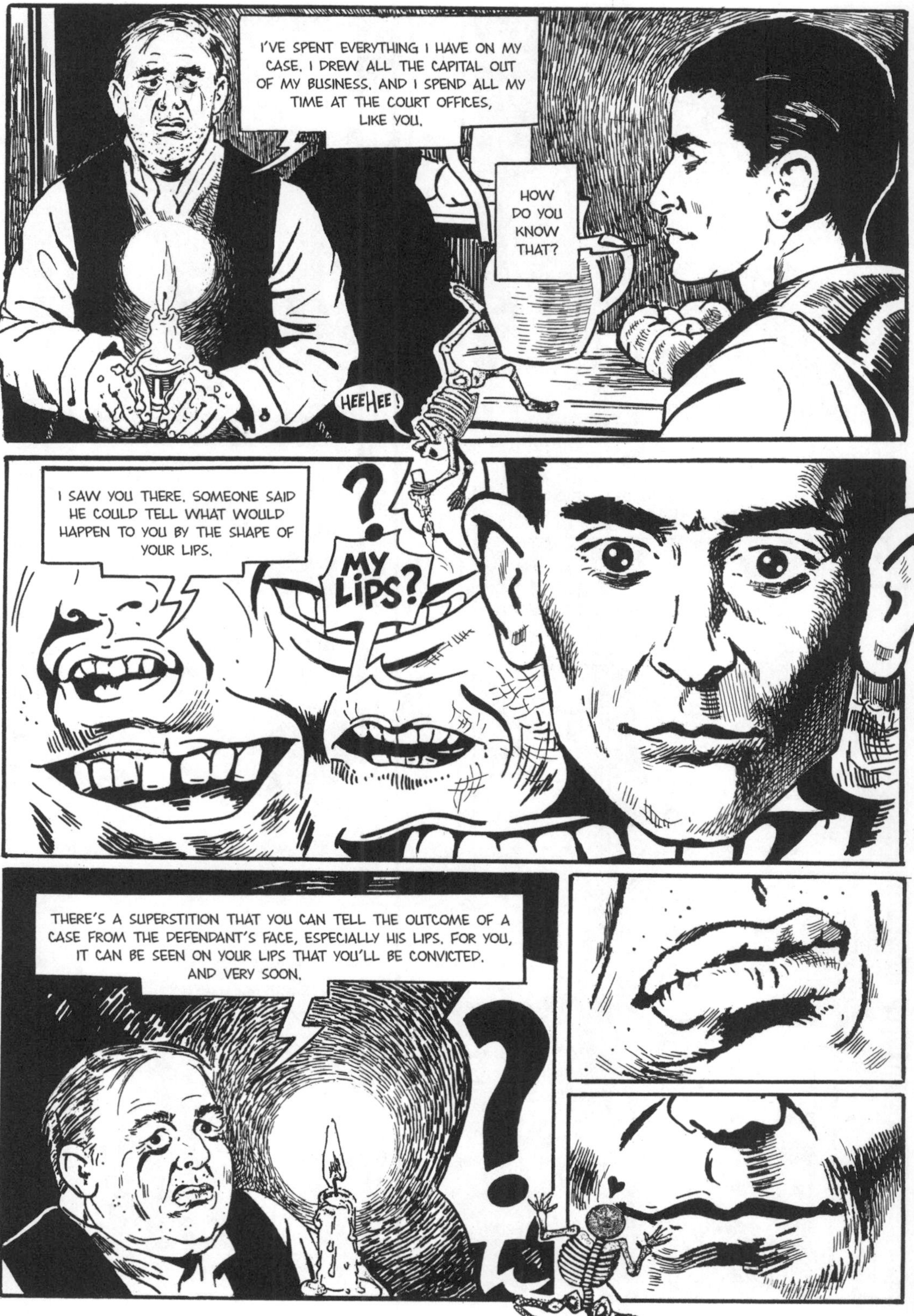
I'VE SPENT EVERYTHING I HAVE ON MY CASE. I DREW ALL THE CAPITAL OUT OF MY BUSINESS, AND I SPEND ALL MY TIME AT THE COURT OFFICES, LIKE YOU.
HOW DO YOU KNOW THAT?
HEEHEE!
I SAW YOU THERE. SOMEONE SAID HE COULD TELL WHAT WOULD HAPPEN TO YOU BY THE SHAPE OF YOUR LIPS.
?
MY LIPS?
THERE'S A SUPERSTITION THAT YOU CAN TELL THE OUTCOME OF A CASE FROM THE DEFENDANT'S FACE, ESPECIALLY HIS LIPS. FOR YOU, IT CAN BE SEEN ON YOUR LIPS THAT YOU'LL BE CONVICTED. AND VERY SOON.
?

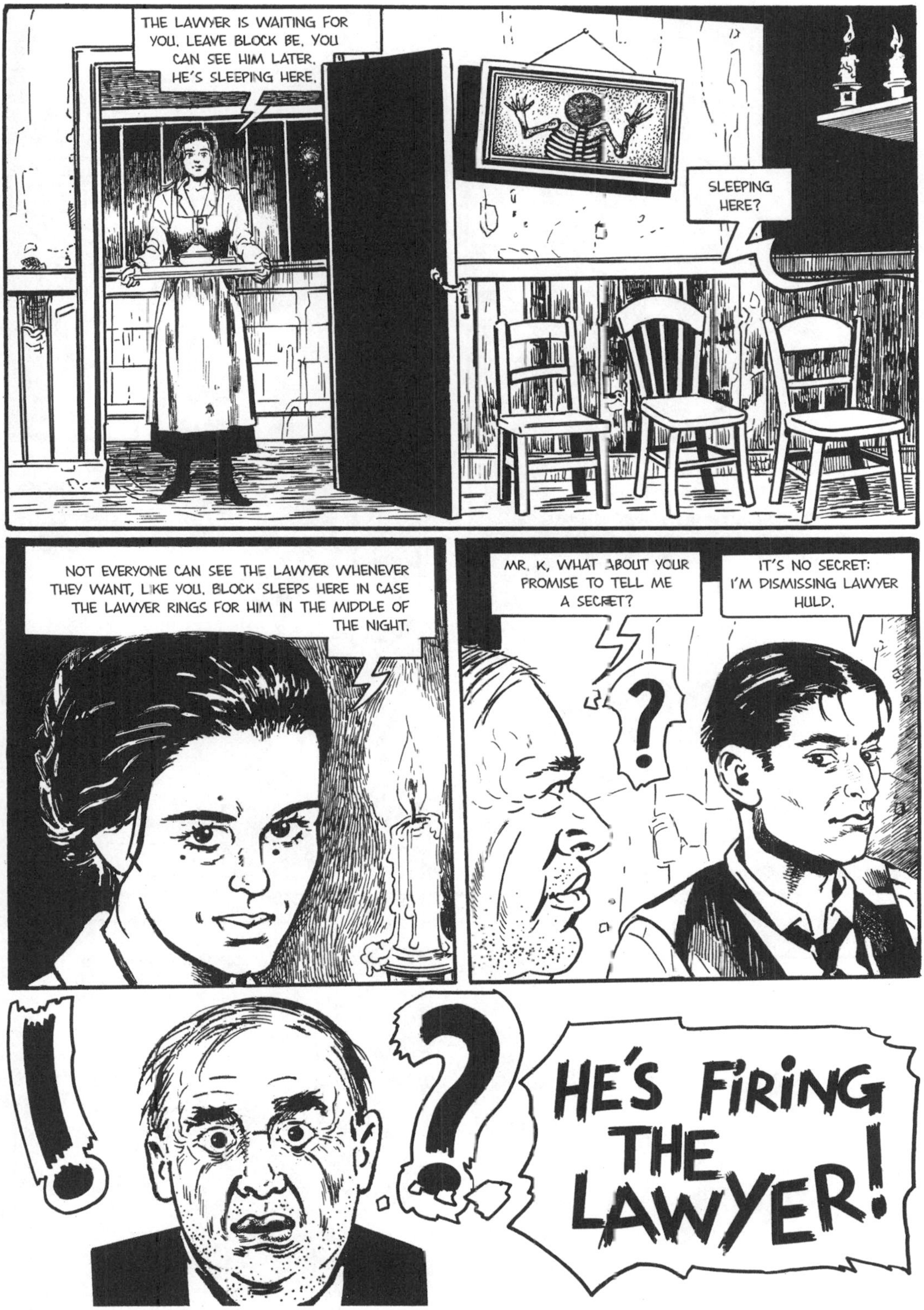
THE LAWYER IS WAITING FOR YOU. LEAVE BLOCK BE. YOU CAN SEE HIM LATER. HE'S SLEEPING HERE.
SLEEPING HERE?
NOT EVERYONE CAN SEE THE LAWYER WHENEVER THEY WANT, LIKE YOU. BLOCK SLEEPS HERE IN CASE THE LAWYER RINGS FOR HIM IN THE MIDDLE OF THE NIGHT.
MR. K, WHAT ABOUT YOUR PROMISE TO TELL ME A SECRET?
IT'S NO SECRET: I'M DISMISSING LAWYER HULD.
?
!
?
HE'S FIRING THE LAWYER!

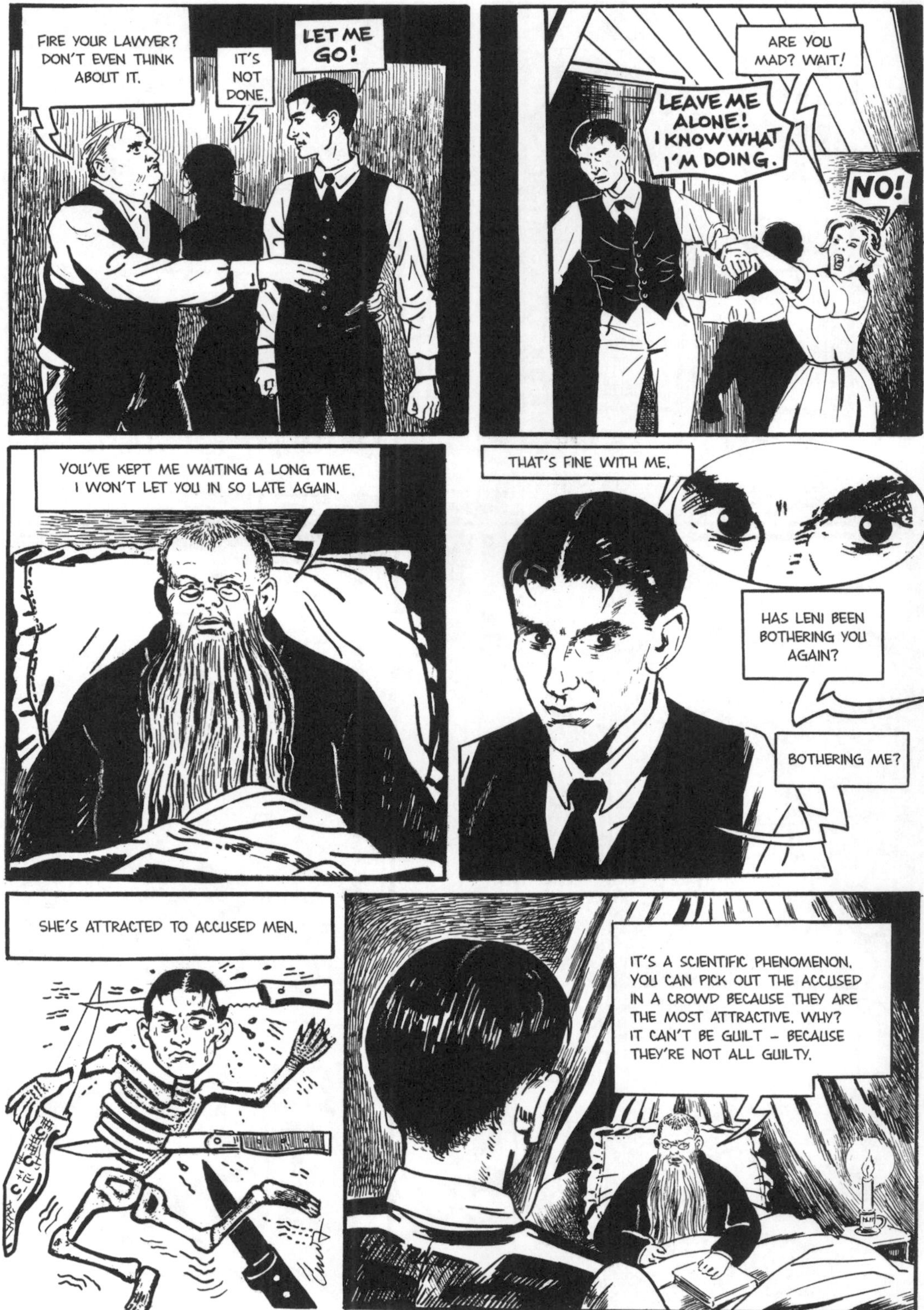
FIRE YOUR LAWYER? DON'T EVEN THINK ABOUT IT.
IT'S NOT DONE.
LET ME GO!
LEAVE ME ALONE! I KNOW WHAT I'M DOING.
ARE YOU MAD? WAIT!
NO!
YOU'VE KEPT ME WAITING A LONG TIME. I WON'T LET YOU IN SO LATE AGAIN.
THAT'S FINE WITH ME.
HAS LENI BEEN BOTHERING YOU AGAIN?
BOTHERING ME?
SHE'S ATTRACTED TO ACCUSED MEN.
IT'S A SCIENTIFIC PHENOMENON. YOU CAN PICK OUT THE ACCUSED IN A CROWD BECAUSE THEY ARE THE MOST ATTRACTIVE. WHY? IT CAN'T BE GUILT – BECAUSE THEY'RE NOT ALL GUILTY.

SO IT MUST BE THE AURA OF THE PROCEEDINGS AGAINST THEM THAT STICKS TO THEM AND MAKES THEM DESIRABLE.

HMM

I'M TAKING MY CASE OUT OF YOUR HANDS.

DON'T BE IN SUCH A HURRY.

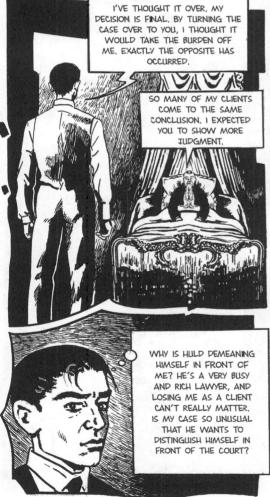

I'VE THOUGHT IT OVER. MY DECISION IS FINAL. BY TURNING THE CASE OVER TO YOU, I THOUGHT IT WOULD TAKE THE BURDEN OFF ME. EXACTLY THE OPPOSITE HAS OCCURRED.

SO MANY OF MY CLIENTS COME TO THE SAME CONCLUSION. I EXPECTED YOU TO SHOW MORE JUDGMENT.

WHY IS HULD DEMEANING HIMSELF IN FRONT OF ME? HE'S A VERY BUSY AND RICH LAWYER, AND LOSING ME AS A CLIENT CAN'T REALLY MATTER. IS MY CASE SO UNUSUAL THAT HE WANTS TO DISTINGUISH HIMSELF IN FRONT OF THE COURT?

I'M GOING!

LIT, D'APRÈS TARDI

83

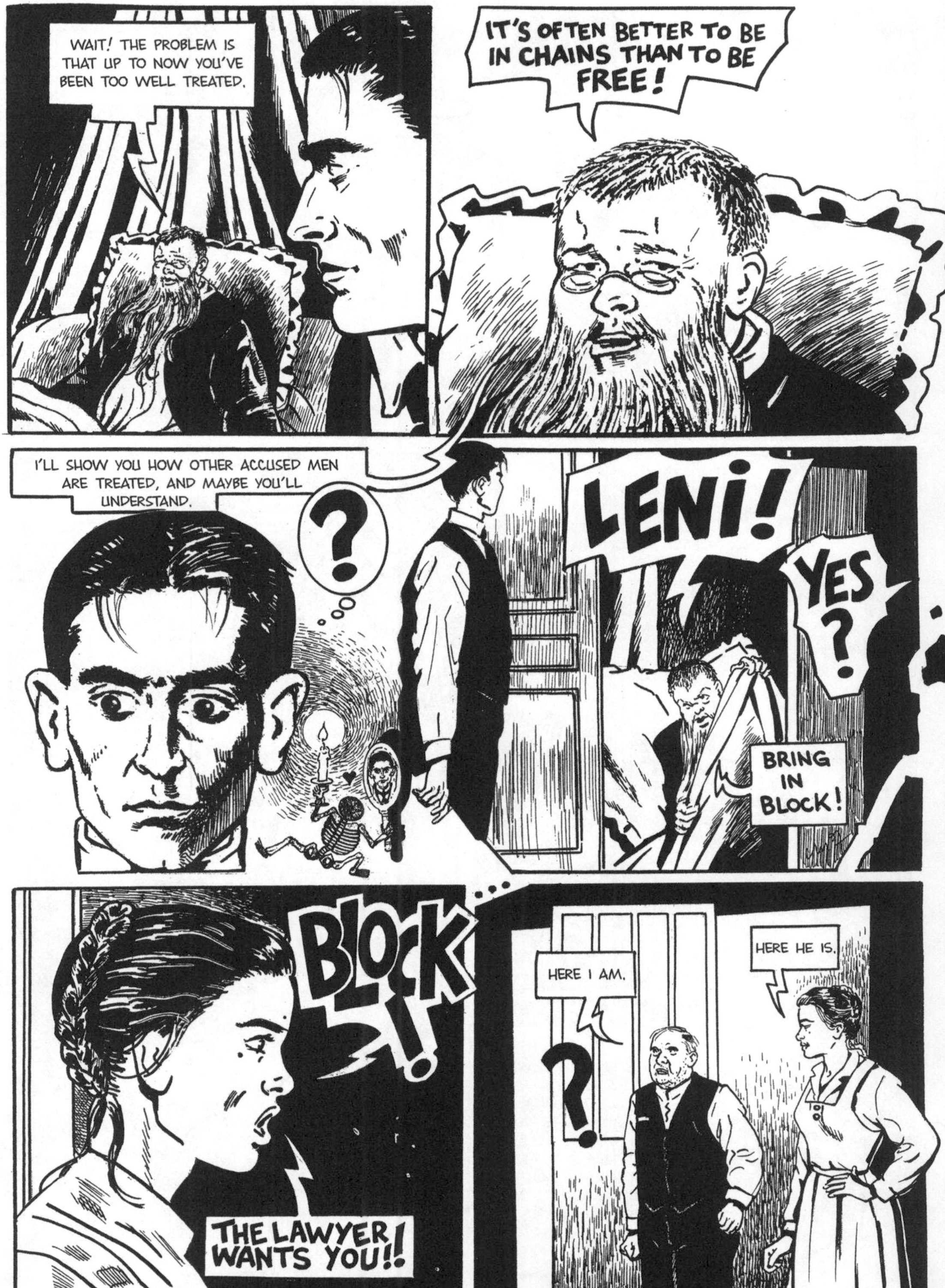
WAIT! THE PROBLEM IS THAT UP TO NOW YOU'VE BEEN TOO WELL TREATED.
IT'S OFTEN BETTER TO BE IN CHAINS THAN TO BE FREE!
I'LL SHOW YOU HOW OTHER ACCUSED MEN ARE TREATED, AND MAYBE YOU'LL UNDERSTAND.
?
LENI!
YES?
BRING IN BLOCK!
BLOCK!
THE LAWYER WANTS YOU!!
HERE I AM.
?
HERE HE IS.

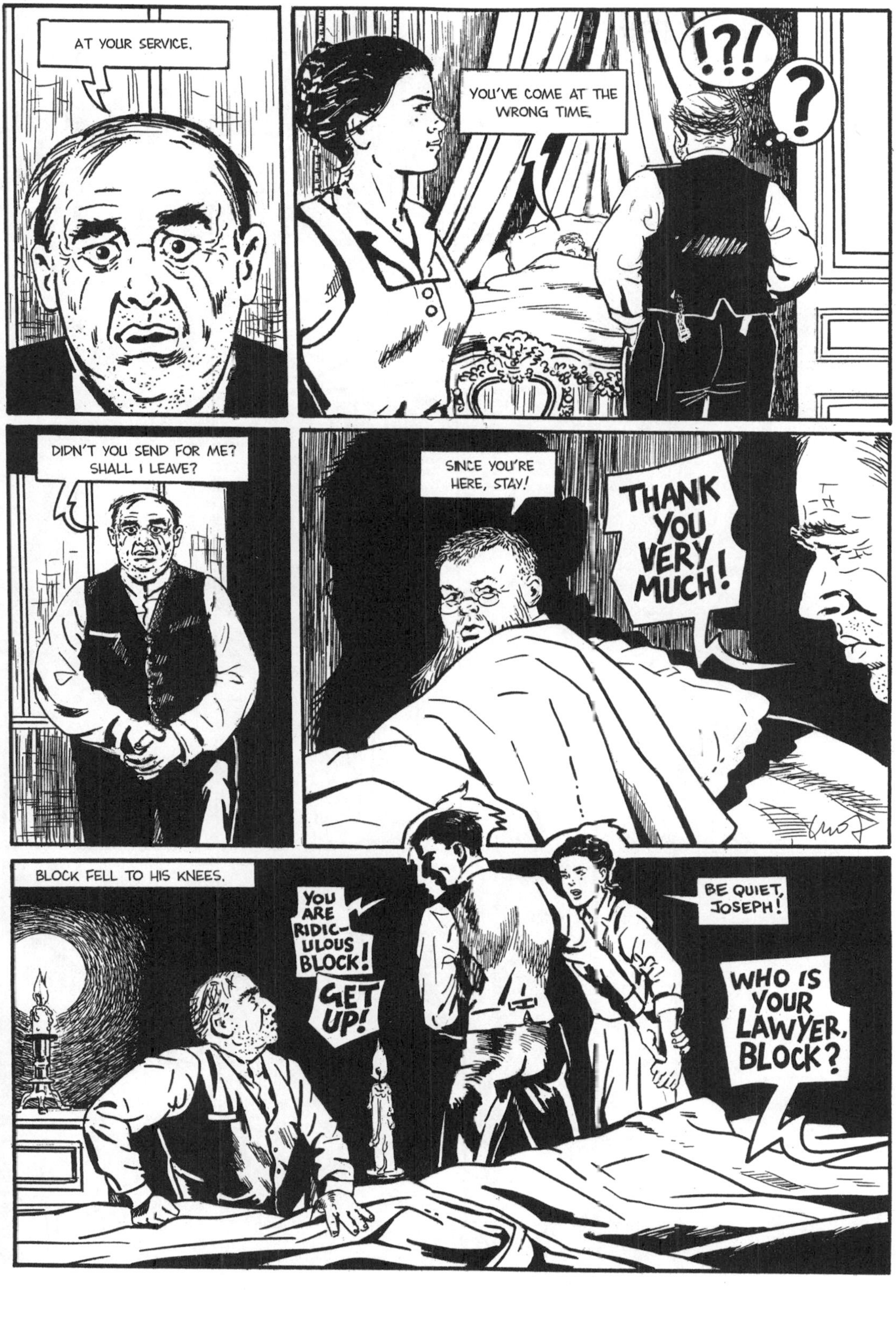

AT YOUR SERVICE.
YOU'VE COME AT THE WRONG TIME.
!?!
?
DIDN'T YOU SEND FOR ME? SHALL I LEAVE?
SINCE YOU'RE HERE, STAY!
THANK YOU VERY MUCH!
BLOCK FELL TO HIS KNEES.
YOU ARE RIDICULOUS BLOCK!
GET UP!
BE QUIET, JOSEPH!
WHO IS YOUR LAWYER, BLOCK?

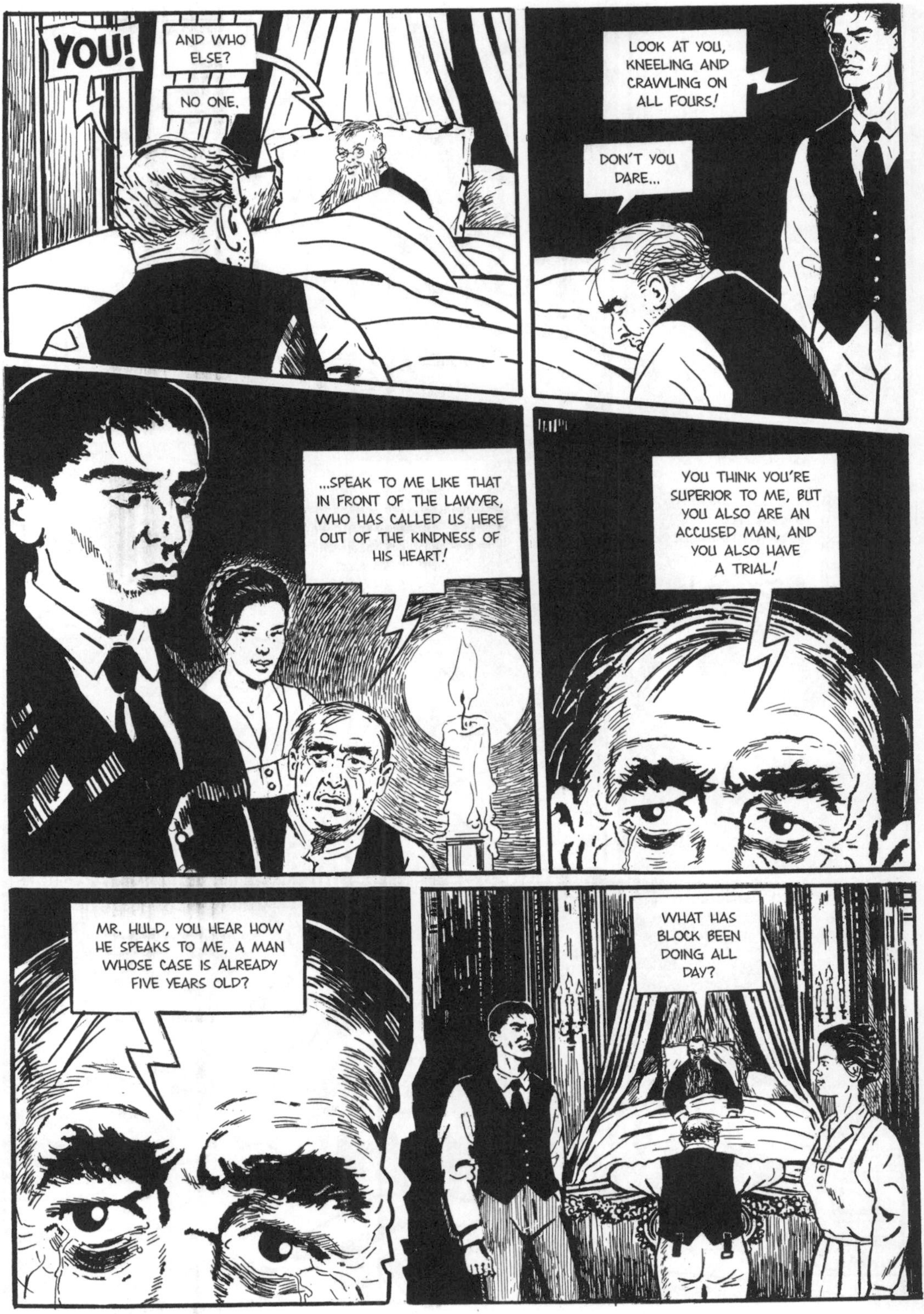
YOU!
AND WHO ELSE?
NO ONE.
LOOK AT YOU, KNEELING AND CRAWLING ON ALL FOURS!
DON'T YOU DARE...
...SPEAK TO ME LIKE THAT IN FRONT OF THE LAWYER, WHO HAS CALLED US HERE OUT OF THE KINDNESS OF HIS HEART!
YOU THINK YOU'RE SUPERIOR TO ME, BUT YOU ALSO ARE AN ACCUSED MAN, AND YOU ALSO HAVE A TRIAL!
MR. HULD, YOU HEAR HOW HE SPEAKS TO ME, A MAN WHOSE CASE IS ALREADY FIVE YEARS OLD?
WHAT HAS BLOCK BEEN DOING ALL DAY?

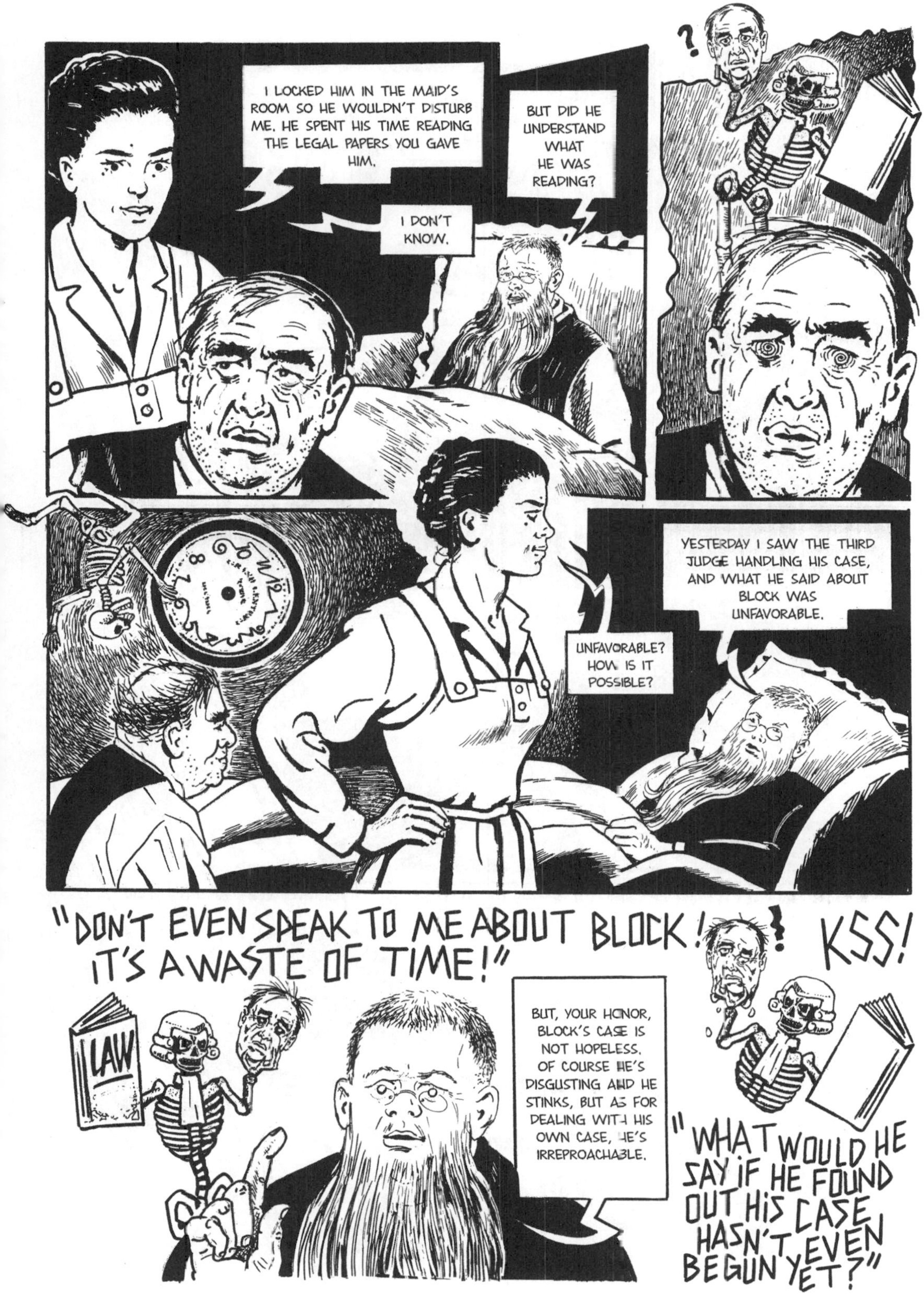
I LOCKED HIM IN THE MAID'S ROOM SO HE WOULDN'T DISTURB ME. HE SPENT HIS TIME READING THE LEGAL PAPERS YOU GAVE HIM.
BUT DID HE UNDERSTAND WHAT HE WAS READING?
I DON'T KNOW.
?
YESTERDAY I SAW THE THIRD JUDGE HANDLING HIS CASE, AND WHAT HE SAID ABOUT BLOCK WAS UNFAVORABLE.
UNFAVORABLE? HOW IS IT POSSIBLE?
"DON'T EVEN SPEAK TO ME ABOUT BLOCK! IT'S A WASTE OF TIME!"
KSS!
LAW
BUT, YOUR HONOR, BLOCK'S CASE IS NOT HOPELESS. OF COURSE HE'S DISGUSTING AND HE STINKS, BUT AS FOR DEALING WITH HIS OWN CASE, HE'S IRREPROACHABLE.
"WHAT WOULD HE SAY IF HE FOUND OUT HIS CASE HASN'T EVEN BEGUN YET?"

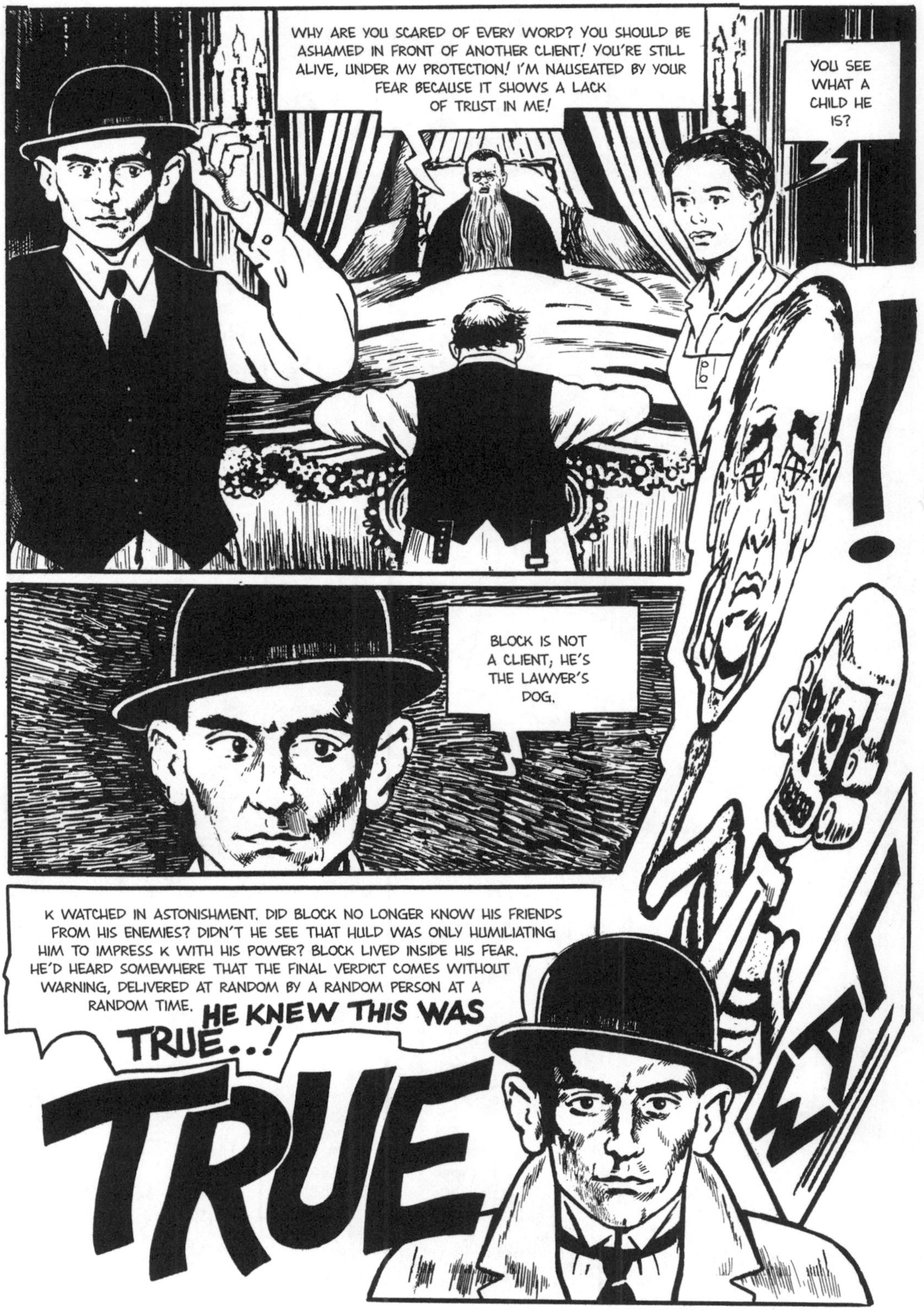

WHY ARE YOU SCARED OF EVERY WORD? YOU SHOULD BE ASHAMED IN FRONT OF ANOTHER CLIENT! YOU'RE STILL ALIVE, UNDER MY PROTECTION! I'M NAUSEATED BY YOUR FEAR BECAUSE IT SHOWS A LACK OF TRUST IN ME!
YOU SEE WHAT A CHILD HE IS?
BLOCK IS NOT A CLIENT; HE'S THE LAWYER'S DOG.
K WATCHED IN ASTONISHMENT. DID BLOCK NO LONGER KNOW HIS FRIENDS FROM HIS ENEMIES? DIDN'T HE SEE THAT HULD WAS ONLY HUMILIATING HIM TO IMPRESS K WITH HIS POWER? BLOCK LIVED INSIDE HIS FEAR. HE'D HEARD SOMEWHERE THAT THE FINAL VERDICT COMES WITHOUT WARNING, DELIVERED AT RANDOM BY A RANDOM PERSON AT A RANDOM TIME. HE KNEW THIS WAS TRUE...!
TRUE

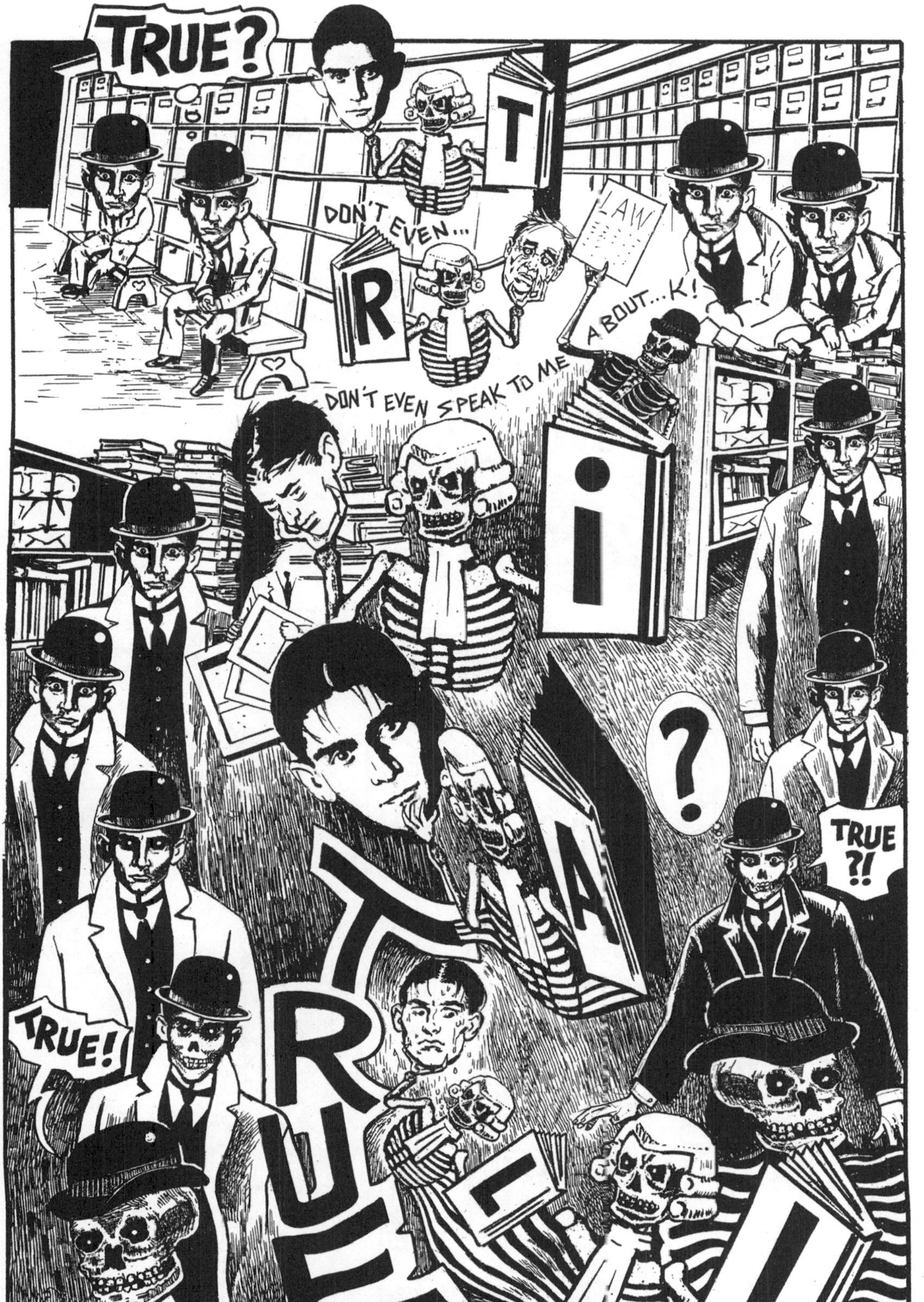
TRUE?
T
DON'T EVEN...
LAW
R
DON'T EVEN SPEAK TO ME ABOUT...K!
i
?
A
TRUE ?!
TRUE!
TRUE
!

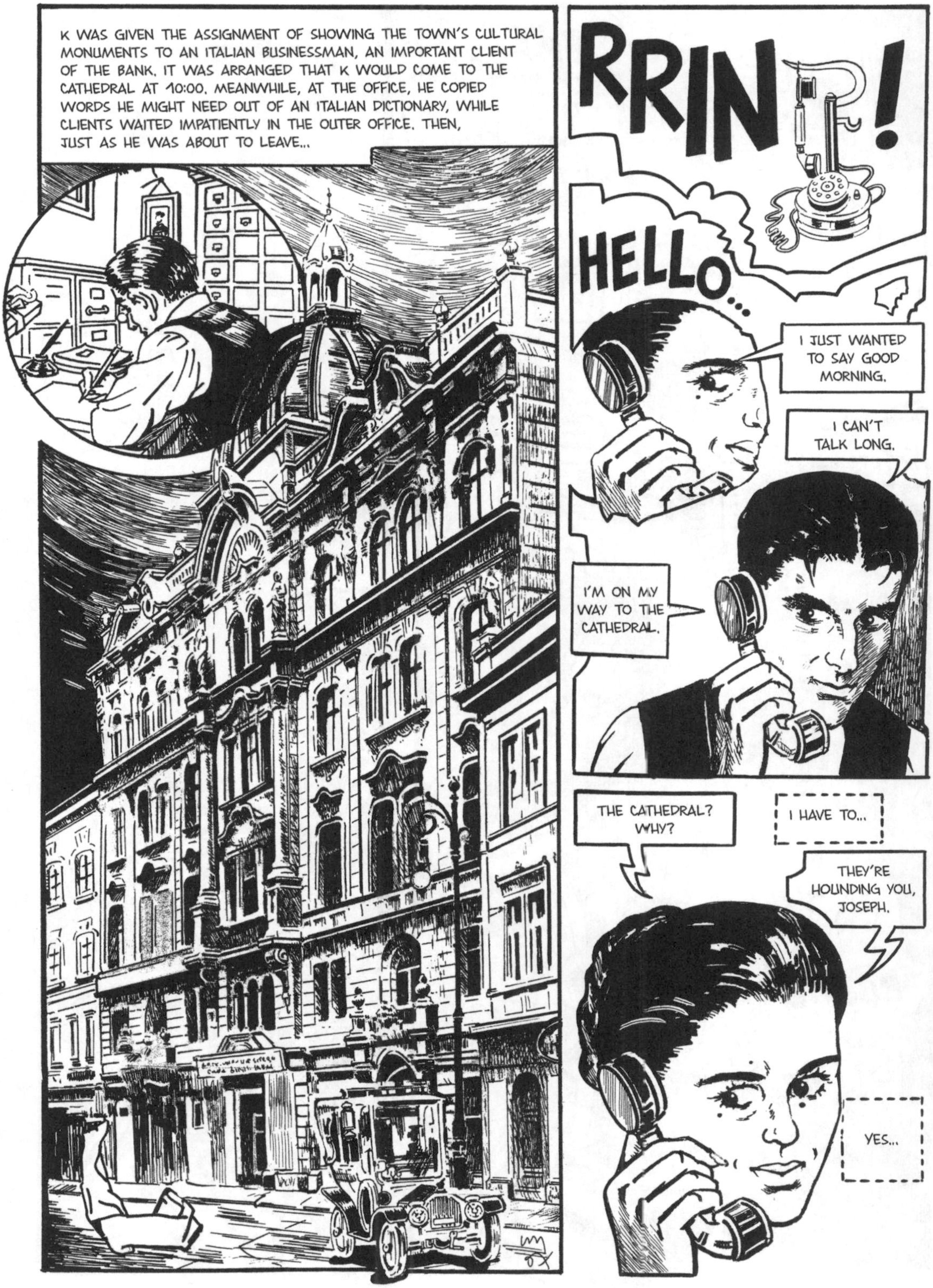
K WAS GIVEN THE ASSIGNMENT OF SHOWING THE TOWN'S CULTURAL MONUMENTS TO AN ITALIAN BUSINESSMAN, AN IMPORTANT CLIENT OF THE BANK. IT WAS ARRANGED THAT K WOULD COME TO THE CATHEDRAL AT 10:00. MEANWHILE, AT THE OFFICE, HE COPIED WORDS HE MIGHT NEED OUT OF AN ITALIAN DICTIONARY, WHILE CLIENTS WAITED IMPATIENTLY IN THE OUTER OFFICE. THEN, JUST AS HE WAS ABOUT TO LEAVE...
RRING!
HELLO...
I JUST WANTED TO SAY GOOD MORNING.
I CAN'T TALK LONG.
I'M ON MY WAY TO THE CATHEDRAL.
THE CATHEDRAL? WHY?
I HAVE TO...
THEY'RE HOUNDING YOU, JOSEPH.
YES...

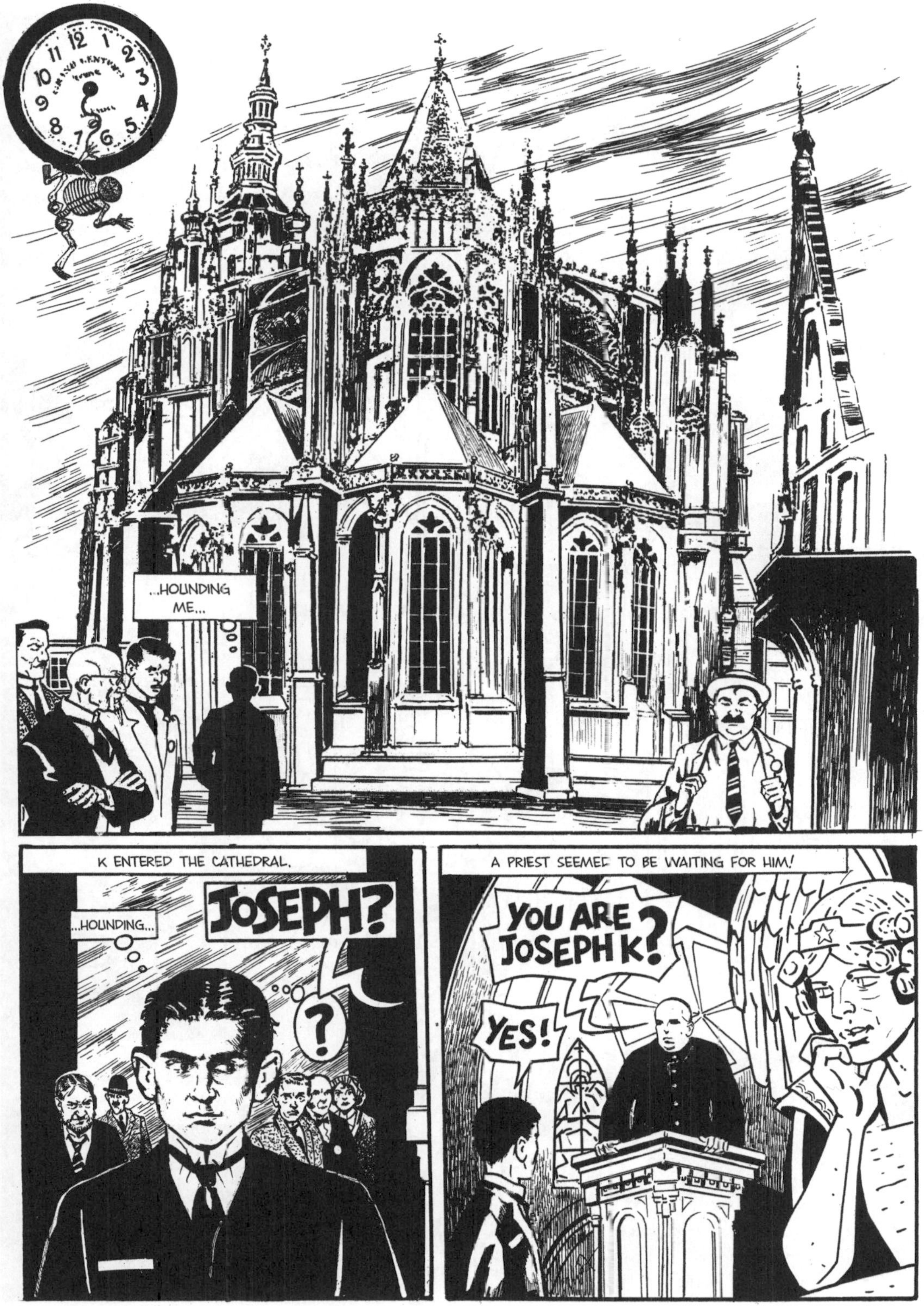
...HOUNDING ME...
K ENTERED THE CATHEDRAL.
...HOUNDING...
JOSEPH?
?
A PRIEST SEEMED TO BE WAITING FOR HIM!
YOU ARE JOSEPH K?
YES!

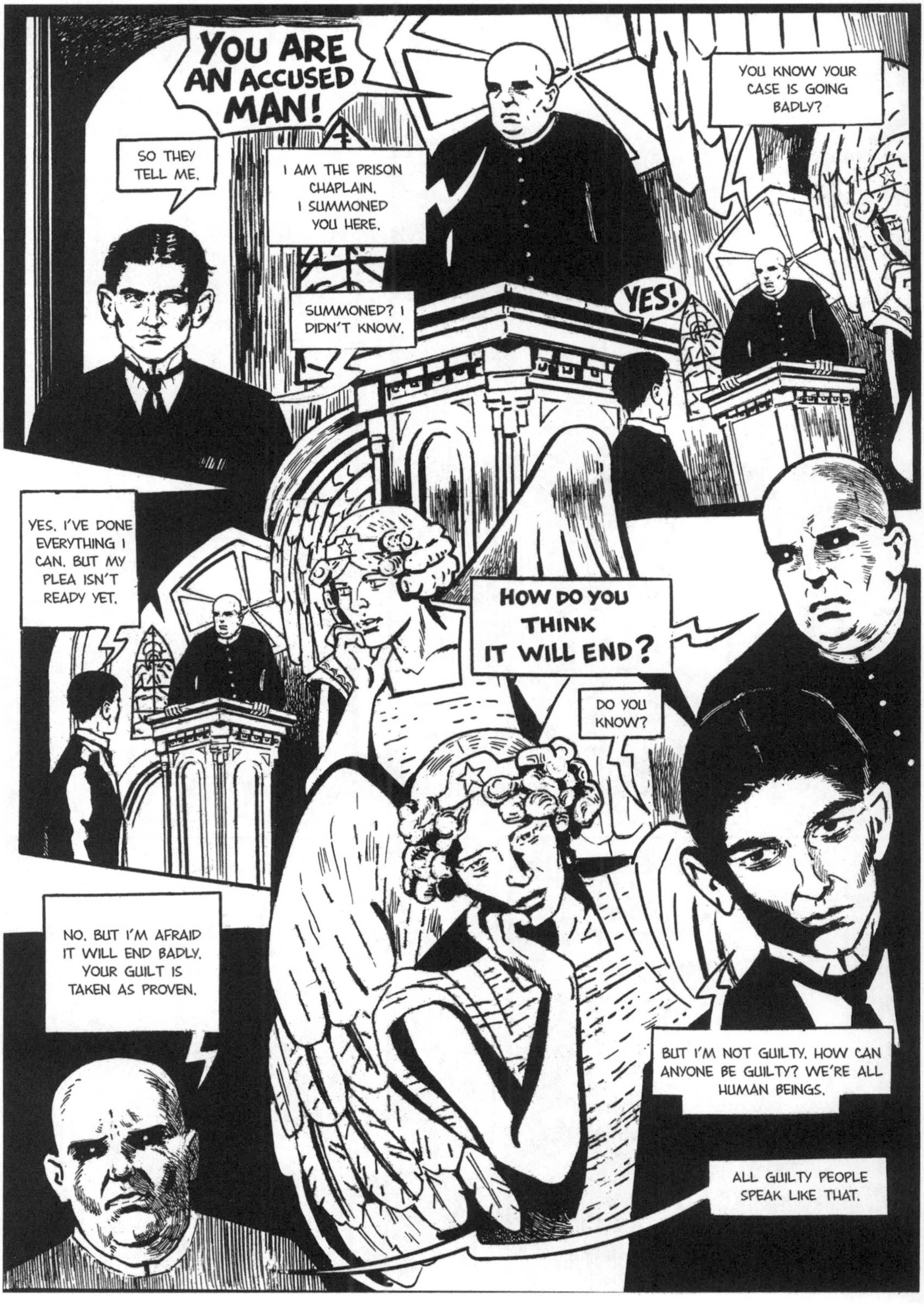
YOU ARE AN ACCUSED MAN!
SO THEY TELL ME.
I AM THE PRISON CHAPLAIN. I SUMMONED YOU HERE.
SUMMONED? I DIDN'T KNOW.
YES!
YOU KNOW YOUR CASE IS GOING BADLY?
YES, I'VE DONE EVERYTHING I CAN, BUT MY PLEA ISN'T READY YET.
HOW DO YOU THINK IT WILL END?
DO YOU KNOW?
NO, BUT I'M AFRAID IT WILL END BADLY. YOUR GUILT IS TAKEN AS PROVEN.
BUT I'M NOT GUILTY. HOW CAN ANYONE BE GUILTY? WE'RE ALL HUMAN BEINGS.
ALL GUILTY PEOPLE SPEAK LIKE THAT.

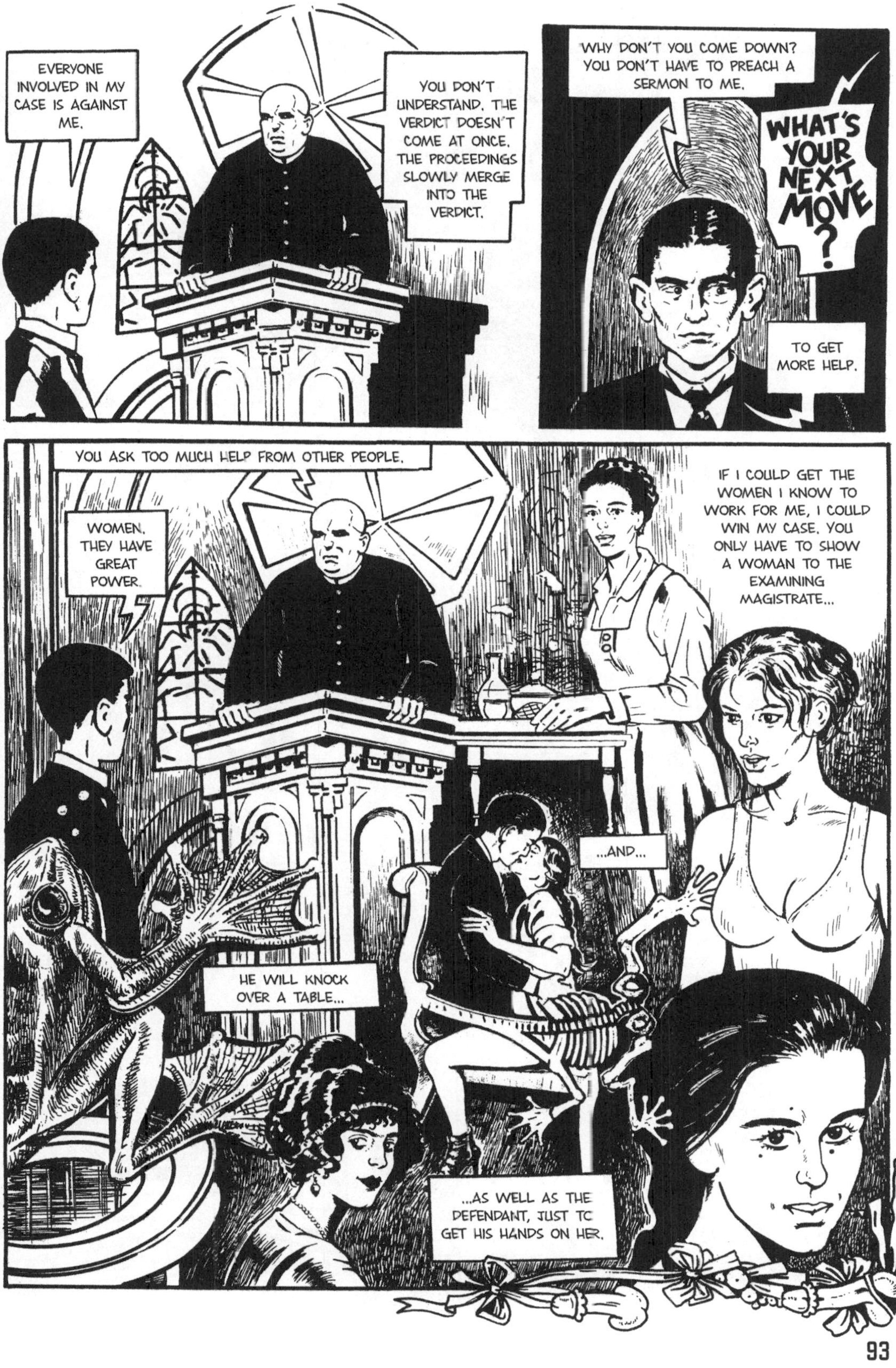
EVERYONE INVOLVED IN MY CASE IS AGAINST ME.
YOU DON'T UNDERSTAND, THE VERDICT DOESN'T COME AT ONCE, THE PROCEEDINGS SLOWLY MERGE INTO THE VERDICT.
WHY DON'T YOU COME DOWN? YOU DON'T HAVE TO PREACH A SERMON TO ME.
WHAT'S YOUR NEXT MOVE ?
TO GET MORE HELP.
YOU ASK TOO MUCH HELP FROM OTHER PEOPLE.
WOMEN. THEY HAVE GREAT POWER.
IF I COULD GET THE WOMEN I KNOW TO WORK FOR ME, I COULD WIN MY CASE. YOU ONLY HAVE TO SHOW A WOMAN TO THE EXAMINING MAGISTRATE...
...AND...
HE WILL KNOCK OVER A TABLE...
...AS WELL AS THE DEFENDANT, JUST TC GET HIS HANDS ON HER.

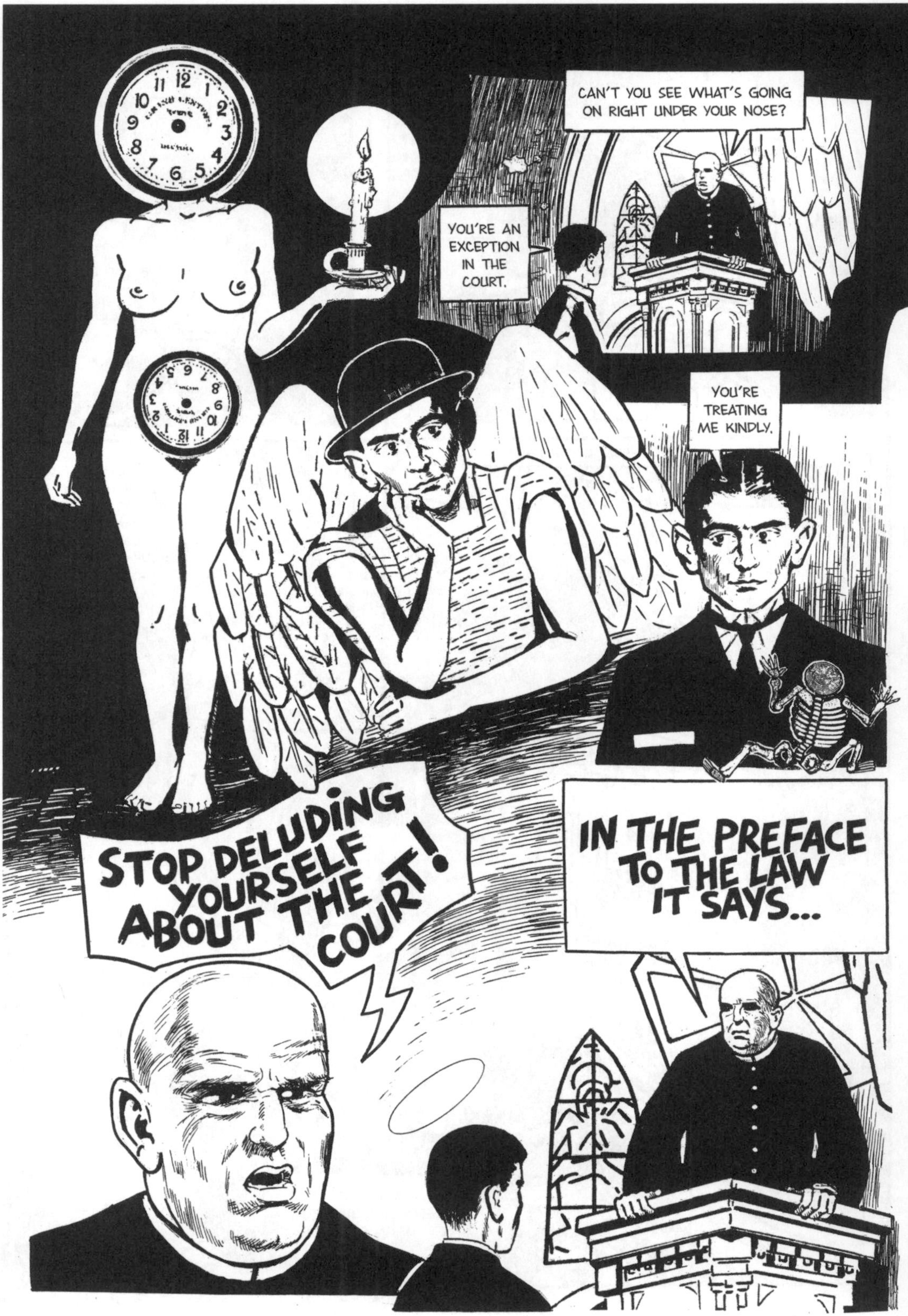
CAN'T YOU SEE WHAT'S GOING ON RIGHT UNDER YOUR NOSE?
YOU'RE AN EXCEPTION IN THE COURT.
YOU'RE TREATING ME KINDLY.
STOP DELUDING YOURSELF ABOUT THE COURT!
IN THE PREFACE TO THE LAW IT SAYS...

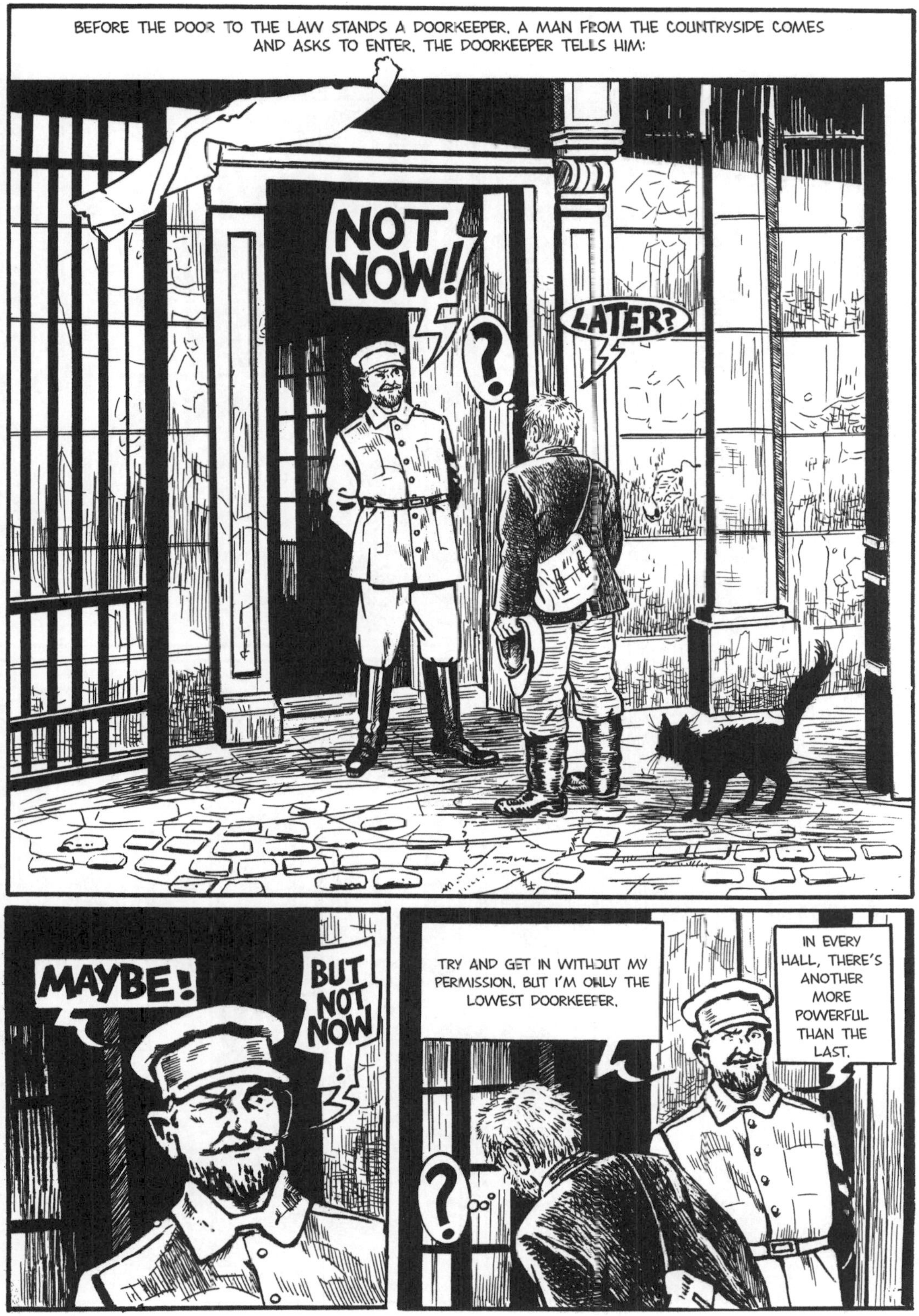
BEFORE THE DOOR TO THE LAW STANDS A DOORKEEPER. A MAN FROM THE COUNTRYSIDE COMES AND ASKS TO ENTER. THE DOORKEEPER TELLS HIM:
NOT NOW!
?
LATER?
MAYBE!
BUT NOT NOW!
TRY AND GET IN WITHOUT MY PERMISSION. BUT I'M ONLY THE LOWEST DOORKEEPER.
IN EVERY HALL, THERE'S ANOTHER MORE POWERFUL THAN THE LAST.
?

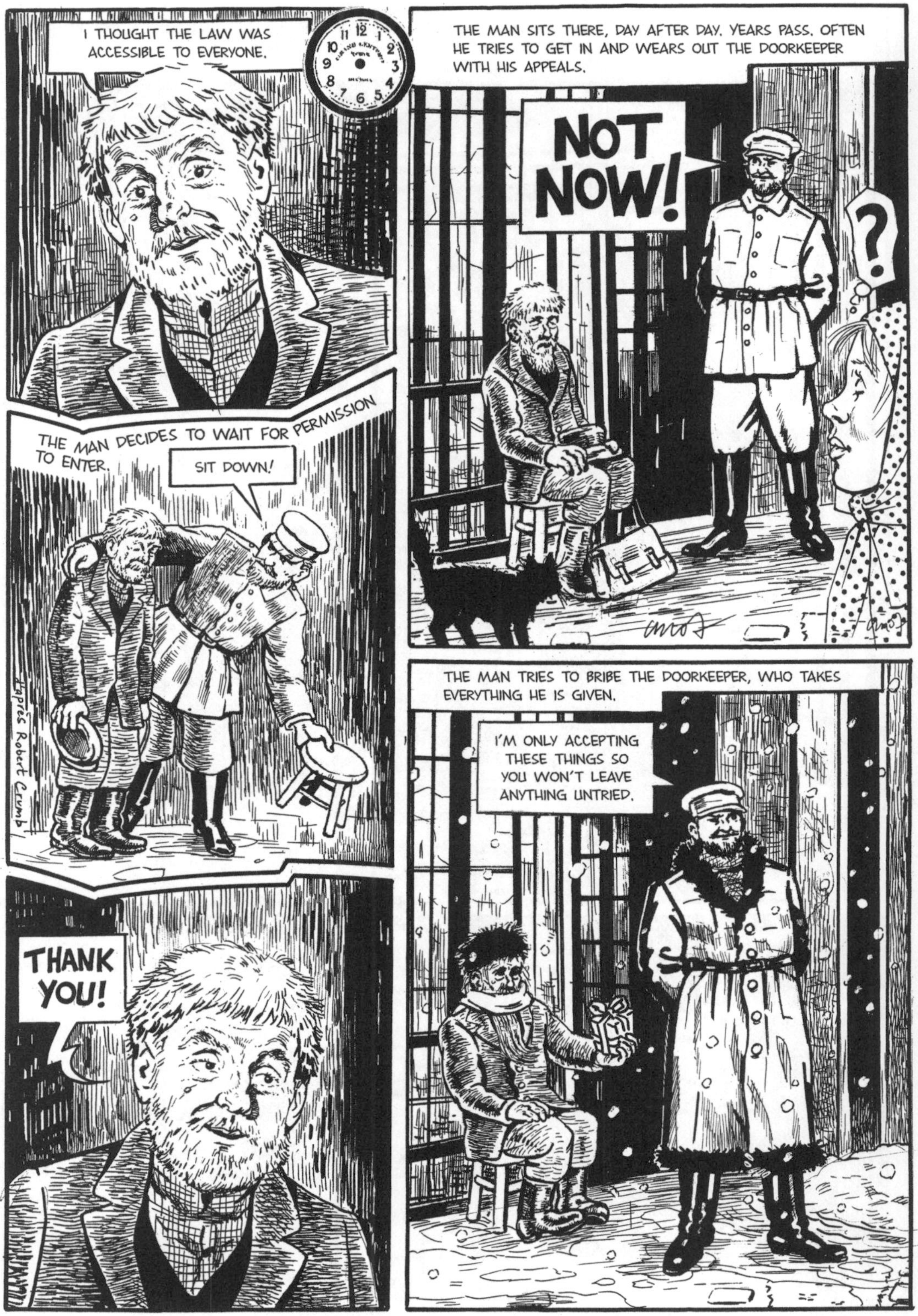

I THOUGHT THE LAW WAS ACCESSIBLE TO EVERYONE.
THE MAN DECIDES TO WAIT FOR PERMISSION TO ENTER.
SIT DOWN!
d'après Robert Crumb
THANK YOU!
THE MAN SITS THERE, DAY AFTER DAY. YEARS PASS. OFTEN HE TRIES TO GET IN AND WEARS OUT THE DOORKEEPER WITH HIS APPEALS.
NOT NOW!
?
THE MAN TRIES TO BRIBE THE DOORKEEPER, WHO TAKES EVERYTHING HE IS GIVEN.
I'M ONLY ACCEPTING THESE THINGS SO YOU WON'T LEAVE ANYTHING UNTRIED.

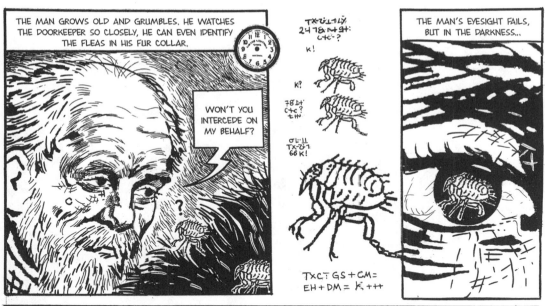

THE MAN GROWS OLD AND GRUMBLES. HE WATCHES THE DOORKEEPER SO CLOSELY, HE CAN EVEN IDENTIFY THE FLEAS IN HIS FUR COLLAR.

WON'T YOU INTERCEDE ON MY BEHALF?

THE MAN'S EYESIGHT FAILS, BUT IN THE DARKNESS...

...HE SEES A GLOW COMING FROM THE DOOR TO THE LAW. HE IS GOING TO DIE SOON, BUT IN HIS MIND...

THERE'S ONE QUESTION I NEVER ASKED ALL THESE YEARS.

WHAT DO YOU WANT NOW? YOU'RE INSATIABLE!

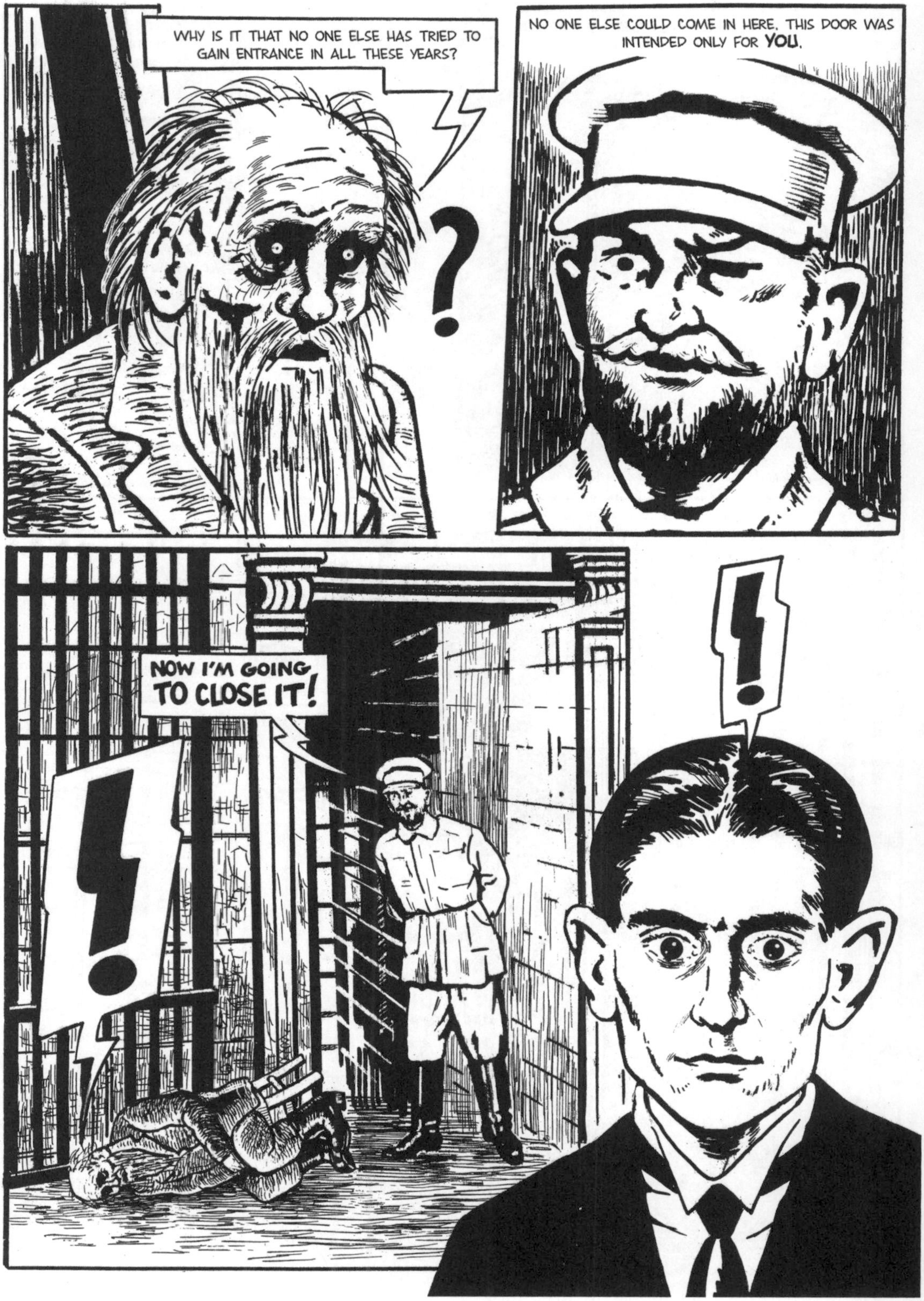
WHY IS IT THAT NO ONE ELSE HAS TRIED TO GAIN ENTRANCE IN ALL THESE YEARS?
?
NO ONE ELSE COULD COME IN HERE. THIS DOOR WAS INTENDED ONLY FOR YOU.
NOW I'M GOING TO CLOSE IT!
!
!

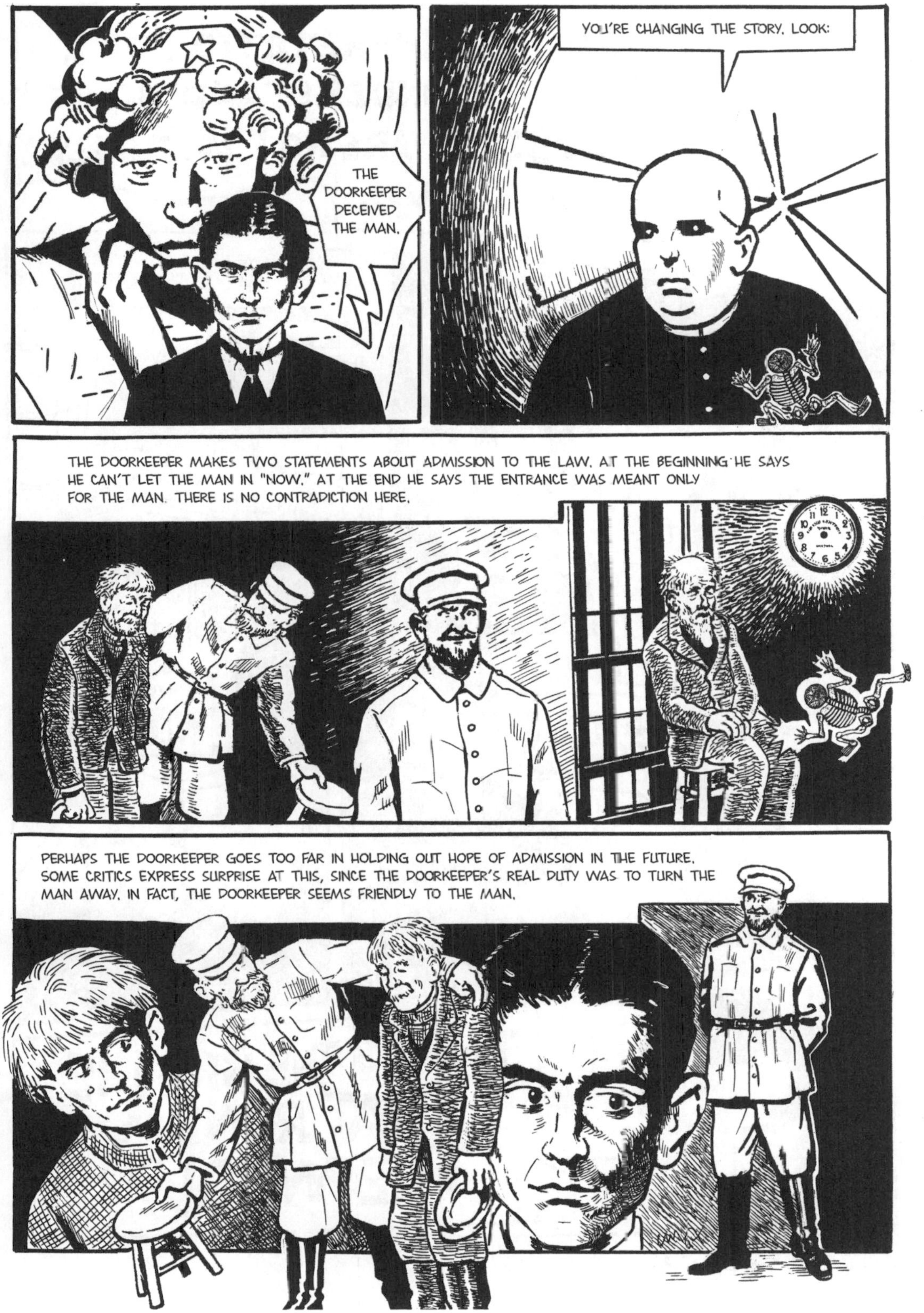
THE DOORKEEPER DECEIVED THE MAN.
YOU'RE CHANGING THE STORY. LOOK:
THE DOORKEEPER MAKES TWO STATEMENTS ABOUT ADMISSION TO THE LAW. AT THE BEGINNING HE SAYS HE CAN'T LET THE MAN IN "NOW." AT THE END HE SAYS THE ENTRANCE WAS MEANT ONLY FOR THE MAN. THERE IS NO CONTRADICTION HERE.
PERHAPS THE DOORKEEPER GOES TOO FAR IN HOLDING OUT HOPE OF ADMISSION IN THE FUTURE. SOME CRITICS EXPRESS SURPRISE AT THIS, SINCE THE DOORKEEPER'S REAL DUTY WAS TO TURN THE MAN AWAY. IN FACT, THE DOORKEEPER SEEMS FRIENDLY TO THE MAN.

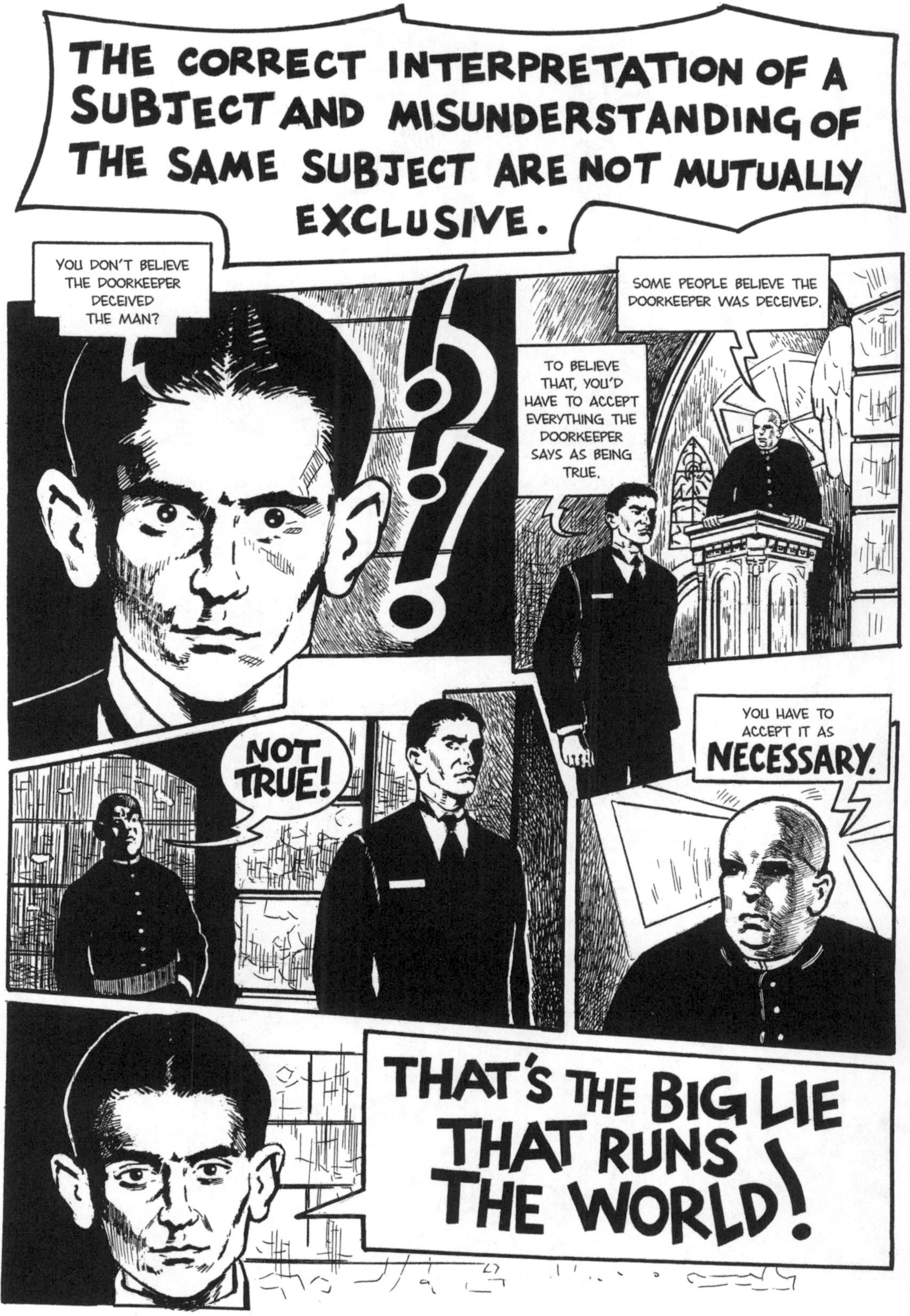
THE CORRECT INTERPRETATION OF A SUBJECT AND MISUNDERSTANDING OF THE SAME SUBJECT ARE NOT MUTUALLY EXCLUSIVE.
YOU DON'T BELIEVE THE DOORKEEPER DECEIVED THE MAN?
?!
SOME PEOPLE BELIEVE THE DOORKEEPER WAS DECEIVED.
TO BELIEVE THAT, YOU'D HAVE TO ACCEPT EVERYTHING THE DOORKEEPER SAYS AS BEING TRUE.
NOT TRUE!
YOU HAVE TO ACCEPT IT AS NECESSARY.
THAT'S THE BIG LIE THAT RUNS THE WORLD!

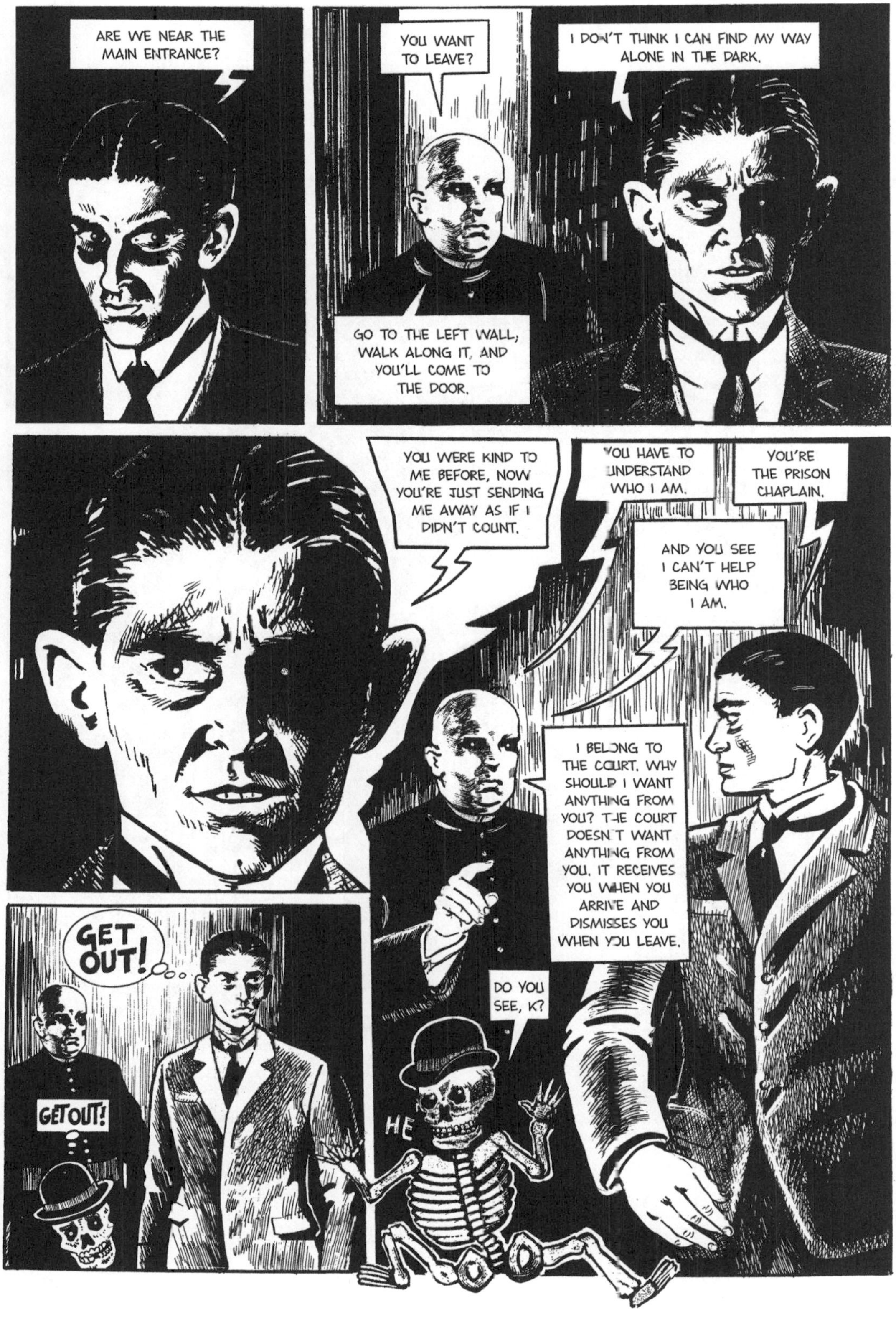
ARE WE NEAR THE MAIN ENTRANCE?
YOU WANT TO LEAVE?
I DON'T THINK I CAN FIND MY WAY ALONE IN THE DARK.
GO TO THE LEFT WALL; WALK ALONG IT, AND YOU'LL COME TO THE DOOR.
YOU WERE KIND TO ME BEFORE, NOW YOU'RE JUST SENDING ME AWAY AS IF I DIDN'T COUNT.
YOU HAVE TO UNDERSTAND WHO I AM.
YOU'RE THE PRISON CHAPLAIN.
AND YOU SEE I CAN'T HELP BEING WHO I AM.
I BELONG TO THE COURT. WHY SHOULD I WANT ANYTHING FROM YOU? THE COURT DOESN'T WANT ANYTHING FROM YOU. IT RECEIVES YOU WHEN YOU ARRIVE AND DISMISSES YOU WHEN YOU LEAVE.
GET OUT!
GET OUT!
DO YOU SEE, K?
HE

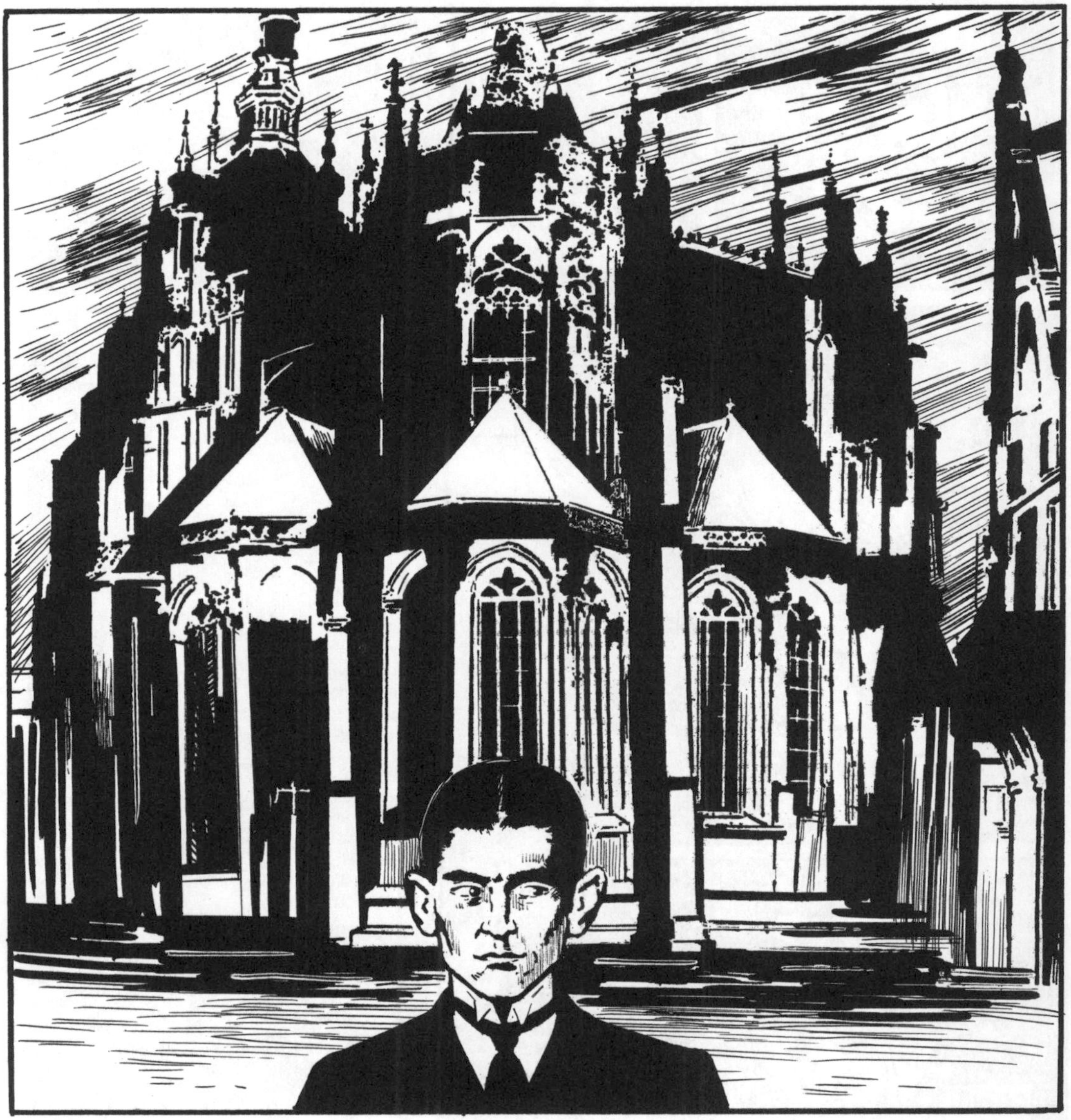

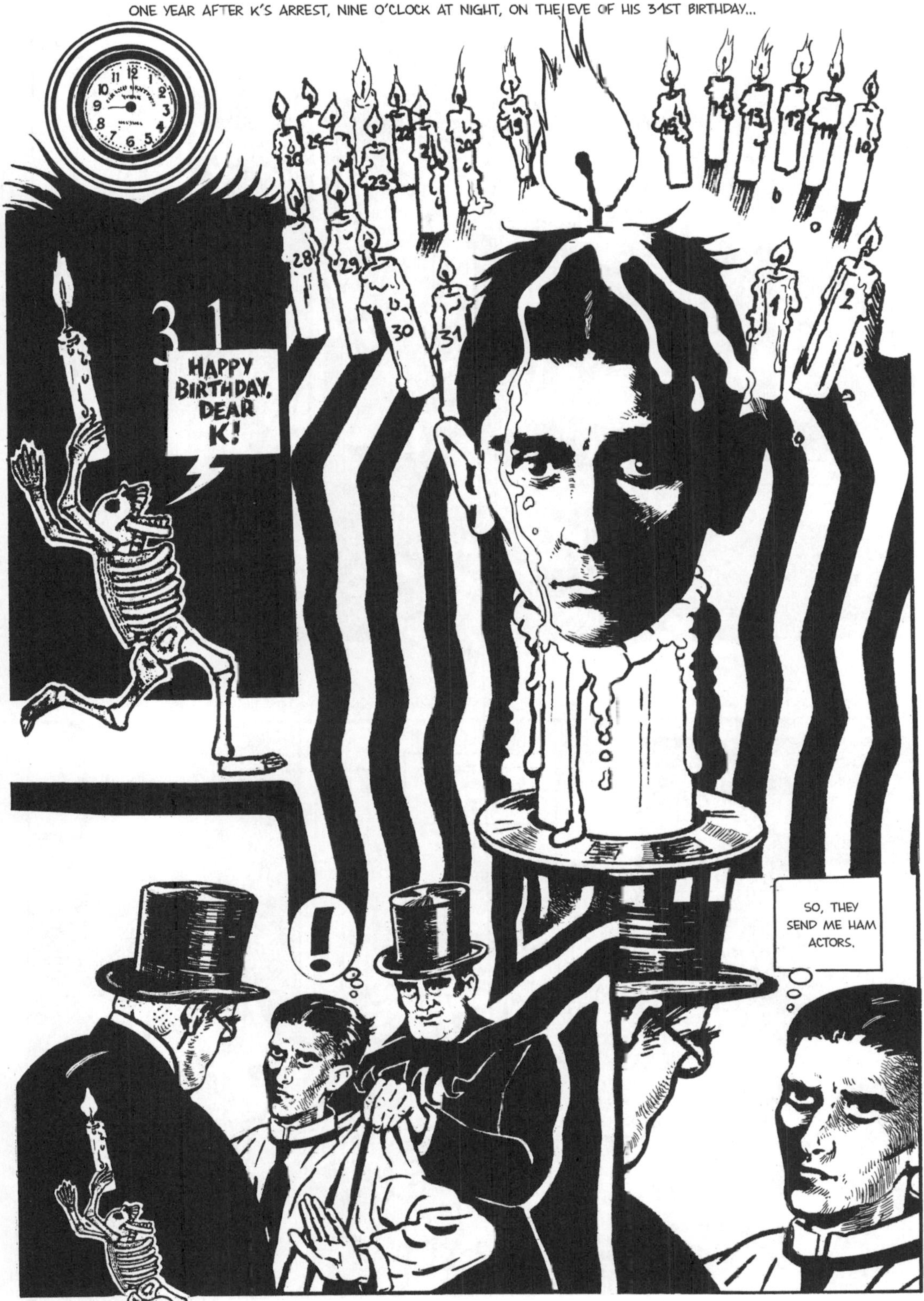
ONE YEAR AFTER K'S ARREST, NINE O'CLOCK AT NIGHT, ON THE EVE OF HIS 31ST BIRTHDAY...
31
HAPPY BIRTHDAY, DEAR K!
!
SO, THEY SEND ME HAM ACTORS.

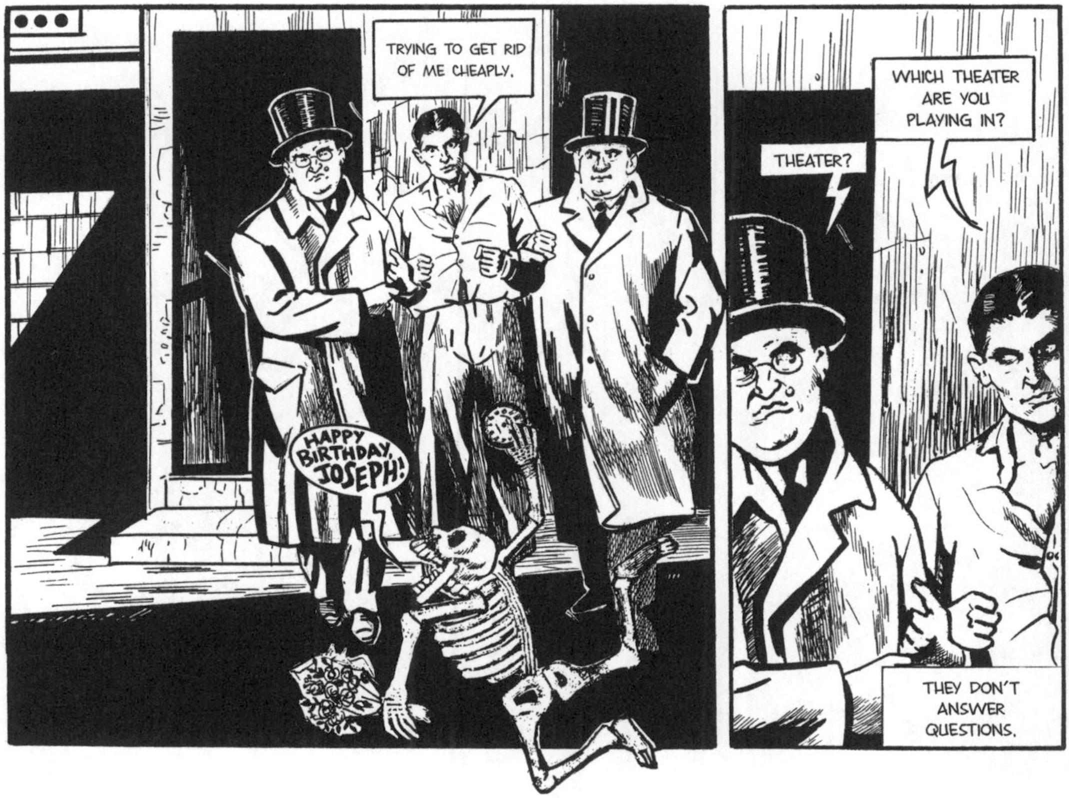
TRYING TO GET RID OF ME CHEAPLY.
HAPPY BIRTHDAY, JOSEPH!
WHICH THEATER ARE YOU PLAYING IN?
THEATER?
THEY DON'T ANSWER QUESTIONS.

CHAPTER 9

TOGETHER THEY BECAME THE KIND OF ENTITY USUALLY FORMED BY LIFELESS MATTER.

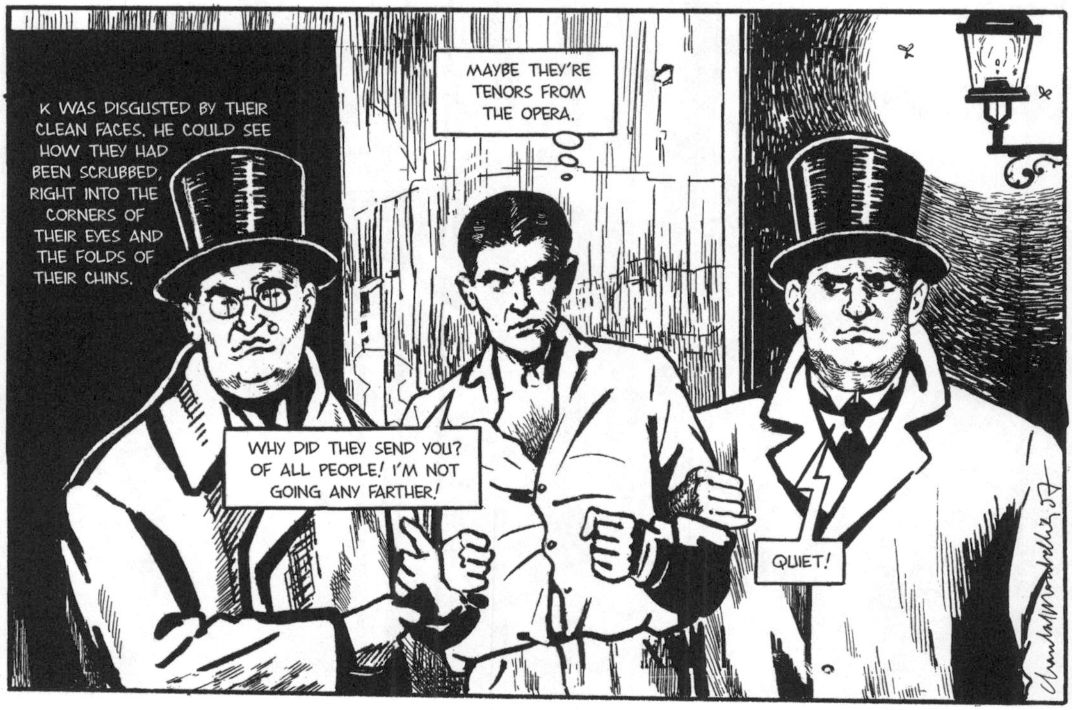
K WAS DISGUSTED BY THEIR CLEAN FACES. HE COULD SEE HOW THEY HAD BEEN SCRUBBED, RIGHT INTO THE CORNERS OF THEIR EYES AND THE FOLDS OF THEIR CHINS.
MAYBE THEY'RE TENORS FROM THE OPERA.
WHY DID THEY SEND YOU? OF ALL PEOPLE! I'M NOT GOING ANY FARTHER!
QUIET!

I MAY AS WELL USE MY STRENGTH NOW. I WON'T NEED IT ANY MORE AFTER THIS.

K WAS REMINDED OF FLIES TEARING OFF THEIR LEGS, TRYING TO ESCAPE FROM FLY-PAPER.

?

! HELP!

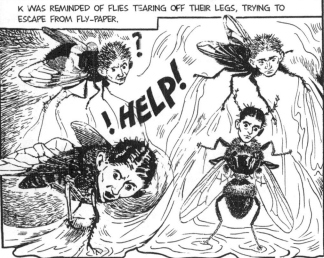

MISS BÜRSTNER!

K WAS NOT REALLY SURE IT WAS MISS BÜRSTNER, AND IT DIDN'T REALLY MATTER IF IT WAS OR WAS NOT. HE REALIZED THERE WAS NO POINT RESISTING THESE MEN OR KEEPING LIFE GOING BY PUTTING UP A STRUGGLE.

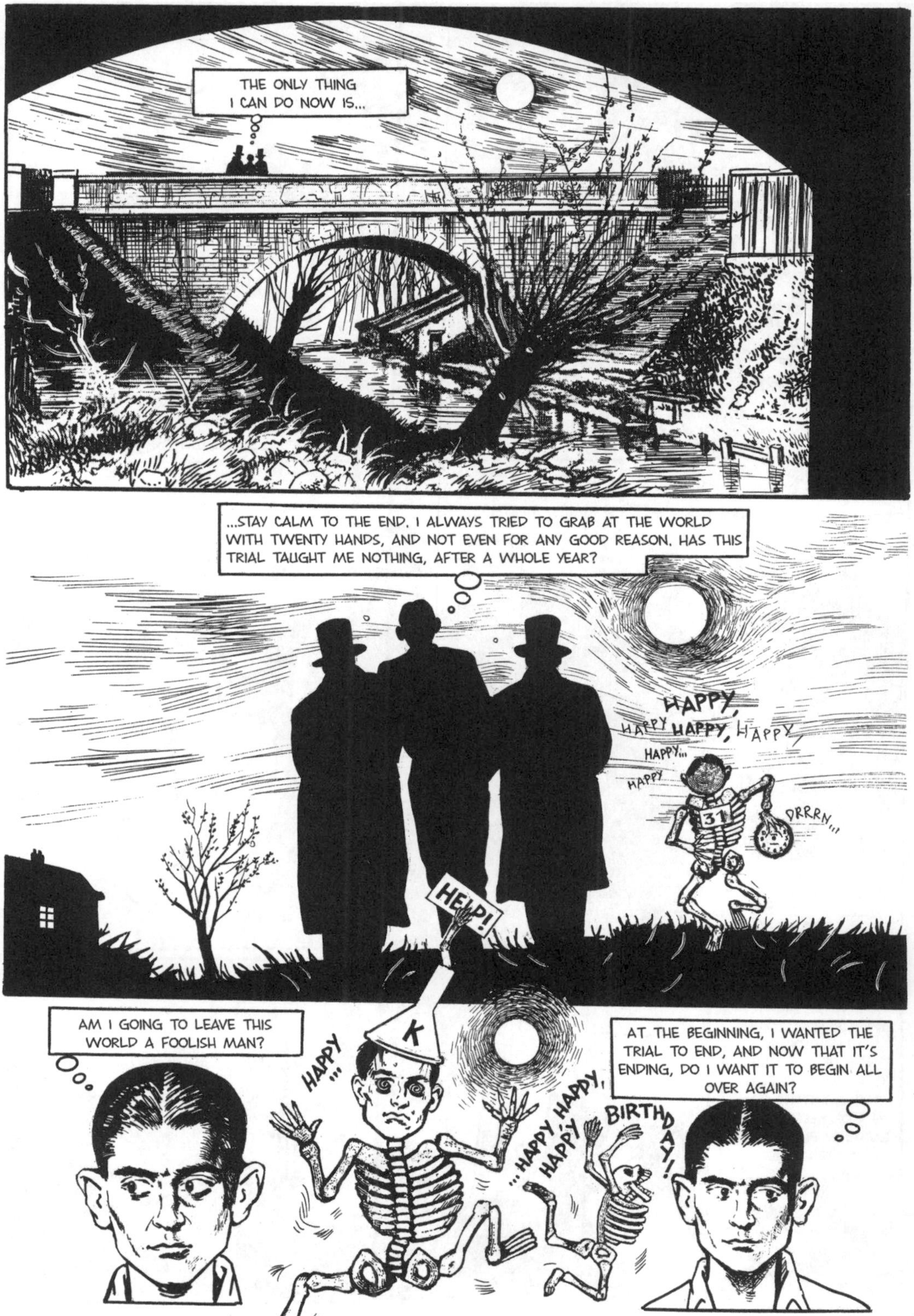
THE ONLY THING I CAN DO NOW IS...
...STAY CALM TO THE END. I ALWAYS TRIED TO GRAB AT THE WORLD WITH TWENTY HANDS, AND NOT EVEN FOR ANY GOOD REASON. HAS THIS TRIAL TAUGHT ME NOTHING, AFTER A WHOLE YEAR?
HAPPY, HAPPY HAPPY, HAPPY, HAPPY... HAPPY
31
DRRRN...
HELP!
AM I GOING TO LEAVE THIS WORLD A FOOLISH MAN?
K
HAPPY...
...HAPPY, HAPPY, HAPPY BIRTHDAY!
AT THE BEGINNING, I WANTED THE TRIAL TO END, AND NOW THAT IT'S ENDING, DO I WANT IT TO BEGIN ALL OVER AGAIN?

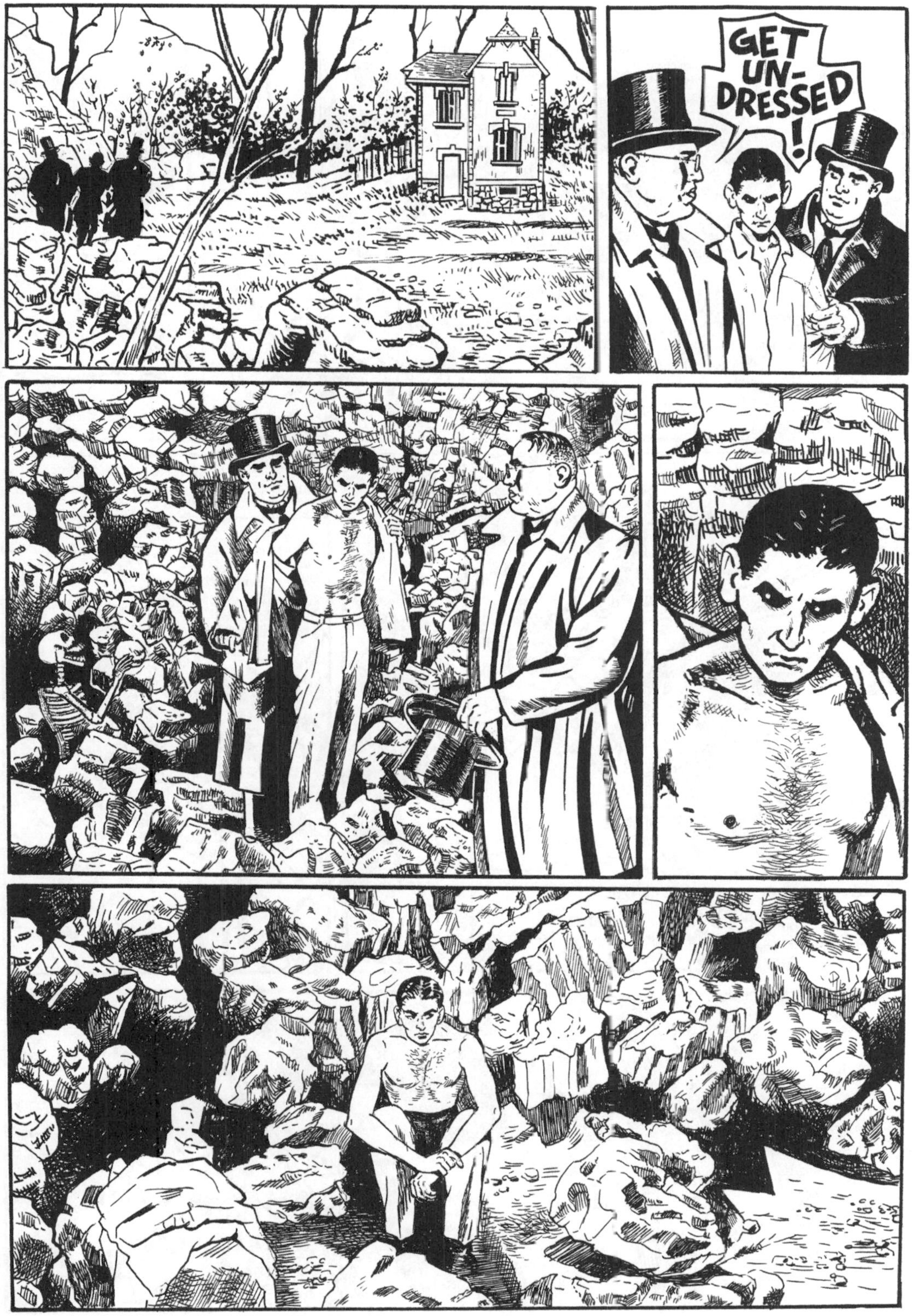
GET UN-DRESSED!

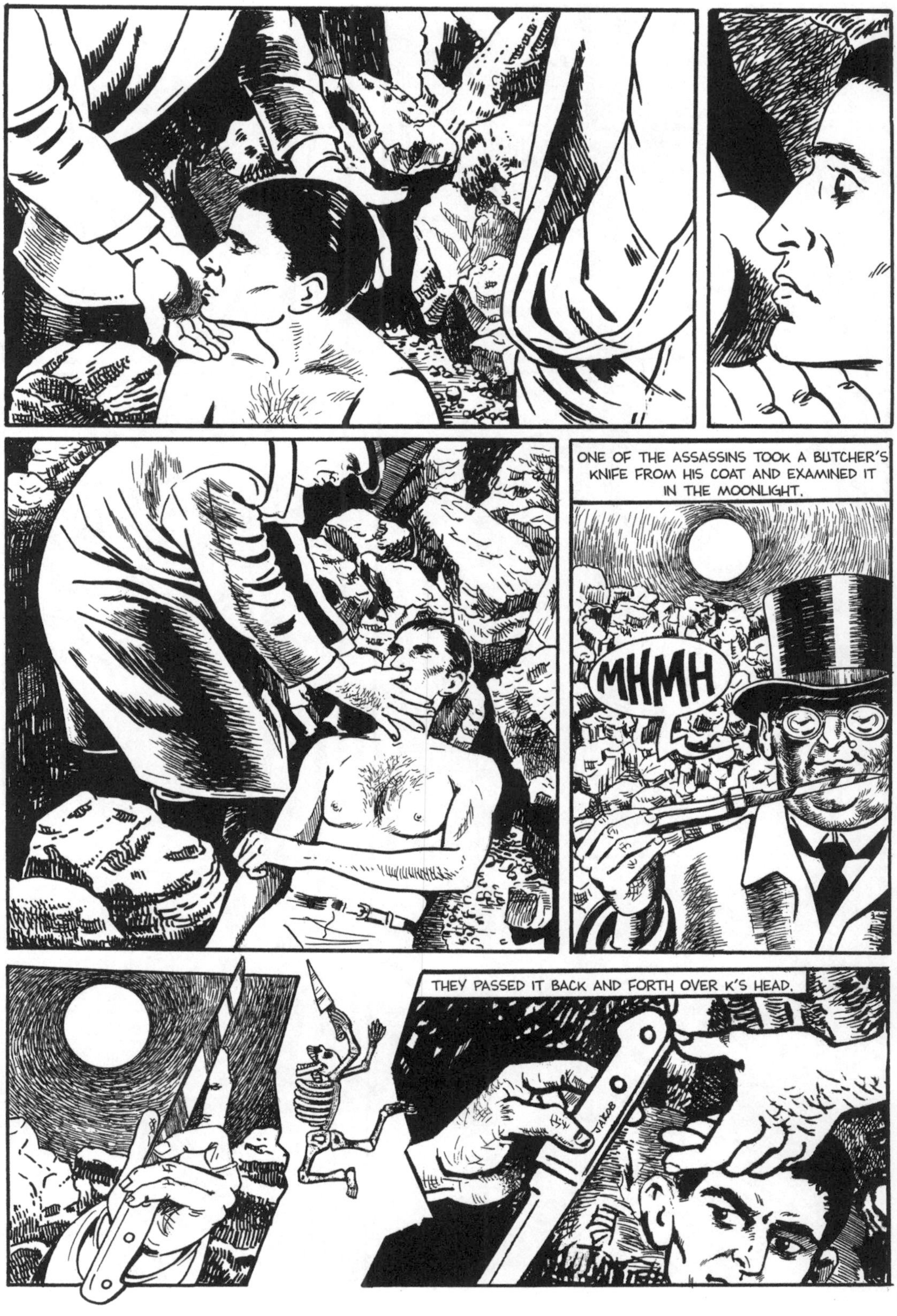
ONE OF THE ASSASSINS TOOK A BUTCHER'S KNIFE FROM HIS COAT AND EXAMINED IT IN THE MOONLIGHT.
MHMH
THEY PASSED IT BACK AND FORTH OVER K'S HEAD.
JAKOB

K REALIZED NOW...

...THAT **HE** SHOULD GRASP THE KNIFE AND PLUNGE IT INTO HIMSELF, BUT HE WOULD NOT DO THE AUTHORITIES' JOB FOR THEM. THIS WAS BECAUSE THEY HAD TAKEN AWAY FROM HIM THE STRENGTH NECESSARY TO PERFORM THE ACT.

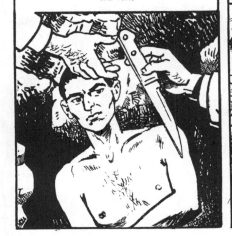

K'S GAZE FELL ON A HOUSE NEAR THE QUARRY.

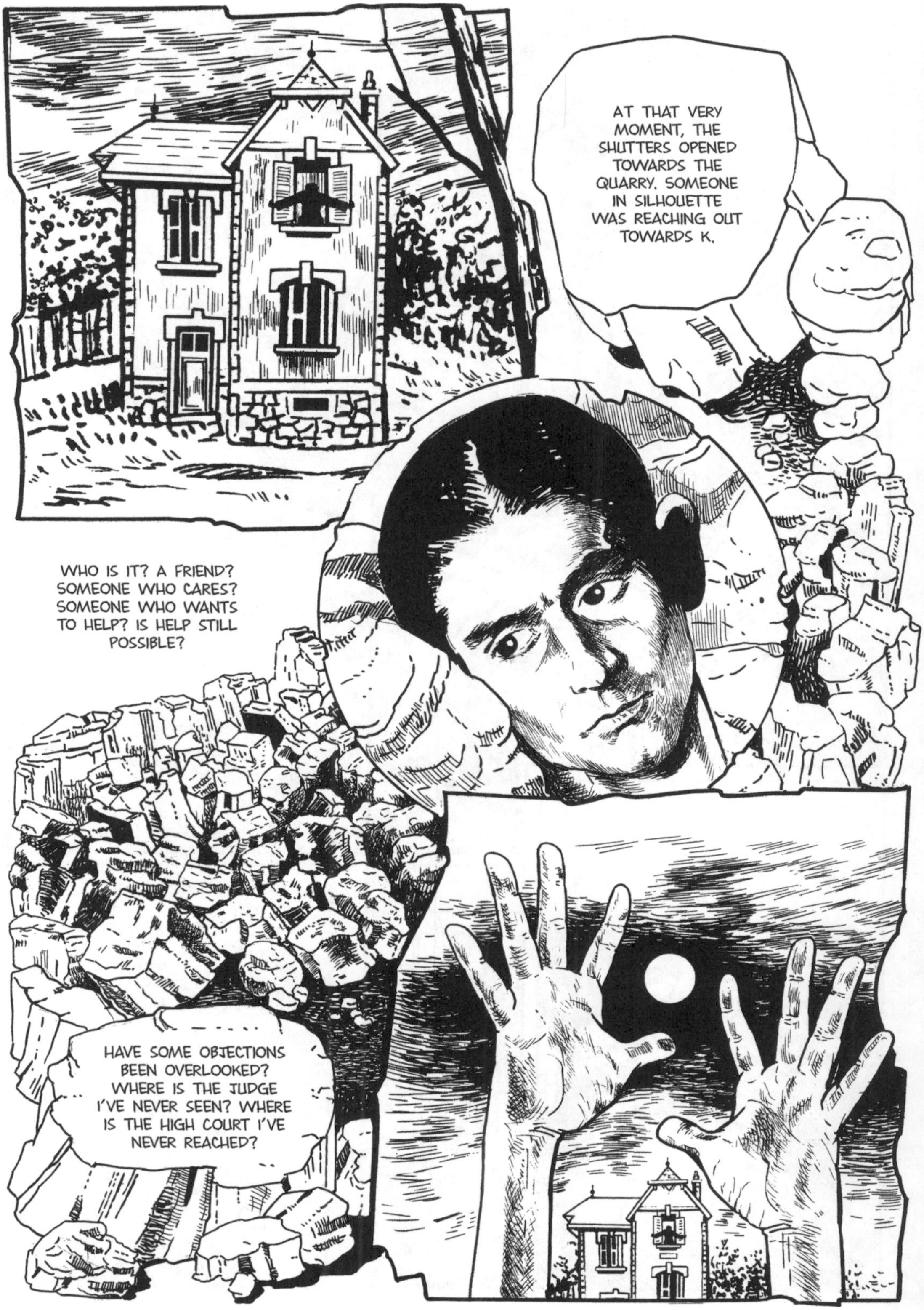
AT THAT VERY MOMENT, THE SHUTTERS OPENED TOWARDS THE QUARRY. SOMEONE IN SILHOUETTE WAS REACHING OUT TOWARDS K.
WHO IS IT? A FRIEND? SOMEONE WHO CARES? SOMEONE WHO WANTS TO HELP? IS HELP STILL POSSIBLE?
HAVE SOME OBJECTIONS BEEN OVERLOOKED? WHERE IS THE JUDGE I'VE NEVER SEEN? WHERE IS THE HIGH COURT I'VE NEVER REACHED?

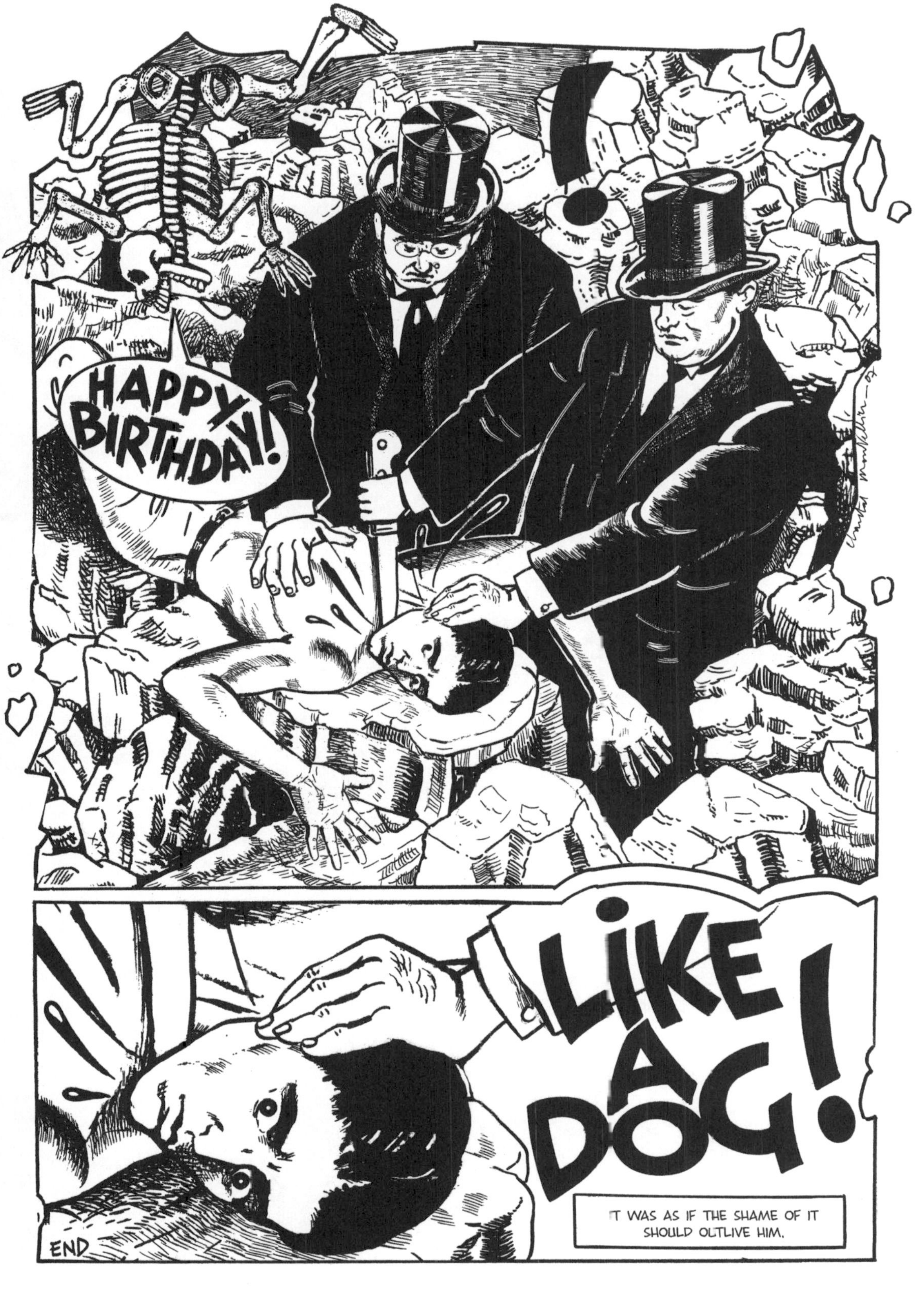
HAPPY BIRTHDAY!
LIKE A DOG!
IT WAS AS IF THE SHAME OF IT SHOULD OUTLIVE HIM.
END

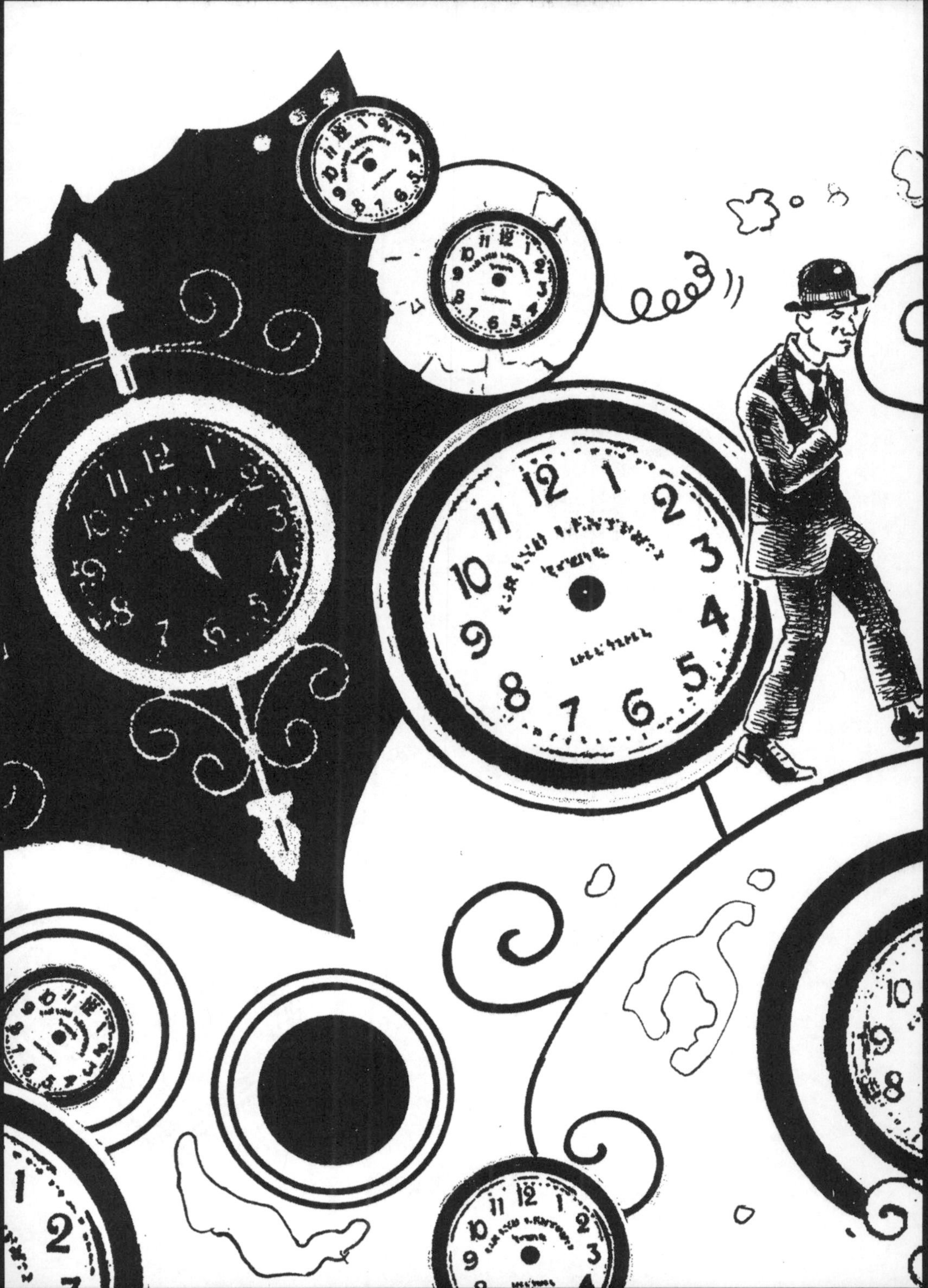

LIKE KAFKA'S OTHER TWO NOVELS—"THE CASTLE" AND
"AMERIKA"—"THE TRIAL" WAS NOT PUBLISHED DURING KAFKA'S
LIFETIME. BEFORE HE DIED FROM TUBERCULOSIS AT THE AGE OF
FORTY, KAFKA ASKED HIS CLOSE FRIEND, THE JOURNALIST MAX
BROD, TO DESTROY ALL HIS UNPUBLISHED WORKS AFTER HIS
DEATH. BROD, HOWEVER, DECIDED TO OVERRIDE KAFKA'S LAST
WISH AND BEGAN PREPARING THE MANUSCRIPT OF "THE TRIAL"
FOR PUBLICATION, ORDERING KAFKA'S BUNDLE OF UNNUMBERED
CHAPTERS, SOME OF THEM MERE FRAGMENTS, INTO A FIRST
EDITION IN 1925.

THROUGHOUT HIS LIFE, KAFKA WROTE SPORADICALLY, AND
OFTEN INTENSIVELY, THROUGH THE NIGHT. ENCOURAGED BY
BROD, WHOM HE MET AT UNIVERSITY IN 1902, HE PUBLISHED
MANY STORIES, MOST FAMOUSLY "METAMORPHOSIS" (1915) AND
"IN THE PENAL COLONY" (1919), WHICH HE WROTE WHILE
STILL WORKING ON "THE TRIAL." IN THE SAME PERIOD, HE
ALSO WROTE THE STORY "BEFORE THE LAW," WHICH APPEARS
IN "THE TRIAL" AS THE PARABLE RECOUNTED BY THE PRIEST.

ELEMENTS OF KAFKA'S INNER LIFE, WITH ITS UNRESOLVED
SEQUENCE OF FRUSTRATIONS, ANXIETIES, AND THWARTED
RELATIONSHIPS, FIND THEIR WAY INTO JOSEPH K'S NIGHTMARISH
EXPERIENCE IN "THE TRIAL."

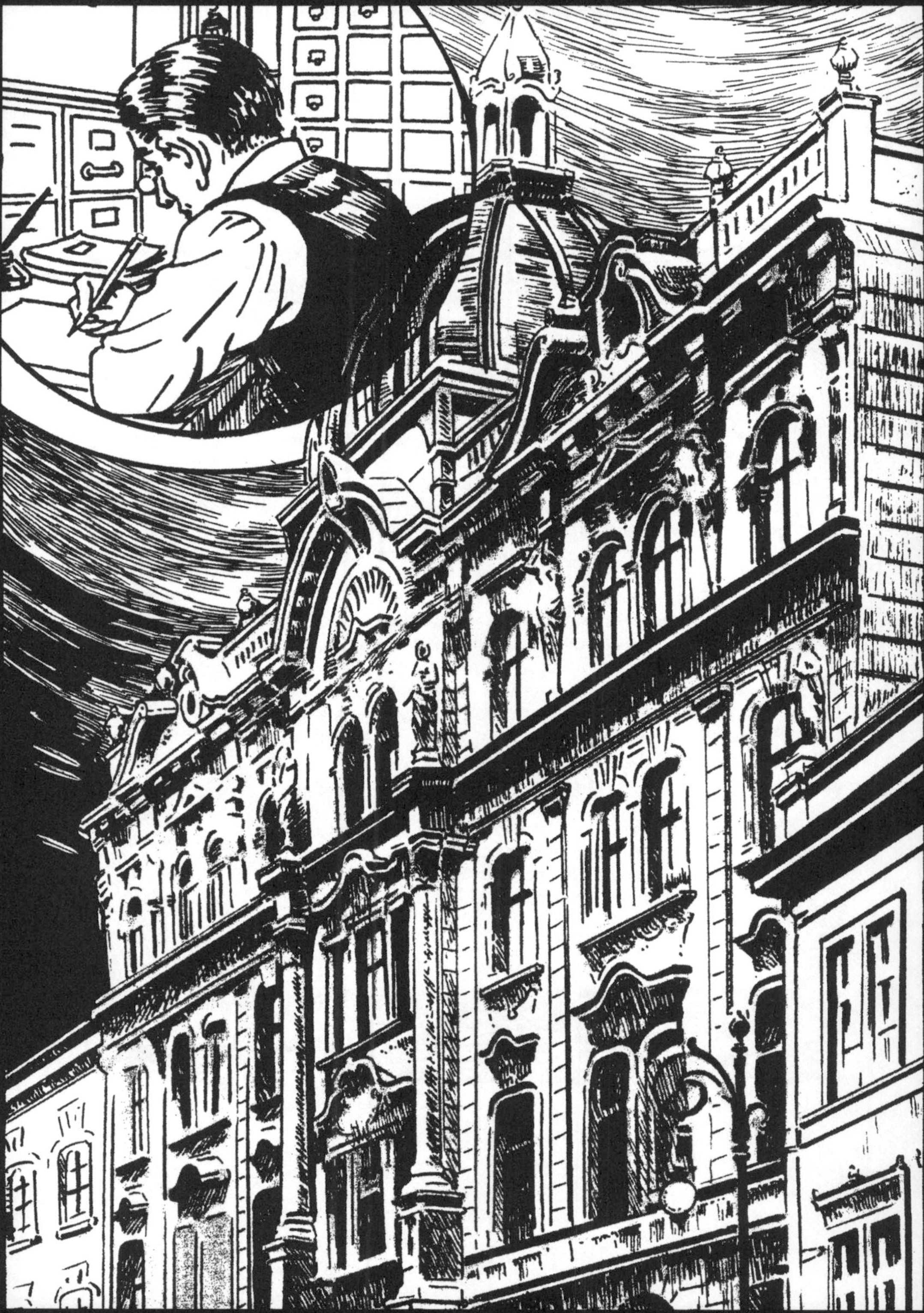

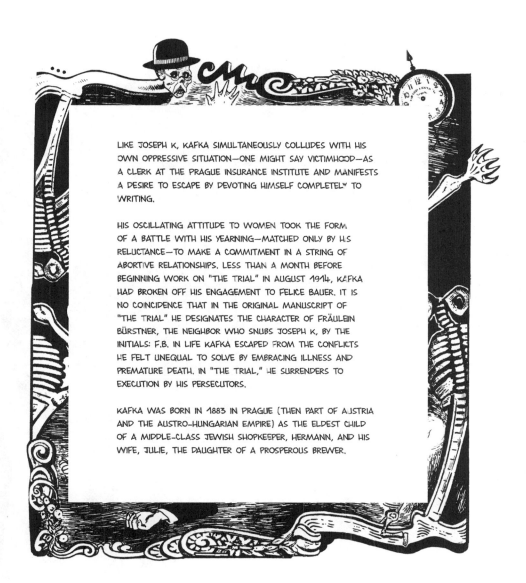

LIKE JOSEPH K, KAFKA SIMULTANEOUSLY COLLUDES WITH HIS OWN OPPRESSIVE SITUATION—ONE MIGHT SAY VICTIMHOOD—AS A CLERK AT THE PRAGUE INSURANCE INSTITUTE AND MANIFESTS A DESIRE TO ESCAPE BY DEVOTING HIMSELF COMPLETELY TO WRITING.

HIS OSCILLATING ATTITUDE TO WOMEN TOOK THE FORM OF A BATTLE WITH HIS YEARNING—MATCHED ONLY BY HIS RELUCTANCE—TO MAKE A COMMITMENT IN A STRING OF ABORTIVE RELATIONSHIPS. LESS THAN A MONTH BEFORE BEGINNING WORK ON "THE TRIAL" IN AUGUST 1914, KAFKA HAD BROKEN OFF HIS ENGAGEMENT TO FELICE BAUER. IT IS NO COINCIDENCE THAT IN THE ORIGINAL MANUSCRIPT OF "THE TRIAL" HE DESIGNATES THE CHARACTER OF FRÄULEIN BÜRSTNER, THE NEIGHBOR WHO SNUBS JOSEPH K, BY THE INITIALS: F.B. IN LIFE KAFKA ESCAPED FROM THE CONFLICTS HE FELT UNEQUAL TO SOLVE BY EMBRACING ILLNESS AND PREMATURE DEATH. IN "THE TRIAL," HE SURRENDERS TO EXECUTION BY HIS PERSECUTORS.

KAFKA WAS BORN IN 1883 IN PRAGUE (THEN PART OF AUSTRIA AND THE AUSTRO-HUNGARIAN EMPIRE) AS THE ELDEST CHILD OF A MIDDLE-CLASS JEWISH SHOPKEEPER, HERMANN, AND HIS WIFE, JULIE, THE DAUGHTER OF A PROSPEROUS BREWER.

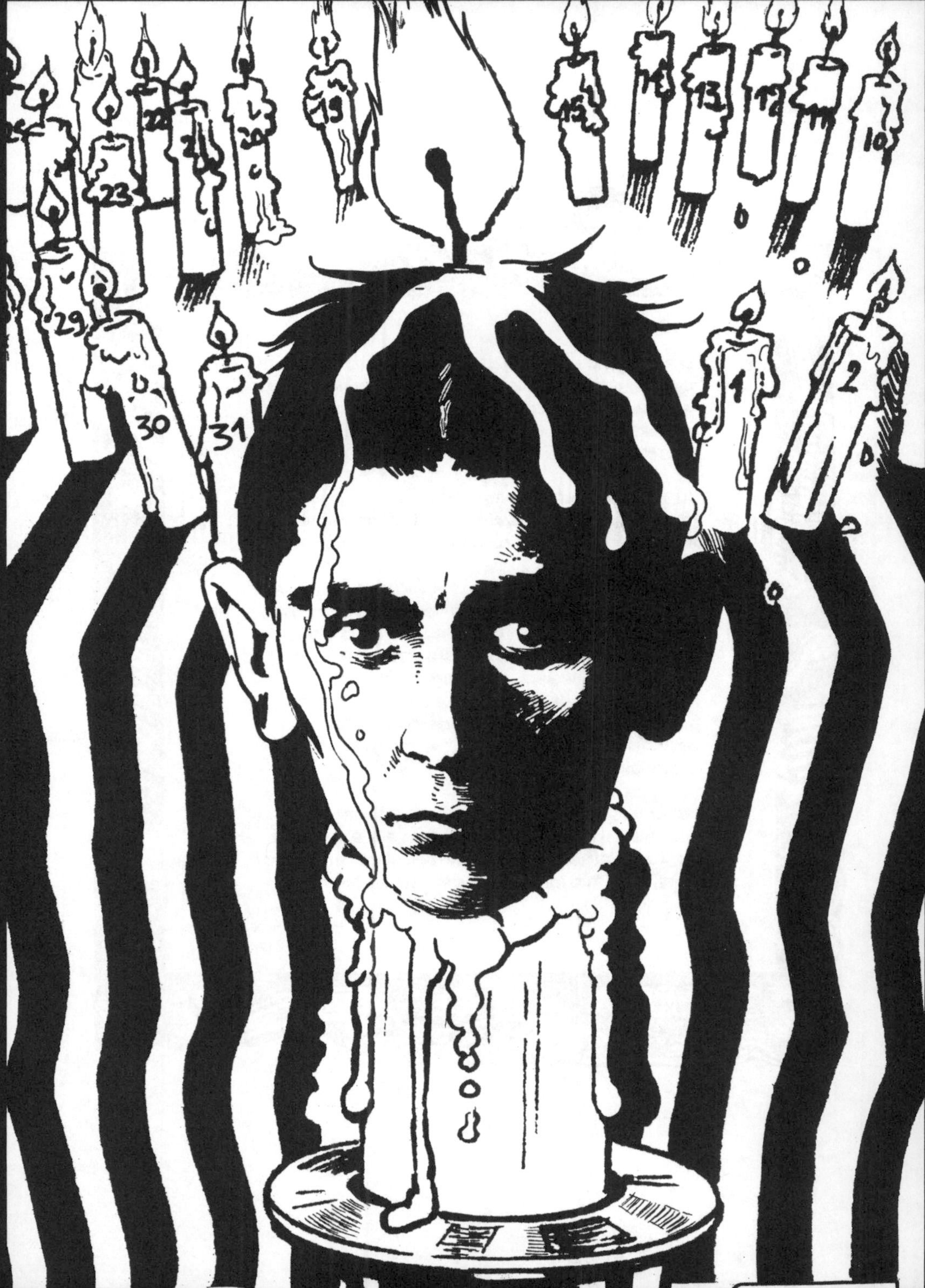

29
23
19
15
14
13
12
10
30
31
1
2

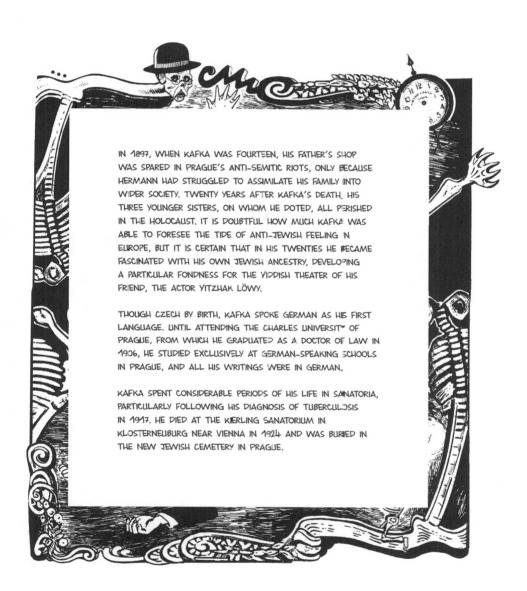

IN 1897, WHEN KAFKA WAS FOURTEEN, HIS FATHER'S SHOP
WAS SPARED IN PRAGUE'S ANTI-SEMITIC RIOTS, ONLY BECAUSE
HERMANN HAD STRUGGLED TO ASSIMILATE HIS FAMILY INTO
WIDER SOCIETY. TWENTY YEARS AFTER KAFKA'S DEATH, HIS
THREE YOUNGER SISTERS, ON WHOM HE DOTED, ALL PERISHED
IN THE HOLOCAUST. IT IS DOUBTFUL HOW MUCH KAFKA WAS
ABLE TO FORESEE THE TIDE OF ANTI-JEWISH FEELING IN
EUROPE, BUT IT IS CERTAIN THAT IN HIS TWENTIES HE BECAME
FASCINATED WITH HIS OWN JEWISH ANCESTRY, DEVELOPING
A PARTICULAR FONDNESS FOR THE YIDDISH THEATER OF HIS
FRIEND, THE ACTOR YITZHAK LÖWY.

THOUGH CZECH BY BIRTH, KAFKA SPOKE GERMAN AS HIS FIRST
LANGUAGE. UNTIL ATTENDING THE CHARLES UNIVERSITY OF
PRAGUE, FROM WHICH HE GRADUATED AS A DOCTOR OF LAW IN
1906, HE STUDIED EXCLUSIVELY AT GERMAN-SPEAKING SCHOOLS
IN PRAGUE, AND ALL HIS WRITINGS WERE IN GERMAN.

KAFKA SPENT CONSIDERABLE PERIODS OF HIS LIFE IN SANATORIA,
PARTICULARLY FOLLOWING HIS DIAGNOSIS OF TUBERCULOSIS
IN 1917. HE DIED AT THE KIERLING SANATORIUM IN
KLOSTERNEUBURG NEAR VIENNA IN 1924 AND WAS BURIED IN
THE NEW JEWISH CEMETERY IN PRAGUE.